D0172270

# THE SECOND MIRACLE

- "THE PEACE OF NON-RATIONAL UNDERSTANDING"

"THE TEACHING OF FUNDAMENTAL RELATIONSHIP"

"THE ADVENTURE OF THE UNKNOWN"

"TRANSFORM - NOT PERFORM"

"LESS SELF PROTECTIVE"

"DISTRACTS OF FEAR"

JOY-HURT - BY YOSEMITE

"IF YOU ARE THINKING YOU ARE RUNNING FROM FEAR"

DOUBT - ANGER - FEAR
  |          |        |
MIND    HEART    BODY

BODY
  |
FEELING

# THE
# SECOND
# MIRACLE

*Intimacy, Spirituality,
and Conscious Relationships*

by

Richard Moss, M.D.

CELESTIAL ARTS
*Berkeley, California*

Copyright © 1995 by Richard Moss, M.D. All rights reserved. No part of this book may be reproduced in any form, except for brief review, without the express permission of the publisher. For further information, you may write to:

Celestial Arts Publishing
P.O. Box 7123
Berkeley, California 94707


Cover Design: Blue Merle Graphics
Text Design and Composition: Star Type

Printed in the United States of America

Library of Congress Cataloging-in-Publication Data

Moss, Richard M., 1946–
       The second miracle / by Richard Moss.
           p.    cm.
       ISBN 0-89087-765-3
       1. Spiritual life.   2. Self-actualization (Psychology)—Religious aspects.   I. Title.
       BL624.M675   1995
       291.4—dc20                                    95-17541
                                                          CIP



First Printing, 1995

1   2   3   4   5   /   99   98   97   96   95

*To my wife, Ariel,*
*with whom I have learned so much*
*about loving and intimacy,*
*side by side with*
*Andreas, Maria, and Tassos.*

*To my friend Yvan Amar,*
*whose life and teaching*
*so eloquently integrates relationship, love,*
*and the sacred.*

*In honor of Franklin Merrell-Wolff,*
*who was the first to show me a life well-lived*
*in service to Consciousness.*

# TABLE OF CONTENTS

# ACKNOWLEDGMENTS

This book would not be what it is without the intelligent questioning and devoted assistance of my wife, Ariel. She has been both editorial companion and a major contributor to the integrity and clarity of the text.

Several people have read and commented on the manuscript at different stages and have given me helpful feedback as well as loving support. My love and gratitude to Anne Hillman for her enthusiasm, Julia Press, Roberto Solari, Agueda Gonzalez, and Avis Ballard for their thoughts, Eugene Trimboli for copy editing as well as asking important questions, Gabrielle St. Claire for her clarity and playfulness, and Michael Plesse for his quiet intelligence. Most especially, I want to thank Aster Barnwell for taking the time to make detailed criticism and commentary that, I feel, has significantly enriched this work. Each of you are more than friends; you are peers whose friendship and work with me over the years has greatly enriched my own teaching.

I am especially grateful to my publisher, David Hinds, for his continued support of my work, and to Leana Alba, for her careful reading, thoughtful questioning, and intelligent editorial assistance. Many thanks to my secretary, Tammi Clanton, for the umpteen pages she printed out and the corrections she carefully entered into the computer.

This book was written over several years in many locations. I am grateful to many friends who provided me with quiet surroundings and support, as well as to many others who unknowingly, through a turn of phrase or in speaking of their lives, pointed my thoughts in a particular direction that eventually found its way onto these pages.

Finally, this teaching would never have come into being without the many people who have participated with me in my work. I owe each of you a great debt. Together we have lived the exloration that has made this work alive. It is your dreams, your love, your courage, and your suffering that gives substance to all that I have said. I often imagine that in the last instant of my life it will be your essence, as well as that of my close loved ones, that will be breathed into Infinity with me.

# INTRODUCTION

This book invites you on a journey into the essential teaching of fundamental relationship. To awaken this teaching in myself and in each of us is my deepest quest and the passion of my heart and soul. For more than twenty years I have taught constantly all over the world about the indivisible oneness of our relationship to ourselves, each other, and the great mystery that we call God. This is the fundamental relationship, where we meet the divine in ourselves, see the divine reflected in the mirror of the other, and live this in our daily lives. This is far more than philosophy; it is deeply diving into life itself. This relationship must be realized in our deepest core, so that it pulsates in our cells, and radiates from our hearts, transmitting itself through the silence, clarity, and strength of our presence. This connection is what underlies everything: our personal lives, our business lives, our sense of vitality, our energy, our health, our genius. Everywhere I have traveled, in North America, Europe, Australia, South America, the call can be heard irresistably and urgently: Listen to your deepest essence and open your hearts to the Larger Intelligence that is forever seeking, in so many ways, to awaken through each of us. The music of this call cannot be ignored anymore; we would be fools to refuse the greatest privilege that life offers us.

I use the term teaching in the ancient and revered sense of being called to the privilege of initiation into a path of discipleship—not to a person, or an ideology, but to self-realization and service to Life. Together we become members of a growing community of individuals who, via various paths, are remembering our deeper nature and submitting our lives to that Truth. I believe, at this point in our human existence, it is very helpful, indeed it may be essential, that we consciously regard ourselves as students, or more aptly disciples. Discipleship is not a term that is much appreciated any longer in the modern world. Yet, if we would but shift our perspective, we would recognize that we are, and can be nothing else than, disciples of Life. Life, Existence, the Universe—whatever word we use to refer to the Great-Mystery-That-Is—is *the* Teaching made manifest; our conscious relationship to It is our personal discipleship, the individual path that we walk and share. I have found that as soon as we embrace ourselves, our world, and each other as fellow disciples of the Teaching, in whatever way that comes to have meaning for us, we begin to think and act with more humility and a healthy sense of obligation. Then our spiritual journey begins to become much fuller, more intelligent, and equally important, gentler. This is crucial now, as the energy seeking to awaken in us is quickening and intensifying, demanding our full and humble attention. To deny it, or approach it, in any other way risks grave consequences.

I have divided this book into three parts. Each part is somewhat like a symphonic movement that has a particular rhythm or feeling rather than marking a true division of the content or the flow. Part One: The Condition, begins with looking at the First Miracle, what we learn through it, the strengths we have developed and the inherent limitation of this basic consciousness. Then it describes the coming of the Second Miracle—the fundamental shift in the basis for our identity that we are being called to, and what this means for each of us and our world. Part Two: The Teaching, goes on to discuss what I consider certain key aspects of our Western mystical heritage in terms that help us recognize the spirituality we are already living and the great invitation of a life in faith. Part Three: The Life, brings the teaching into daily life. It explores the three keys to self-healing and the four pillars of spiritual practice. Specifically, it discusses the healing of childhood trauma, transmuting suffering, transforming body consciousness, working with energy, dreams, meditation, and prayer, and how, when we approach our lives through our feeling and in faith rather than through our thinking, we begin to truly incarnate a higher level of consciousness. Most important, it is about how through the consciousness we bring to all our relationships, we begin to live a path of enlightenment.

I suggest that this book be read in the sequence of the chapters, because some of the metaphors and terminology important to understanding the later chapters are introduced and explained early on. In coming to terms with the question of voice gender, I alternated between he and she, rather than what are, to me, awkward constructions such as s/he, his/her, and so on. The word God is also, understandably, a problem for many people whose deeper essence was often dishonored by the dogmatic interpretations of religion they were exposed to in early life. Also, it is no longer appropriate (if it ever was) for God to be perceived as The Father, an exclusively masculine imprinting. God, as I use the word in this book, is a notion refering to That which is always prior to any gender, characteristic, or quality, or concept whatsoever. I have gradually become deeply sensitive to the generalized devaluing of the feminine over the last many millennia, and especially the pain of it in my own life and in the lives of the people with whom I work. It is one of the central issues of our time and I feel deep resonance with the resurgence of the notion of Goddess within the specific context of righting that imbalance. However, to me, a deeper psychology of consciousness embraces rather than discriminates between male/female, God/Goddess. There is a certain point where attempting to be politically and spiritually correct becomes almost too egoistically fixated, and our deeper work is to try to understand ourselves in ways that relax our egos so that we can be available to That which is what we are calling God. Perhaps I am naive in this, but I have chosen to use the word God with the understanding that I am including God-the-Father and God-the-Mother, or Goddess, within the simpler construction.

One of my intentions is that this book can be read aloud, that first and foremost it be musical rather than intellectual. Words are important to me, both in the cognitive sense of what they say, but equally in the subliminal sense of what they convey. Over the years, in my teaching, I have seen that when people struggle to understand the words before they have reached the deeper intuition from which the words flow, they obstruct their capacity to receive the energy riding on and between the words. The result is the sense of not understanding. But if the reading is undertaken like listening to music, or like listening to the rain on the roof, meaning arises in another way. I urge the reader to let the words flow, to pause from time to time and let the mind drift, to take a deep breath and meet the words from an easeful, spacious place in your body. I feel that many words are not meant to imprison us, but rather, are a way of pointing our attention. God is one of those words, but so is he, she, love, meditation, prayer, faith, ego, intellect, consciousness, and so forth. Truly, I often use these words from a place of partial intuition and understanding, and in the very act of speaking or writing about them discover new meanings. I believe this process has no real limit. Therefore, while you have the right to expect a certain degree of accuracy and consistency, there is no way, ultimately, to use certain words consistently or concretely.

In a time when Eastern mysticism and spirituality has made so many valuable contributions to the Western soul, I feel that it is crucial that we reappreciate the profound mystical heritage of the West. Specifically, the principal voice I regularly quote in this book is the voice of Jesus. Most of the quotes come from a Gnostic text called The Gospel According to Thomas, one of many tracts from an extraordinary Coptic library lost for sixteen centuries and discovered in 1945 in a ruined tomb near Nag Hamadi, Upper Egypt. This text is one of the earliest manuscripts relating to the New Testament and is, according to the translators, based on an earlier work written in Greek around 140 A.D. It is possible that it contains genuine words of Jesus, and it has the crucial advantage, for me, of having escaped much of the proselytizing and fictionalizing of his life that distorts the New Testament gospels. The Gnostic Gospels restore the emphasis to the nature of the new consciousness rather than to the miraculous attributes that occasionally manifest themselves as a consequence of this consciousness. Wherever I quote from this text I include the number of the specific maxim, called logia in the text, so that readers can find it for themselves.

The Jesus I propose is not the Christ we have castrated with our egos by deifying him and raising him so far above ourselves that his teaching becomes uprooted from an immediate aliveness we all can and will, eventually, incarnate. The Jesus you will meet here is nothing short of our evolutionary destiny vividly and explicitly calling to us and inviting us to give ourselves to the living work of realizing a new consciousness. Unfortunately, for too many people, Jesus' teaching has become part of an archaic religious language perceived by the modern soul as repressive, or regressive, a language that too easily loses the subtlety, paradox, and rich ambiguity of the living journey. The result is that many people feel betrayed by their religion and unable to find the inner psychical intimacy with Jesus that a deeper part of the soul truly needs. Regardless of what religion we are born to or adhere to, Jesus as The Christ is one of the crucial archetypes of the human soul, particularly in the West. As we seek to make the radical inner transformation through the discontinuity between the First and Second Miracle, the old and new consciousness, he is one of the crucial symbols and energies that can sustain us through that transition. Therefore, I have undertaken an interpretation of Jesus' teaching to help invigorate a contemporary and living mystical psychology.

Despite my frequent references to Jesus, I am not an advocate of Christianity over other religions. Indeed, I am cautious of all institutional religions simply because they too easily succumb to dogmatic interpretations of what must always remain profound mystery. What I do advocate is sincere spirituality, an irrevocable commitment to consciousness. I also quote from other religious traditions and mystics, particularly Walt Whitman, but Jesus is unquestionably one of the world's most important spiritual figures. His teaching as it is presented in the Gnostic Gospels is, in my experience, an eloquent and very accurate description of both the process of awakening to, and the essence of, the Second Miracle. Anything that assists this Jesus in being accessible to our souls at this time can strengthen, particularly for a Westerner, the capacity to embrace the radical transformation of consciousness that is gradually happening in us all.

In *The Second Miracle* I have tried to remain true to my own experience, which continues evolving in many ways over the years. While this book stands alone and can be read without familiarity with my former writings, it is a further expression of a body of work that I have recorded in three previous books. The important change in my own life reflected in this work has been a new marriage with the addition of three stepchildren in my family. Eight years ago I was living a contemplative lifestyle, with many hours of quiet solitude each day and sleeping alone. I was the central figure of a community dedicated to exploring the transformation of consciousness. But for the past eight years, I have become a family man and have ceased to live in a localized spiritual community. While I have continued to teach during these years, the hectic nature of family life has been the principle environment for my own growth, and it has greatly influenced how I share myself and my work.

Primarily, what family life has taught me is that a higher state of consciousness means very little until it can be embodied in everyday living. My stepchildren (ages six, twelve, and fourteen when we began living together) didn't care a lot about my spiritual credentials; they responded directly to the quality of how I communicated my feelings, needs, and limits, and how I responded to theirs. Needless to say they challenged me over and over again in ways I never suffered while leading a spiritual community. In the mirror they held up, and in the gift of reliving my childhood through them, came greater appreciation for my parent's struggles in raising me. Equally important, I saw firsthand, how our consciousness evolves from the "openness" of childhood to the "boundedness" of adulthood. For this and more, our time together has been a true blessing.

Their mother, my wife Ariel, is not only a wonderful partner, she is equally a disciple of the teaching. We first met through my writings and conference work, but in our intimate life together her gifts to me have been many, especially the quality of her mothering, her wisdom about the body, and her uncommon intelligence about people's emotional natures. In insisting that we meet each other as unique people and not as objects, and in being an intimate mirror for the fears and conditioning that unconsciously cause us to withhold relationship, she has been an important teacher for me. Together we have learned a great deal about conscious relationship. The journey, at times, has not been easy, but she and our family have had a profound effect on how I have come to answer for myself the question "What really matters?"

A true Teaching is liberating precisely because it obligates us to live from a far deeper level of ourselves. As we make the challenging descent to these depths we realize our own I-amness, a place of being that says "yes" to life even in times of greatest hardship. We become the authors of our own lives, taking our stand in Truth no matter what the consequences. No longer can our humanity be held ransom by fear or our goodwill stripped from us by stress and suffering. Life's difficult challenges will always remain, but we are no longer victims. We are the disciples of all that life presents to us; we do not forget our true home.

Millennia of fear for survival has made us ingenious takers. We consider it our privilege to take from life, to take from the land, from the forests, from the seas, from each other, even from the angels, and from God. But to be conscious is not only a miraculous privilege, it is also an obligation. It is an obligation to evolve, to give back to Evolution by becoming servants of That which is forever seeking to awaken in us. Here is a journey we all must take, a journey that demands utmost maturity while, paradoxically, granting it at the same time. In choosing to answer this call we become servants of Life's deeper intelligence; the great stricture closing our hearts at last relaxes. All along, all we had to do was accept the obligation of consciousness, and by grace we begin to drink from the fountain of real joy. It is my deepest hope that this book will serve you in realizing that joy for yourself.

Richard Moss
February, 1995

# THE
# CONDITION

*Crave to know that from which all beings take birth,*
*that from which being born they live, and that towards which they*
*move and into which they merge.*

—Taittiriya Upanishad

# CHAPTER I

# THE CALL TO CONSCIOUSNESS

An epochal event is unfolding within each of us. It is a miraculous demonstration of the intelligence of the Universe, yet very few people actually realize the essence of this miracle or the magnitude of what is at stake. Often, quite unconsciously, we become victims of the apocalyptic struggle in which this new possibility is being born within us. We react habitually in ways that weaken us and threaten our very survival instead of engaging this great movement as disciples of life's deepest impulse.

The soil upon which this epochal struggle is being waged is our own consciousness. It is not a question of good versus evil; it is an evolutionary shift in our actual capacity for consciousness. Realizing this shift in ourselves, or in the very least becoming servants to that possibility, is the most important thing we can individually do with our lives. At stake is our capacity to love, to celebrate life, to care for each other, and to steward our planet. It seems likely that our very survival is at stake. For while Evolution itself is presenting us with this new possibility, we are by no means assured of embodying it soon enough. The choices and behaviors that are rooted in our old consciousness threaten to engulf us all. There is a work to be done, a teaching to be lived, and no one is exempt.

Right now, as we look out upon our world, there is a great sense of foreboding. The Earth's human population is growing at a tremendous rate, threatening the environment in every habitat and even in its most basic capacity to sustain life. Our unique minds have liberated technologies of immense power, while our emotional, psychological, and spiritual maturity lags behind in the capacity to utilize these powers wisely. The challenge for each of us personally, given the immensity of the problem, is how to respond. Uncertain of the next step, and fearful of the unknown, we are like adolescents unconsciously soiling the home nest, making things intolerable in order to propel ourselves outward to a new age of accountability and maturity. Now, with so much at stake, we are standing on the threshold of a great awakening, but we don't quite know what is being asked of us. What is desperately needed is a clearer perception of what this next step really is, what is involved in living it, and how we can commit ourselves to support the highest possibility.

There is one certainty and that is that all of us will die; none of us can escape this simple truth. Yet a great mystery is that few of us consciously live as if this were the case. We pretend that we can protect ourselves, we pretend that all that matters is our own happiness, we imagine we can transcend our bodies, we lie to ourselves and hide behind fictions. The first step that we must take is to recognize that our lives are brief. What distinguishes our brief individual moment on Earth is that we do not hide in delusion, that we choose to wake up and, rather than expecting our lover, our possessions, our science, our government, our religion, or our God to save us and fulfill us, we assume this responsibility for ourselves.

4  We have all grown up hearing of the horrors of the Holocaust, as well as hearing of inspired and heroic lives connected with that event, such as Oskar Schindler's. In my first visit to Germany some years ago, as the train crossed the border from Austria, a sense of darkness and distrust closed over me. I realized that it

wasn't the Germans I distrusted, it was myself. Even as a child I never felt I could judge the Germans. Looking into my own heart, dread would well up—could I too do such terrible things? How is one human being lured away from his own humanity while another is lifted toward saintliness? When will we finally take a stand in our highest nature and let the alchemy of that commitment begin to undo the old fearful self and transform us?

Imagine asking a group of Germans whether they now unshakably trusted themselves to never again become victimized by fear, to never again be manipulated to endorse cruelty, racial hatred, political or spiritual zealotry, to never again allow themselves to commit or tolerate genocide as their parents, and even some of them, had. Indeed, more than merely asking these questions, imagine urging each of them to speak a deeply felt prayer that would affirm their accountability to themselves, a prayer for ruthless self-honesty, a commitment to never give themselves away to any leader, or any collective movement that betrays their humanity. This is precisely the opportunity I had some years ago while teaching in Germany.

The circumstance was during a pre-dawn ceremony I was leading called a sweatlodge. A sweatlodge is originally a Native American purification ritual. The form of the ceremony, as I focus it, is very simple. We sit together on the bare earth inside a low hut made from flexible branches covered with blankets. Rocks, heated red hot in a fire, are carefully brought inside and placed in a central hole. When the entrance flaps are sealed closed, the hut is completely dark; it is like crawling into a collective womb. Water is then periodically poured onto the rocks, producing steam, and the lodge becomes very hot.

Essentially, this kind of ritual consciously invites suffering in order to face, and pass through, the layer of deep instinctual fear that easily closes our hearts. Before beginning, the spiritual and psychological context is carefully and profoundly invoked. Every participant understands that the ritual is consecrated: First, to opening our hearts in acknowledgement and compassion for life's suffering; second, in gratitude for all that we have received from

5

life and for all the people, living or dead, that have served us; third, in forgiveness for our endless tendency to withhold our love due to fear; and finally, in affirmation of conscious relationship, the commitment to risk living from our deepest sense of truth and unprotected openness with every person. To bring this consecration personally alive, each person is invited to offer a spontaneous and heartfelt prayer out of the deepest prompting of his or her soul. Between the rounds of prayer, we open the flaps for fresh air, drink some water, and rest. The sense of community and the shared recognition of the universality of our suffering, our gratitude, and our longing for conscious service to life, make these rituals a profoundly beautiful honoring of oneself, each other, and life's deepest invitation.

That morning in Germany, in the translucent darkness and heat of the lodge, I was feeling into the prayers. Voice after voice was praying for forgiveness for wounds they had brought to their children and parents, asking for the courage and strength to face fear and suffering, asking for health for their loved ones, for support in dealing with family problems. I know such prayers are important and beautiful; I have made such prayers myself, but given the agony I could sense in the souls of many of these people, these prayers were still on the surface. I had the disturbing sense that unconsciously, we were still trying to take for ourselves, still self-involved, as if we imagined God as some ultimate parent, rather than seeing our responsibility to a more mature relationship to God and discovering the deeper joy that comes with it. This is the joy that comes from accepting the obligation to really see ourselves, to become as fully conscious as we can and then offer ourselves in service to life. A powerful voice spoke from within me, summoning each of us to face our own essential accountability, to face how we have abandoned our humanity and might do it again, to really see where our souls are rooted. It was not a call to shame or guilt for the actions of the past, but an invocation to realize the connection to our deepest self, what I call our I-amness. It is this most essential and solitary place within, where we encounter our own and life's terrible potential for good and evil and finally reconcile these in a fundamental commitment to Truth. The consequences when we fail to honor this central place of our being are all too apparent throughout human history.

Slowly and hesitantly, new voices were heard in the sweat-lodge. They came from the same people, but there was a new energy. There was sobbing and tears and deep anguish as the prayers began to come from the depths of their souls. The terrible wound of the past war and the concentration camps was there, but also in that honest agony was a new resolve, never to give up one's own authority to anybody. People prayed never to abandon or demean their own fragile humanity and the humanity of others. They prayed to stand up for their hearts' knowing, and not be seduced by fear or by great fantasies for the future.

The answer to how we are so easily stripped of our humanity is tragically simple; we've scarcely known it. The usual explanations for Man's inhumanity—poor parenting, poverty, early childhood abuse, poor education, social injustice and so on—undoubtedly contribute, yet many people rise above these circumstances. To me these are symptoms; the root of the problem is far more fundamental. It has to do with the nature and activity of our basic consciousness, what I call the First Miracle, and specifically, how we invest our attention. The question of I-amness is a matter of attention. It is a matter of what our hearts are really listening to, of how we sense our own bodies, of how we perceive others, of what we invest with meaning and imbue with value. The cumulative effect of how we invest our attention determines whether we put down roots deep into the bedrock of our essence from which we may be bent but not uprooted, or onto a foundation of ideas and beliefs from which we can be easily dislodged by the storms of life's fierce challenges. This is the essence of the spiritual struggle within our souls.

There is a growing agony in the soul of the modern person and this agony is a direct result of the triumph of intellect. Over thousands of years intellect has succeeded in increasingly protecting us from the vicissitudes of nature. But now spawned by the ceaseless inventiveness of our intellects, there is an ever-increasing

7

number of man-made distractions competing for our attention, seducing us away from our essence. We are in, or so it is called, the Information Age, but what we are bombarded by is far more than information. We are literally drowning in endless images and sounds. Radios, televisions, stereos, magazines, newspapers, billboards, even books, fill us with other peoples' ideas, other peoples' opinions and all kinds of fantasies that, intentionally or not, manipulate our desires and needs. The ubiquitous cellular telephone is perhaps the newest in an endless list of objects increasingly intruding into our precious little solitude and capacity for self-reflection. There is more and more information communicated, but at the expense of genuine contact. Of course, some of this information barrage has real value and can expand our understanding of our world. But to a large degree, most of this input conspires for our mediocrity, revolving around simplistic issues of right and wrong, or overtly seducing our weaknesses, vanities, and fears. Our culture blinds us to paradox, to the truth that life is neither black nor white. It disempowers us, making us feel that we are defined by a ceaseless procession of things outside of ourselves, or by implying that we are, in fact, all-powerful.

What all this input represents is an assault on our souls. It excites our attention toward innumerable materialistic dreams that only a privileged few can ever actually attain: Dreams in any case that do not, ultimately, fulfill us. Worse, in this ceaseless excitation we become numbed to the real magic of living, the real wealth that we can each discover in ourselves and in our communities. Where in all this is our own organic rhythm with the flow of nature? Where is our ease and trust in our body's intelligence? Where is the richness of our own inner landscape? Where is our own music, our own dreams, our own fantasies, and visions? Our attention is so fragmented, so superficial; we are rarely plumbing our depths. In a few humans, this is tragic; in billions it is catastrophic. Modern culture is failing to imbue us with the capacity to recognize what really matters. And this is fundamental: If each of us cannot answer the question "What really matters?" from the depths of ourselves, by what stars do we navigate the complex seas of life?

We can no longer afford to be naive; there is no such thing as a casual or innocent use of our attention. Everyday, moment by moment, how we invest our attention gradually creates who we are and our awareness of the world. Values and actions follow accordingly. If we continue to be passively seduced by the ceaseless excitation of modern life, we will never meet our inner wealth, never have enough, never feel fulfilled. If we keep choosing the promise of happiness, of the quick fix, of easy answers, instead of a real commitment to spiritual substance, we live in true poverty for which our materialism and compulsive consumerism is but a compensation for inner emptiness. The maxim "as we sow, so shall we reap" becomes the touchstone for modern life. Spiritual mediocrity breeds social decay and collapse. Refusing to face into ourselves, protecting our egos, worshipping security and happiness while pandering to fear, we can all too easily forfeit our humanity.

It is possible to draw an analogy between Europe in the 1920s and 30s and the situation today as we approach the third millennium. At that time, many Europeans, particularly Jews, could not allow themselves to believe the danger they were in. The signs were there, but the implications of acting on them seemed too threatening. To do so meant upheaval and emigration. It meant trusting the validity of their own intuition of danger, facing despair and loss, accepting radical change, arguably without sufficient empirical proof. Of course, once these conditions were confirmed it was too late.

Similarly today, will we truly read and face the signs of the times? Is global warming an imminent reality? Are the loss of countless species, the pollution of the seas, the catastrophic collapse of the great fisheries, the denuding of the rain forests, really a threat? Is it reasonable to be releasing, in a few centuries, the carbon that nature took hundreds of millions of years to safely store beneath the surface of the earth? Is the barring of our windows and barricading of our doors against robbers and violence an acceptable price for society as it is? The behemoth consumer culture is like a cancer consuming energy and resources without regard to the balance of life on Earth. The United States and other First

9

World countries are the primary tumor, but the cancer is rapidly metastasizing to all the developing nations of the world. Dare we let ourselves feel the nightmare of what human consciousness is creating? Indeed, do we risk staring into the abyss within our own souls, and wonder whether we too are dissociating ourselves, even now, from something we dare not deny? Who or what really owns our souls? While the rational ego waits for sufficient empirical proof that there is real danger, will we, like the Jews, find ourselves on planet Auschwitz?

Today, the debate addressing and the controversy surrounding this terrifying possibility is extensive. Yet, I believe there is something fundamental that we are not seeing, not understanding. It is that our basic consciousness that looks out and perceives the problem and would attempt any number of rational solutions is *itself* part and parcel of the problem. I am not saying that sane, rational decisions—recycling, ecological conservation, and so forth —aren't helpful. Indeed, they are absolutely necessary and central to the dawning age of accountability. Yet—and here is the real issue—they may not be enough. It is possible that our very consciousness, at our present stage of evolution, and not just the misuse of intellect, or human greed and fear, is itself the deeper cause of our growing global catastrophe.

This dilemma is similar to the situation many of us face when we become ill. One part of us recognizes that we are sick and takes steps to make lifestyle changes and obtain help. But after many years of exploring medicine, self-healing, and the psychoenergetics of spiritual transformation, it has become clear that the part of us that wants to heal (or wants to evolve spiritually) and undertakes various regimens to do so, is often an older and larger pattern of consciousness of which the disease is, itself, but one manifestation. What often is needed for true healing is a fundamental shift of consciousness that releases the energy from the old pattern and allows a new one to begin. The paradox of such a radical approach to healing is that it has nothing to do with healing; it has to do with being, with I-amness. Healing proceeds naturally and often in quite unexpected ways out of our I-amness.

There is profound hope for all of us because of this spontaneous process of self-healing, the spontaneous evolution to a new level of consciousness. The problem for our rational egos is that it cannot be undertaken simply through our intellects or motivated by our personal will. We are incredibly naive when we believe that we can bring about this change through methodologies that we ourselves devise and pursue. The best any of our methodologies can do is set the stage for our receptivity to a deeper intelligence; our rational minds cannot direct the process that is being called forth from us now. There is a mysterious alchemy, a quality of grace, of unpredictability, to this kind of change that does not bow to the urgency or even the sincere efforts of our ego-driven selves. Above all, it rarely emerges from actions born of fear; it grows from our inner stillness. To be sure, we may not feel still; today, more and more of us feel threatened even if we can find no reason in our own lives. But we must learn to rest in the stillness, to not be seduced by our fear. The deep healing that we seek is fundamentally a spiritual process, and in spiritual territory we are the disciples, not the masters. Above all, we are in the domain of faith, a completely new relationship to our whole experience of being.

The very real possibility that, given our present level of conscious activity, we may not be able to heal ourselves is, I believe, the great wound to the modern soul. As in the line by Walt Kelly in his Pogo cartoon, "We've met the enemy and he is us," we are the disease. In whatever arena we look—our personal lives, in business, in government, at the environment—the old consciousness that has led us so successfully to this point has, itself, become the disease. And though we keep pretending that we can heal and change ourselves, we really do not know how. Indeed, all we may be able to do is to face into ourselves, into this wound, with ruthless self-honesty and approach the threshold of faith in which that new potential of consciousness is always waiting to meet us. This potential, in all the varying ways we each find our way to it, is what I refer to as The Second Miracle.

To even consider this possibility takes great courage, but it is only the first step. We must reach the point in the depths of our

11

being where we can go no further on our own efforts. This, from the point of view of our ego-selves is the deepest, most fundamental wound, a wound that we endlessly try to avoid with all the cleverness of our intellect and force of our self-will. Paradoxically, it is a sacred wound, a gift of evolution itself, for it has the power to radically transform us and even heal us if we let it enter us deeply enough. It has this power precisely because it is the wound the ego cannot heal.

These are sober thoughts, not the stuff of popular best-sellers. But I am not in the least a pessimist or doomsday prophet. On the contrary, it is because I have seen the incredible wonder and miracle of the awakening human soul that I have faith. Everywhere, more and more people are awakening to the inner call of spirit through a process that is often, at the same time, the most profound wounding and miraculous dawning of a new life. To be wounded deeply enough, in a way that our egos cannot ultimately remedy, is to be brought to a new level of consciousness, a new level of being-ness in which we are called back to our true home. This is more than hope; this is the promise of life itself, the promise of evolution.

I am not saying that we must intentionally suffer in order to grow. Life is filled with the possibility of delight, but it is not our joy and genuine inner peace that limits us; it is our capacity to meet suffering. The truth is that most of us will not look beyond our old consciousness until, for whatever reasons or under whatever circumstances, it categorically fails us, and we are, indeed, suffering. If we will but open our eyes and our hearts, we discover that we have been brought face-on to a deeper mystery. To imagine that we can sidestep suffering and follow a path of peace is a ploy of our egos that keeps us from taking an honest look at how we are feeling, a fresh look at what is actually taking place in our lives, at all the change, all the upheaval and even the cruelty, all the uncertainty that hints at a deeper process that we must learn to trust and to make room for in our lives. It may not feel to each of us, in the darkness of our own personal struggle, that this is an evolutionary shift, but it can be if we consecrate ourselves to it. The difference between being an angry or unhappy victim, or an awakening disciple, is all the difference in the world. As we each, one by one, begin to take responsibility for allowing the grace of the evolutionary process to occur, we discover the real potential for inner peace, and the real power to act as midwives to an emerging new possibility for life on Earth.`

One of the most fundamental truths of this mystery is that we are all interconnected. As each of us takes a step closer to the new consciousness, similar steps becomes easier for everyone else. Jesus, Buddha, Walt Whitman, Mother Mary, Mary Magdalene, Simone Weil, and many others have pioneered the way; now it is our turn. We are each being called to a new level of consciousness, The Second Miracle. Regardless of whether we ever have any great spiritual breakthroughs, just knowing that we are responding to this call imbues our lives with rich meaning and an authentic sense of joy. We have embarked on a journey of incredible aliveness, a journey of community-building and hope. Here, indeed, is the possibility of a life well-lived, in which we each are the vessel for an evolving consciousness that uplifts the whole web of being for everyone and everything.

# CHAPTER 2

# THE FIRST
# MIRACLE

*Human beings are that aspect of Nature
becoming conscious of Itself.*
—Thomas Berry

Everywhere we look humanity swarms over the earth observing, inquiring, discovering, mimicking, learning. Once we admired birds soaring on updrafts and dreamt of flight. Now people hang glide and great airships cross the continents. We watched seals and dolphins riding waves. Now exhilarated surfers do the same and hydrofoils speed from seaport to seaport. Imagine the more than ten billion human eyes everywhere gathering impressions. Think of the ten billion human hands touching, probing, digging, uncovering, grasping, wielding an almost limitless array of devices formulated to interact with our world or to give expression to our inner world. But the eye and ear and hand and nose were not enough. We peer through microscopes and telescopes; radar and sonar extend our senses, increasing the range of our perception beyond anything imaginable even a few generations ago. We are everywhere: drilling miles down into the Earth's body, ascending its highest mountains, following ever more challenging routes. We have traveled to the moon, split the atom, sent probes to nearly all the planets of our solar system, and are deciphering and mapping the genetic code. Anything that we can perceive we are interacting with. And the cumulative activity and information goes beyond the capacity for any of us individually to begin to comprehend.

Why is it so hard to stand outside of all this activity and not see the obvious? You and I, all of us together, now and in the past and doubtless for as long as we continue to exist, are, as Thomas Berry writes, "that aspect of Nature becoming conscious of itself."[1] The notion of Nature becoming conscious—I savor it. How simple, how eloquent. And what a profound shift of perspective, compared to all those years in school being told that the human race is special because, unlike almost all other creatures, we are self-aware. Instead of seeing ourselves as the product of Nature, we are taught to think that we are above her. I know that I came away from my education being told that I, as a human being, was a member of the dominant species, a special case. And while it was not said directly, the implication of the science, history, and religion we were taught was that planet Earth was ours to use for our own ends.

Is this why I felt so miserable, so isolated?

We are infatuated, hypnotized by the uniqueness of our consciousness. We think of ourselves, both individually and as a species, as an end in itself. Yet clearly, we are but one of millions of species. Are we really the dominant species? Aren't we, as the others, more truly servants of the great impulse of life? We are life's eyes and ears. We are that part of God thinking about the creation, seeing it, touching it, tasting it, revealing it, naming it, explaining it, transforming it. It is an extraordinary privilege, but it bears, also, significant sacrifice and great responsibility.

Jesus said, "The foxes have their holes, and the birds have their nest, but the Son of Man has no place to lay his head and to rest" (Logia 86). This speaks directly to our nature. Unlike other creatures that remain relatively unself-conscious and which act primarily through instinct, we human beings are much more complex. The Garden of Eden story is an allegory about the development of a special new consciousness evolving in the creature

15

Homo sapiens and in our early predecessors. It tells about the essential nature of this new consciousness: our ability to stand outside ourselves and be self-aware. It shows how, as we became self-aware, we developed an ego, a separate sense of self. Through our egos we began to perceive ourselves as autonomous. For the first time we could observe our own behavior, we could recognize our own nakedness, our own physicality. Gradually we could feel pride and shame. The Garden myth is the story of The First Miracle, the story of the birth of ego and its servant intellect, of the amazing capacity to evaluate, name, categorize, and judge. With this birth came our ability to symbolize, to give names to objects, to develop complex language and speak to each other. With the miracle of personal autonomy, some things become good and others evil, depending on their impact upon us or upon our own subjective requirements. In this movement into subjectivity we are changed forever. We become in a limited sense like God, responding and creating out of ourselves, no longer unconsciously following the dictates of Nature, no longer unconsciously obedient to the larger coherence or intelligence of the universe. Never again will we be satisfied with a den, a nest, or a cave. We have been chosen for another destiny: consciousness.

And there can be no rest. No sooner have we defined ourselves, the boundaries of our world, our politics, our science, before our intellect springboards off of the new revelation. This kind of intelligence is forever inventive, compulsively inventive. We will see anew, we will redefine. No matter what it is we think we have grasped about ourselves, we will be forever surprised. There will be "no place to rest our head," in our thinking. This means that we have no final identity. We are forever evolving in our perception of ourselves and everything else. In this sense we are, indeed, "created in the image of God."

This is our blessing, our destiny, our service to Life. It is also our cross. We pay dearly for the privilege of self-awareness, this level of consciousness I call the First Miracle. As the Eden story so clearly depicts, the price for our specialness is to become exiled from the kingdom of nature. Other creatures belong; we observe.

In fact, it is impossible to become conscious of something without, at first, being separate from it. Think for a moment of the wind. If you are moving at the speed of the wind you cannot feel it. To become conscious of the wind you must resist it, push against it. This is what the ego is: the "I" that pushes against the All. It is a closing down of unobstructed intimacy with Existence so that, paradoxically, we can begin to become conscious of Existence. Ego is born out of contrast; it requires being separate; it requires interaction. It gives birth to self-will and the first discernment, yes or no. And, it can be threatened.

Separation becomes our essence and with it comes suffering and all we do to avoid it. To be an organism that can taste and smell, that can feel pleasure and delight is also to be able to experience pain. But pain is not suffering. Suffering is a level of pain in which the integrity of our ego feels threatened; we are divided from the usual sense of our own being. In fact, we can say that until we became self-aware there may have been pain, but only minimal suffering. We obeyed the law of the jungle: We lived and died like any other creature. Our emotions were rudimentary and reflexively oriented around survival and procreation.

But consciousness is like a question being placed to each of us moment by moment: How much reality can you bear? When the amount of stimulation entering our self-awareness is greater than we can organize into the familiar feeling of ourselves, it has exceeded what we can bear. This is suffering. This is the great sacrifice and wound of self-consciousness: Our capacity for subjective self-awareness, for a personal identity, brings with it vulnerability to suffering. We can feel fundamentally threatened by nature's unpredictability, overwhelmed by loss, agonized by shame, driven to despair by life's real or apparent cruelty. Every step upward on the ladder of consciousness implies a greater capacity to suffer. It also provides the means, through our growing intelligence, of attempting to avoid it. Because suffering is intolerable to the subjective ego, it is, rightfully, to be feared.

Without our actually realizing it, almost all the activity of intellect is marshalled to support the ego or defend it against suffering.

The dilemma of First Miracle consciousness is that the more we attempt through intellect to protect ourselves from suffering, or even from the sense of lack, the more we create an identity and a way of life that can be threatened in new and unforeseen ways. Eventually what we do to protect ourselves from one level of suffering leads us, once again, to suffering. Often the problem has now become even more complex, more insidious. The threat to our environment is precisely this. The escalating effect of our collective effort to protect our egos threatens to cause us to devour our own world. It is a form of blindness that grows fundamentally from our sense of separation, our sense of exile from nature and from ourselves.

In becoming conscious we enter a cycle in which suffering defines the limits of our self-awareness. It is our capacity to suffer that defines how much reality we can bear. It defines, as well, our capacity for our relationship or immediacy with God or Vastness, and the limits to what we will face in ourselves and be open to with each other. We are Nature becoming conscious of Itself, but we are also Nature awakening to feeling. We are therefore Nature's suffering as well. This insight holds the key to one of the most perplexing notions at the heart of Christian mythology, the story that God brutally sacrificed his own son, Jesus, supposedly to redeem the sins of mankind. This makes absolutely no sense if God, as Jesus and many religions have claimed, is a loving Being. How can a supposedly loving God be so horrible?

But if we see this allegory from the perspective of the evolution of consciousness, it suggests a profound new understanding of the relationship of mankind to Mystery, and especially as we are called to Mystery in our suffering. God, or in the manifest form on Earth—Nature—is not cruel; it is that there is no way that Nature (or God) can become conscious of Itself without creating an instrument for that consciousness. You and me (or more accurately our egos), are that instrument, but in developing an identity, we also automatically become vulnerable to suffering. The difference between Jesus and the average person is that Jesus had realized a new level of consciousness, The Second Miracle, in which the relationship to suffering became conscious in a new way. He understood self-awareness as the cross we each must carry as servants of an awakening universe.

In the less conscious person, suffering is perceived as coming from outside, threatening the ego, and is reflexively defended against in every way possible. This defense against suffering, or more accurately against the expansion of consciousness that can embrace suffering in a new way, is also, unknowingly, a defense against the very movement of evolution. This defense, which can be metaphorically spoken of as disobedience, is the "sin" of humanity at the level of our First Miracle selves. Jesus represents the Second Miracle, the understanding of the inherent vulnerability of First Miracle consciousness *and* the capacity to engage a new relationship to Existence in which this suffering is no longer resisted as before and we become conscious servants of the evolutionary process.

We might well be tempted to say, the hell with it. Who wants a conciousness in which suffering is inevitable? Yet, the paradox is that the evolutionary step into the First Miracle that gives rise to ego, intellect, and suffering, also opens us up to the greatest bounty of life, our ability to learn, to grow, and most especially, to experience love. Paradoxically, as we are able to accept our relationship to suffering we grow in our capacity for love.

The first step toward love as a conscious experience requires the development of the ego, with the simultaneous splitting of *self* from *other*. A baby does not say "Mama" until he has also become aware of a sense of his own self-existence. As the baby further develops, this awareness becomes more layered, more complex. Now he can begin to discern and judge, cherish or despise, act for or against. With the capacity to perceive the separation of self from other, the potential for cruelty, deceit, greed, generosity, honor, compassion and, ultimately, love comes into existence. In fact, the potential for every quality of relatedness and behavior, high or low, all are born together. The argument over genetic imprinting versus upbringing and social conditioning as the cause for the enormous spectrum of human behavior is important, but it is

19

secondary to this fundamental phenomenon: All our behavior, from saintliness to genocide, becomes possible the moment there is the split between self and other, the split between the subject "I" and the objects: you, them, it. This is the first great epochal moment in human evolution, The First Miracle. Without this kind of subject-object consciousness only instinctual relationship is possible and while we do not really suffer in the instinctual state, neither are we free to really learn to love.

This then, suggests a very different interpretation of Original Sin. The root of the word sin derives from Old English and means "a dangerous illness or disease."[2] For creatures imbedded in nature, responding mostly by instinct, there can be no sin. Their existence is not a disease to them or to any other creature. Their existence just is, and all their interactions within their environment remain relatively unchanging, regulated, and balanced by Nature's inherent homeostasis, millennia after millennia. But once there is the split between subject and object, ego emerges and begins to mediate our perception both of ourselves and of our world. We lose our innocent state of belonging, of unconscious absorbtion in existence. Now nothing can remain the same. Indeed, this is "a dangerous illness," because intellect, as the servant of the ego's fear, can interfere with everything without first recognizing the underlying connectedness. Intellect perceives and creates through mental abstractions that, by their very nature, are not integrated. Yet, the implication of wrongness that accompanies the common meaning of sin is false. We are not inherently malevolent or beneficent; rather, we are becoming conscious.

In a certain sense we can say that in order for our egos to become fully conscious we must relearn or recapitulate all the work that it took for the universe to evolve the infinite complexity of relationships and energy that comprise its wholeness. For example, violence as instinct is innocent, a necessity of survival. Violence in a developing ego can be exaggerated to evil or repressed to impotency and sickliness. In order to become conscious of the nature of violence, some of us inevitably have to perpetrate both extremes, thereby creating contrast so that all of us can observe the consequences. The caring of a mother bear for her cubs is limited by instinct; you could not really call it moral. But the moral caring of one human being for another reflects our growing awareness of our inherent relatedness; we can be nurturing or abusive, sensitive or indifferent, according to whether we perceive connectedness or not. The building of a nest by a bird is instinctual and integrated with the environment. The conscious fabrication of a home by human beings is a complex response to individual fears, aesthetics, values, needs, plus social conditioning, environmental characteristics, economics, and on and on. But the consequences of billions of such homes is potentially disastrous precisely because the intellect, at least in its early evolutionary expression, is the disciple of our separated egos. It will not submit to being the servant to life in the larger sense, until it truly recognizes that to do so is the only viable path. This is exactly why the birth of intellect out of subject-object consciousness is, initially, a truly dangerous disease.

But is our compulsive inventiveness and our reflexive avoidance of suffering really a sin? At the level of First Miracle consciousness, we cannot become conscious of something without contrast, which inevitably means somehow manipulating everything we perceive, interfering with it even if we don't mean to. Even our own survival is not exempt. We are only now beginning to understand that we are part of a vast interdependent ecosystem precisely because we are disrupting it so severely. And here we see the crux of the problem—there is an unconsciousness in our consciousness. This is the crisis of our time. Human consciousness is all pervasive, and intrudes into every aspect of the natural order. Knowledge is growing exponentially. We are more conscious today of our universe than ever, yet for the first time the collective impact of our way of life threatens the existence of millions of creatures, ourselves included. If there is one single most important thing that we must do, it is this—we must become more conscious of the nature of our own consciousness.

Perhaps the first step we must take is to accept forgiveness. We can do evil, but we are not evil. We did not choose this unique consciousness, Nature did. For all we know it is an aberration, a mutation that was never meant to be and that will not survive. I don't believe this, but whether or not it is the case, it was not our

21

doing. It is Nature itself over billions of years that has generated the potential of our unique kind of consciousness. We are but the expression of this potential and its servant. In the reception of this burden we are faultless; Original Sin is no sin at all. We are caught in an extraordinary dilemma. We are a creature that in becoming conscious of itself can become the eyes and ears of Nature, the feeling heart of God. Yet in the very miracle of attaining this consciousness we become separated from the infinite subtlety of interconnected wholeness that is the Universe. Now, to protect our own integrity of consciousness we begin, both consciously and unconsciously, to violate that wholeness. At the level of the First Miracle, the prime concern is that our egos must not be overwhelmed or dissolved back into unconsciousness. It is our sacred duty to resist suffering or any force, even God or wholeness, if merging into this state compromises our capacity for separate self-awareness. But evolution demands that we enter the darkness, enter the place where we are torn from our consciousness. We must make the darkness light. Should it surprise us then that eventually some human beings would be called upon to renounce suffering, that is, to give a new name to suffering. To renounce suffering is not to repress or deny it, but to become conscious of ourselves within it. This is an entirely new level of consciousness, an entirely new recognition of our own nature and the nature of the Infinite. It does not necessarily have to be suffering either that is renounced; Buddha renounced Nirvana, the all-devouring bliss that, if entered completely, dissolves all self-awareness. Jesus renounced suffering by consciously meeting it in a new way. In this sense Nature, or God, did give Her son, Jesus, to be crucified. But this was not an act of cruelty; it was the evolutionary expansion in our capacity for consciousness. Now, for the first time our egos begin to descend into the dark. No longer must we be threatened in the old way. No longer must our intellect be the servant of fear.

22

Evolution moves at its own pace. While it is time we take a ruthlessly honest look into our own hearts and acknowledge that as conscious creatures there is much that we have done and are doing that deserves criticism, we should remember that we are but children. The first ancestors of Homo sapiens began to emerge perhaps four million years ago. We began to use rudimentary tools only a million or so years ago. The foreshadowings of The First Miracle are hard to guess, but the earliest cave art dates from about forty to fifty thousand years ago. The first written languages, along with the domestication of plants, is barely ten thousand years old. Psychologist Julian Jaynes argues that introspection is merely three thousand years old. Clearly, the Second Miracle is only now in the last few thousand years beginning to emerge in the human drama. We are hardly out of kindergarten as far as consciousness is concerned. For all we know, given our youth, we are unfolding this gift as well or better than any creature endowed with self-awareness in the universe.

Jesus said: "Blessed is the lion which the man eats and the lion will become man; and cursed is the man whom the lion eats and the lion will become man" (Logia 7). We must no longer allow ourselves to be devoured by our egos. The ego is a gift of evolution that allows us to enter conscious relationship with our world, to learn, to acquire knowledge. But when we are eaten by it everything becomes an object, an abstraction, including ourselves. We lose our sense of wholeness as an organism. We lose our sensual participation with our bodies, our deep sense of connection to each other and with our world. We become rational instead of re-lational. We become manipulative and controlling, obsessed with power, and ruled by fear. Then our wonderful intelligence is employed to dominate rather than to worship this magnificent world. In this way we are cursed.

It is time, therefore, that we begin to cherish and respect our terrible inheritance. This, to me, is the larger meaning of the cross: Not that one special man suffered and died, but that each of us can, and must, receive in ourselves the wound of consciousness, and then purposefully assume the responsibility of consciousness.

23

1. Berry, Thomas, *The Dream of the Earth,* Sierra Club Books, 1988.

2. Partridge, Eric, *Origins,* Macmillan, 1977.

# CHAPTER 3

# TO BE AS LITTLE CHILDREN

Many years ago, before I had much experience with children, I was entrusted with the care of a little boy for a few hours. Little did I know how momentous this encounter would be for me. I have told this story in my book *The I that Is We,* but I am repeating it here because it helps to illustrate subsequent insights. I was sitting with him in my bedroom. He was about a year old and was crawling awkwardly over my bed, which was Japanese style and close to the floor. I could sense his tentativeness toward me; I was unfamiliar. Where was his mother? I, too, felt awkward and uncertain of how to be with him.

In my discomfort, I decided to do something good. At that point in my life, I had learned that if I let the focus of my attention become soft and opened my heart, I could, at least with adults, create an environment of trust. I decided to project love to the baby.

Instantly, the screams were deafening. Not just blubbering discomfort but full fledged howls. LOUD. I was sure his mother would come crashing through the door any second ready to rescue him. I was embarrassed and confused. How could my love have triggered this reaction? Of course, I tried to undo it. Self-consciously, I shut down the energy field I had momentarily projected toward the baby.

Louder screams.

I was mortified and humiliated. I realized I hadn't the slightest idea how to be naturally open and loving with a child.

Even as these reflections flashed across my mind, the shock pushed me back to receptivity; I fell into the genuine state of openness that I call the virgin moment. The baby was wailing, but in the midst of that he noticed his own hand wave in front of his eyes. As his eyes followed the fleeting movement, his expression changed and his cries ceased. All at once I understood.

I lifted my arm and let my hand pass in front of my open gaze. As the hand entered my field of vision, rather than think, "Now my hand is in front of my face," I just experienced: Hand not there…hand there. Simple perception without self-consciousness. A different universe. My sense of reality shifted. Precisely at that moment, the baby giggled.

The feedback of that giggle was a cosmic Yes! I joined the baby on the floor, bringing my eyes to its height to more readily experience what he was experiencing. For the rest of that time we crawled around on the floor, pushing at dust balls, twanging the spring doorstop…being. He giggled from time to time, but he didn't cry again. And me? I was completely at peace.

I realized what had happened. Letting myself see as the baby saw, my hand was no longer an object outside that I observed. For a moment the spatial changes, the alteration in depth of field, the newness of the panorama was simply perceived without the distance of the observing ego. I understood that feeling awkward with the baby had intensified my self-consciousness. I had become an object of my own awareness, split-off from myself, "a house divided." In this state, the baby was, of course, perceived as other. The intention to send good energy to him, to do something, rather than just being with him in my awkwardness, was not well-meaning at all. While I thought I was acting consciously, the underlying

25

reason for my action was an unconscious reflex of self-protection perpetrated by my separated ego. I had gone into my head and lost contact with my authentic self because my ego felt threatened. The baby's immediate howl was a cosmic No! When I stop to think of all the times I have done this in my life, and all the times all of us do this, it seems miraculous that we have survived each other this long. Clearly one fundamental step we each must take is to recognize this basic self-contraction and refuse to let it control us. This is the work of opening our hearts. And while it makes us quite vulnerable, I am reminded of a quote from the *Course in Miracles,* "Nothing real can be threatened."

The secret of the radiant innocence and openness of young children, and also the reason they must be cared for for so long by adults, is the prolonged period in which their attention remains undifferentiated. A young child's reality is sensual, emotional, feeling, intuitive, and cognitive all at once. And I would add metabolic, hormonal, and physiologic as well; there is little or no compartmentalization of self-experience, physically, or psychically. The little child feels and knows with his whole organism; mind and body, thinking and feeling, inner and outer are not split. Happiness is gurgling, with big eyes, wide smile, and squirming arms and legs. Unhappiness is a total reverberating howl, with gagging, sweating, and agitation. Most important for our consideration, in very young children the division between subject and object, that is, between self and other that is the hallmark of the adult ego, has not yet differentiated. For a little child there is no separate "I," there is no separate other. This is why Jesus says, "Save as ye be as little children, you shall not enter the Kingdom." The Kingdom, as we shall discuss later, is a state of consciousness very similar to the openness of a little child.

It is from this basically undifferentiated Ground of Being, that the ego (the sense of "I") begins to evolve.[1] The Ground of Being is a hypothetical condition of infinite aliveness, a dynamic state where, from the energetic and psychical point of view, everything is potential, nothing has come into form. The emergence of the ego is an incredible mystery of nature. How is it that from a pool of total potentiality a personal self-reflective pattern can take shape? The First Miracle is, from this perspective, a process of limiting or closing down to a dimension of infinite aliveness and being. It is not repression in a negative sense, but the means by which a personal point of view comes into existence. Of course once we have this point of view we do begin to repress any input that threatens us or which we simply don't know how to integrate. This is where so many problems start. But the initial creation of an ego with a separate point of view is truly a miracle, and while developmental psychologists are gradually describing the stages of this process, the cause remains completely unknown.

The Ground of Being is a state antithetical to a limited and personal ego; therefore it is a state impossible for the ego to know directly. But later in life, whenever we access unusually high levels of energy and the world feels whole and connected, we can say that once again we have dipped into the Ground. The most common experience of this is when we "fall in love," but here we are opening to an impersonal source for very personal reasons. It is also possible, though much rarer, to re-experience the Ground through the dissolution of the personal ego, or more correctly the disillusionment of the illusion of a separate I. This is mystical realization, or the process usually referred to as enlightenment. I prefer to discuss this in its broader evolutionary sense as the Second Miracle.

The little child I was with was at an early stage of ego development, still partially available to the Ground, yet sufficiently differentiated to have a sense of space and be fascinated with the various objects around him. He had sufficient body-ego to have learned to isolate the location and sensations of his own arms and legs, and coordinate their motion for crawling. Yet his mental ego was still insufficiently formed to allow him to remember this episode. His somatic memory might well extend back nearly to conception and be remembered later through dream impressions, visions, or unexplainable feelings, but he did not yet have the capacity to consciously remember our time together. Also, my visitor was still sufficiently open so that my shift of attention was an undefendable disruption of his fledgling personal reality. He taught

27

me that at his level of consciousness, a level we all continue to share but are rarely aware of, we are all telepaths and empaths, we are all energetically interpenetrating with each other.

But this would not be the case for long. The ego coalesces quickly, the basic structure is in place within the first two years. By two years the little boy's telepathy and empathy, his easeful, uninterrupted bath in the Ground of Being would start to diminish. By nine or ten years of age it would be all but gone. It is the most natural thing to make this journey from undifferentiated consciousness to personal self-awareness, yet these first years in which the ego coalesces are perhaps the most crucial in the whole of our lives. This development is so fundamental to the essence of what it means to be human that subject-object awareness evolves whether our parents are nurturing and loving or neglecting and abusive. However, the consequences of how we are parented in these early years are tremendous, especially in the eventual capacity for intimacy and relationship, the true basis for all society.

I knew my visitor's mother only slightly but she seemed like a loving and caring parent. I could imagine this little one in her arms, being nursed, stroked, talked to, and cooed to. Her smell, her movements, her sounds, her constant contact, attention, and responsiveness to him was safely reinforcing and giving structure to whatever innate impulse drives the development of self-awareness. Through her and in relationship to his surroundings he was gradually discriminating his body boundary and his comfort with his own body. More and more, there would be an inner world and an outer one. I could imagine him day after day with his mother as she reinforced each object she touched or pointed to with the word that would come to symbolize it for him.

Gradually, as this young one reached the capacity to name his first word, he would have also become increasingly aware of himself as separate from what he was naming, separate from mother, which is usually one of the first words spoken by a child. With this breakthrough, his vocabulary of named external objects would now grow exponentially. Simultaneously, his repertoire of inner psychical objects, that is, feelings, impulses, ideas, and attitudes,

28

would also grow to make up his personal identity. Now, finally, he would truly be born as a human being, a self-aware creature capable of symbolic thinking, of speech and writing, of making judgments, and labeling some things as good and others as bad. No longer embedded in the Ground, he would be cast out of the Garden of Eden. He will have achieved the First Miracle.

It is one of the truly extraordinary accomplishments of nature. Over millions, perhaps billions of years, comes the emergence of this wondrous phenomenon. Yet each human being recapitulates this incredible journey in a few short years. It is so fundamental to us that we do not see it for the miracle it is. In our blindness we ignorantly, and often arrogantly, take it for granted and fail to appropriately respect this essential process.

All young children are, from an energetic point of view, open systems that respond to everything around them as if it was themselves. They literally absorb the physical and psychological environment provided by their parents, or by relatives or childcare centers, and are highly vulnerable to the emotions and unconscious patterns lived out around them. Fortunately the unfolding of the First Miracle is a very resilient process capable of adapting to most circumstances. When the environment is a loving one, where there is a great deal of continuous positive contact, the probability of healthy ego development is relatively well assured. Some problems are inevitable; even in the best of circumstances, we are all just learning. No parents are fully enlightened. Children will unconsciously absorb their parents' fears and biases and later in life will, one hopes, learn to become conscious of these conditioned attitudes and find ways to release them. This is normal; it is the work we all have to do.

However, despite the natural resiliency of the First Miracle, when the ego is differentiating in an environment of neglect and abuse, the child's developing consciousness can be profoundly compromised, especially in its feeling and emotional expression. Basic intellectual functioning is more hardy than our feeling nature. When a young child lies abandoned, crying alone, or is mistreated, its whole world seems at best indifferent and unresponding, at

29

worst malevolent. How can it build trust? Without trust at the child's core, how can he or she later learn to build mature intimacy? Such a child grows up with an unmeasurable feeling of emptiness and betrayal, a sense that the foundation of the world is uncaring and even dangerous. All of us have this feeling to some degree because our egos exile us from a deeper connection to life. But this loss is lessened when we are raised in a loving and nurturing environment because at the deepest level of bodily memory we feel well and safe. When at this same fundamental level the imprint is one of terrible aloneness and dread there is an enormous wound to overcome.

Paradoxically, for some whose basic egos are strong enough, this will be the wound that leads them beyond the First Miracle to an intuition of a deeper reality. But tragically, for a significant number, the fragility of their compromised ego structure will mean that their true potential may never be realized. Having little experience of safe emotional merging with another, or securely resting in the Ground, as soon as the defended self relaxes and begins to sink toward a larger, more undifferentiated beingness, the person encounters the ancient terror, the somatic memory of abandonment. In this condition the probability of developmental aberration can significantly increase. Perhaps this in part explains the growing violence in our society and why today the incidence of suicide and homicide in children, even children under eight years of age, is becoming so prevalent.

Parenting is the first and premier spiritual path. The second is the basic education we provide for our children. Whatever blessing we may receive from spiritual teachers or masters as we travel through life, the foundation we received through our parents and early education, and the foundation we can foster in our children will always remain the fundamental experience upon which everything else depends. In fact, the vast majority of spiritual and psychological work in our time is to first remedy the deep sense of abandonment that begins in us because humanity has not truly understood and revered the spiritual essence of parenting.

An enlightened society will welcome the crucial obligation

of nurturing and caring for its children so that the psychical and physical conditions for their development totally support their greatest capacity for mind and heart. When Jesus sees the baby suckling and says, "Save as ye be as little children, you shall not enter the Kingdom," the attention immediately goes to the infant and the uniqueness of its unobstructed openness. However, equally important in the image is the mother who, in her absorbtion in suckling her child, can also enter the Ground with her child.

In the larger equation of children, parents, and society as a whole we must support and recognize what is prior to the ego's exile and the immense value and power this place has for our future. This is what it means when Jesus says that "what you have done to the least of these you do to me" (Matthew 25:40). When we compromise the psycho-spiritual integrity of our children, we set up difficult barriers to their ability to realize the Christ Consciousness in themselves, not to mention realizing rich and generous humanity. The consciousness of the mother and parents that meets the child at conception, in utero, during labor, at birth, and in the first five to ten years of life largely determines the degree to which the child evolves out of the undifferentiated Ground fully empowered in his intelligence and deeply safe and nurtured in his body and feeling.

These well-nurtured children have a natural sense of compassion and empathy that emerges very early in their lives. They feel safe in a way that is prior to their egos, securely embedded in their most fundamental sense of being. They are much less afraid of their feelings, much less threatened when their egos are stressed. Their trust in life rests more fundamentally in themselves, in a cellular feeling that is prior to the various outer identities we each acquire in the course of living. They will not know this right away, but as they grow up it will be there to underlie their whole relationship with life. These children will inherently serve the higher possibility because their feeling nature resonates with a more natural intelligence. They intuit the next step of evolution more directly and, I have no doubt, can become vessels for the Second Miracle consciousness far less traumatically than someone

31

who does not have this primal sense of belonging and well-being. Supporting this potentiality in our children is not only essential to their future, it is perhaps the richest experience life offers us as living creatures.

In contrast to the above scenario, if the matrix in which the First Miracle is laid down is one of neglect and abuse, we increase the probability of sociopathic and psychopathic behavior. It is a heartbreaking burden that we cannot afford as a society. To a certain degree this has been true throughout human history, but today such compromised individuals end up more isolated, with less support from the general community and with access to much more dangerous weapons. Some even reach high office in government, business, and religious orders, where their inner woundedness leaves them with the power of their intellect, and even the power of charisma, but without the deeper feeling and intuition to use it wisely. As a society we are now reacting to the consequences of our own irresponsibility, using short-term remedies like prisons and an ever-increasing police force, instead of accepting the primary obligation to raise children who feel truly welcome. If we do not prepare the soil for the First Miracle as consciously and conscientiously as we can, then the dawning of the vast, archetypal energies of the Second Miracle are just as likely to amplify our sense of disconnectedness and madness as they are to bring us home to ourselves and each other in love. Our egos create a false sense of our sovereignty, but in reality we are merely servants. As long as we refuse to accept the fundamental obligation to nurture the seeds of consciousness, exceptional suffering, violence, and fear will continue to be our teachers.

The task may seem daunting, but it begins with each of us. There is something deeply liberating in recognizing that we are not free to do as we please, that there is a deeper intelligence to life to which we must become obedient. Obedience is sometimes a dirty word to our egos, but never to our souls. To be obedient implies that we have become conscious of the natural forces in which we are created, and because there is no other heartfull choice once we are conscious, we live as willing servants of these forces. Moreover, we are not being punished; we are never threatened by an angry God. It is the very righteousness of God (a more contemporary expression would be "the very wholeness of Existence") that increases our suffering when we are, as yet, unable to recognize the path we must walk. Nothing unnatural ever happens in this universe. Ignore the requirements of First Miracle consciousness and we naturally increase the probability of pyschic disturbances of all kinds. Nurture ourselves with intelligence and heart and we naturally increase the probability for genius, love, and a growing community of spirit. The work is clear: With a glad heart and true willingness, we must continue to grow in consciousness.

1. Ground of Being is a term I borrow from Michael Washburn. See *The Ego and the Dynamic Ground,* SUNY Press, 1988.

# CHAPTER 4

# COMING TO OUR SENSES

*The First Miracle and Something More*

I use the expression First Miracle precisely because it invites us to pause and reconsider something that generally we take completely for granted. For example, you take for granted that you are reading right now, or that if your eyes look up from this page, your awareness will immediately catalogue the various things that you see or hear or smell. In the instant that you perceive anything, you have already named it and, in another sense, it has named you. This capacity to be aware of something doesn't only make that something real to us, it makes a particular "us" real to ourselves simultaneously.

Is a very young child real to him or herself? Does it understand its own existence in the way you and I do? Obviously not. And that is why parents are necessary to act as a bridge between the pre-personal undifferentiated state of the infant and its ultimate destiny to become a self-reflective person. Human beings, unlike most or perhaps all other creatures, are born unable to do even the most simple things for themselves. A baby zebra will stand up within minutes of birth and be able to run with the herd shortly afterward if necessary. A baby whale is born with the capacity to swim. But in a human being, it is not until consciousness is sufficiently differentiated so that the sense of I becomes distinct from the Ground of Being that we can begin to function as true individuals. This developmental process is one of nature's most magnificent achievements.

But what if we didn't take this for granted? What if we lost our sight and hearing just as we were beginning to develop First Miracle consciousness, so that we couldn't identify external objects the way our parents do, couldn't hear their words, couldn't see their mouths form the words, couldn't associate a visual image to anything? What if we couldn't hear a laugh or see a smile? What if the wetness flowing from our eyes had no name? And the intense feelings inside of us had no way to be objectified so that we couldn't know that our anger was anger or that the intense ache within us was sorrow? How could we communicate with others? How could we utilize the bridge of our parent's subject-object state if we did not have the sensual basis for objectifying reality as they do? How then could we achieve the First Miracle?

This is precisely the dilemma that faced a young girl named Helen Keller. When I am teaching people about the pre-egoic state of consciousness, I use the wonderful film, *The Miracle Worker*, which dramatizes the story of Helen Keller's struggle to speak and read under the remarkable tutelage of Annie Sullivan. An illness early in infancy had left Helen completely blind and deaf. This occurred at a younger age than my little visitor; Helen's consciousness was still nearly completely undifferentiated.

Now we have to try to imagine her reality. As with all infants, she was immersed in a dynamic pool of sensation that was often wondrously pleasant. But as she grew older, all she possessed in order to interact with the external world were the senses of taste, touch, and smell. These senses tend toward the pole of consciousness that conveys immediacy and connection, but such experience is highly subjective. Helen was able to sensually bond with her mother and identify things she could hold, cuddle, or smell. Without sight and hearing, the senses most important for interacting

35

with the outer world, her ability to objectify her experience in consensus with her family was very limited. As her range of activity naturally grew more active and outgoing, her parents had to deal with an inquisitive, noisy, mobile bundle of energy who understood and organized her own experience so subjectively, in ways that had very little resemblance to how the rest of human kind does things.

Thus, Helen's ability to achieve the consensus First Miracle condition was extremely compromised. By the time she was ten years old her parents had exhausted their ability to help her. In desperation they hired Annie Sullivan, a partially blind young teacher of handicapped children. The alternative was to incarcerate Helen to protect her from the world…and the world from her.

For months Annie courageously persisted, trying to teach Helen to make the connection between an object and a word that represents that object. The language Annie employed was a code of touches on Helen's palm that Annie spoke to Helen every time she gave Helen something to touch. But the leap of understanding from an object to the object-of-consciousness, the word that symbolizes it, is no easy leap, which is why I call it the First Miracle. Like any child, Helen resisted; she was painfully frustrated and angry at being controlled by a stranger without understanding the purpose of the relationship. She wanted to return to her mother, a typical response in a part of each of us when faced with the unknown. Finally, one day while water was spilling from the pump over Helen's hand and Annie was repeating the touch sequence for water over and over again, Helen got it…w a t e r ! Her first word. After that her learning was exponential. She eventually attained a university degree and became an inspiration for people all over the world.

In each of us this moment of our first word is one of the most extraordinary moments in all of existence. We have achieved a fundamental miracle of life, but it has occurred so gradually, emerging from our undifferentiated state, that we cannot remember that moment. However, once the First Miracle is intact, we are essentially exiled from the immediacy that links us to the Ground of Being. Without realizing it we are banished from the Garden. Like Adam who was initially obedient to God,—in the undifferentiated state there is no distinction between ourselves and God's law; therefore, in a manner of speaking, we are always obedient to God—the little child lives in the Kingdom. He simply doesn't know it. Therefore, exile from the Garden is not particularly traumatic; the ego just coalesces as the subject-object state becomes established. Once this occurs we have no intellectual recall of our previous undifferentiated state and our innate harmony with universal law. In effect, our subject-object consciousness rests on nothing.

This is why the ego is basically insecure; it does not know in itself the roots of its own finite existence. And being insecure the ego does the only thing it can do: It tries to make itself safe. This, in a nut shell, is the history of humanity at the level of the First Miracle. Rather than participating with life like other creatures, we are compelled by the sacred wound of First Miracle consciousness to be outsiders. The ego's innate lack of spiritual foundation dooms us to feel existentially insecure and its impulse is to try to control anything and everything that threatens us.

Helen Keller's ego-development was unconventional; therefore, she represents a unique category of being that provides us with a window to look more closely at the First Miracle. She was much older when subject-object consciousness, with the capacity for symbolization and language, took full root in her. In addition, Helen always had to rely primarily on the sense of touch to communicate with others. Thus Helen never fully lost her connection to the more body-centered awareness of the pre-egoic state. There is one story, for example, in which some years after learning to "speak," Helen went for a walk in a cemetery. Quite spontaneously, she was drawn to one of the headstones and lingered there touching it. Then abruptly she ran back to the house in which she and Annie were guests and began to go through the clothes and belongings in her room. Unbeknownst to Helen, she was staying in the room of the hostess' deceased daughter whose tombstone Helen had examined. Excitedly, she demanded to know how the person whose things were in the room could be under the ground in the cemetery? Helen had felt the connection.

This kind of sensitivity represents a heightened receptivity to subtle feeling, of a kind very similar to the sensitivity of my little visitor who could feel the shift of my inner attention. While the openness of the undifferentiated condition is common to early childhood, a similar state is clearly available to adults. This has been demonstrated over and over again by mystics and saints of every religious persuasion. But it is not reserved for them alone; it is a wondrous element of life that all of us can partake of in varying degrees. It is challenging work, but it emerges in us naturally as we begin to answer the call of consciousness to go deeper, to allow our bounded egos to open and merge into a more fundamental level of reality.

Helen became a philanthropist whose life inspired many people. She had the remarkable capacity to recognize people by touching their faces for a few seconds. Months and even years later, if she touched the same person's face again, she would recall them. This capacity for touch goes beyond anything that the average mature adult ever experiences because in our contemporary world we have come to rely on a more abstract (or at any rate, less body-centered) connection to existence dominated by the senses of sight and hearing. This, to me, is what makes Helen so exceptional. Because she could not rely on sight and hearing all of her communication and her relationships always involved her body and a very different kind a attention. She, of necessity, was listening to a space far different than what we "see" through our eyes. Her space tended to have no discrete limits. It was as much a space of feeling and deep intuition as it was a space of physical dimension. She had to carefully attend to her whole sense of being; otherwise she became totally lost.

Jacques Lusseyran, another person who became blind quite young, describes that this kind of listening gave him an inner light:

"Without my eyes light was much more stable than it had been with them. As I remember it, there was no longer the same differences between things lighted brightly, less brightly, or not at all. I saw the whole world in light, existing through it and because of it."

This light enabled him to "see," not as we see with ordinary vision, but with an inner vision that illuminated people's souls; he could feel their connection to themselves, their realness and self-honesty. This inner light also enabled him to "see" and get around in the world as long as he wasn't disturbed in his feeling nature:

> "There were times when the light faded almost to the point of disappearing. It happened every time I was afraid. If, instead of letting myself be carried along by confidence and throwing myself into things, I hesitated, calculated, thought about the wall, the half-open door, the key in the lock...then without exception I hit or wounded myself. The only easy way to move around the house, the garden, or the beach was by not thinking about it at all, or thinking as little as possible. What the loss of my eyes had not accomplished was brought about by fear. It made me blind.
>
> Anger and impatience had the same effect, throwing everything into confusion....When I was playing with my small companions, if I suddenly grew anxious to win, to be first at all costs, then all at once I could see nothing. Literally I went into fog or smoke.... I could no longer afford to be jealous or unfriendly, because as soon as I was a bandage came down over my eyes...a black hole opened, and I was helpless inside it."[1]

Lusseyran could "see" if he relaxed the mental ego and stopped thinking and if his behavior toward others no longer came from the presumption of separation. "So is it surprising," he said, "that I loved friendship and harmony when I was very young?" In essence, Helen and Jacques listened within themselves in order see beyond themselves. This kept them closer to their I-amness and

39

simultaneously closer to the Ground, a state where they innately experienced a greater sense of connection and relationship.

The paradox for the ordinary individual is that given the availability of all one's senses, there is little necessity to achieve a deeper quality of attention in developing the basic ego structure. But without this deeper attention, our egos are closed systems and our senses become weakened and unenlightened. Through the lens of subject-object consciousness, our bodies become objects-of-consciousness instead of centers for feeling and we leave them behind, or essentially ignore them, to live primarily in a world of intellectual abstraction. I feel that whatever our human potential, our reliance on thinking at the expense of a more body-and feeling-centered awareness, cripples us in ways that are difficult for us to recognize once the loss has occurred. It is far more than the loss of the kind of extended sensory awareness that Helen and Jacques demonstrated. It may also represent a fundamental loss in our capacity to intuit relatedness, where the ordinary ego perceives only separateness.

I've noticed that when adults open to, and begin to embody, deeper levels of consciousness, feelings of respect, brotherhood, and compassion are, in varying degrees, universally present. They don't have to be trained in us; we do not need to be intellectually instructed that these are better attitudes. In fact, making these fundamental feelings into concepts before we actually know them in our bodies may mean that they become ideals and abstractions that further distance us from our immediate bodily reality. What we must come to realize is that the higher capacities of consciousness and human nature arise naturally as our attention deepens and that our whole organism is part of this process.

Once we understand this, it is not difficult to begin to retrain ourselves to listen from the deeper body-centered consciousness, which will be discussed more fully later. This means fundamentally renewing our appreciation, understanding, and honoring of the senses as a door to higher consciousness. The alchemy of the senses is not new. It is central to the Eastern tradition of Tantra, which emphasizes opening the doors of perception by a deep honoring of the whole range of human sensuality. When such an exploration is consecrated in wisdom, it leads us to the core of our capacity for feeling and unobstructed perception that is innocent of our social conditioning. Despite great confusion in many religious traditions, there is a deep current in the West that is rich in this understanding, as Blake's "Auguries of Innocence" so simply says,

> "To see a World in a Grain of Sand
> And a Heaven in a Wild Flower,
> Hold Infinity in the palm of your hand
> And Eternity in an hour."

In this vision, the journey is not vertically toward our higher or Christ nature, it is simultaneously toward the primal man and woman, Adam and Eve, perfectly created by Nature—and unconditioned by society—to experience the wonder of life. To approach this experience is central in my work. For example, in one aspect of my work, I employ a series of exercises that were inspired by Helen's extraordinary gifts to experientially demonstrate that there is tremendous intelligence available to us through our most basic senses. First, I ask people to close their eyes and then explore another person's face with touch. As they do so, I remind them to relax, to intuit a child's innocent and undifferentiated awareness and to not interpret the experience, nor strive to attribute meaning to the experience. At the same time, I invite the person being touched to become really receptive, to imagine that the partner touching them has never seen a human face, that this is the only way to be physically "seen." Next, still with closed eyes, I ask them to take their time and smell their partner's scent in the areas around his hair, neck and face. I again suggest that they simply stay present and just experience without defending. They are to try to use smell as an infant smells, without expectation or judgement, without any basis for understanding their experience except the experience itself. After a few minutes the process is reversed to give the other partner an opportunity to do the touching and smelling.

The exercise of smelling a stranger might seem distasteful or

41

rude. However, I always find it remarkable to watch how people will begin quite hesitantly, and then some deeper awareness takes over. The effect of this kind of exploration is a lessening of the usual tendency of the ego to create separation. After a few minutes, a sense of palpable calm arises in the room. You can almost see people's minds slowing down. As paradoxical as it may seem, in this state of enhanced instinctual sensuality our availability to higher potentials of consciousness is also amplified and we are naturally more able to engage emotionally satisfying relationships.

Smell is one of the most archaic of the senses, directly connected to the limbic system, the so-called reptilian brain. Smell reaches into basic instinctual levels of our capacity for intimacy and relationship. Habituated to the distancing inherent in egoic consciousness, direct use of the sense of smell can be quite threatening. But if we allow ourselves to relax the self-protective reflex of thinking about what we are doing, smell invites a fundamental level of relationship. In the exercise, no one is forced to participate and the depth of the experience is highly subjective. But, the result is fascinating: People are surprised how, without conversation, with no apparent rational reason, and even if their partner's odor is not particularly pleasing, they feel inexplicably closer afterwards. It is a kind of pre-rational familiarity that rests in a quality of silence and energy rather than in objective criteria.

As I have already stated, certain senses offer themselves more readily to one kind of consciousness over another. Sight is unquestionably the sense that most undergirds the inherent subject-object separation. When I ask people to sit silently looking at each other, often there is an initial increase in nervousness, followed by restlessness. They describe that their minds begin to wander and soon dissociation sets in. With hearing, the boundary between inner and outer begins to blur. Whereas sight almost exclusively conveys a sense of something external and separate, hearing by itself, without sight, creates a continuity between the inner and the outer. This is why being absorbed in music can convey such a sense of immediacy and be so releasing. In general, it is far easier to tell what a person is feeling by listening to his voice than by only looking at him.

Once we move to touch, we enter a transitional zone. Touch conveys connection far more than either sight or hearing. We rarely make love with eyes open. To be truly savored, love-making almost requires the closing of the eyes so that we can enter the sensations most fully. Once we begin to touch there is an entirely more satisfactory, though less rational experience of relationship. This is because, far more so than sight, touch invokes and conveys a primal feeling of connectedness. And it is feeling more than anything else that conveys the meaning of any moment to us, at least in so far as we are organisms and not just intellects. Touch is fundamental to maturation, especially for the deep preconscious functions of our organism. Infants who are neglected and receive little touch are slow to develop spatial awareness, as well as slow to mature a healthy immune system. Twins in the womb have much more touch and are born more coordinated. They develop spatial awareness faster than a solo fetus. Touch is essential to the healthy development of body ego. Touch and a secure sense of belonging, literally, go hand in hand.

Finally, when we consider the senses of smell and taste, we are back in the most primordial areas of consciousness. It is not by accident that mystics refer to Nirvana and the higher states as "the land of milk and honey." This imagery symbolically recalls the early pre-egoic condition of undifferentiated participation with the Ground of Being, a state very akin to the mystical (as we will discuss in a subsequent chapter). If we try to imagine the quality of consciousness that is primarily mediated by taste, touch, and smell, we are very close to the instinctual somatic reality of the infant and our earliest condition of being at-one. This is why during religious and healing ceremonies, incense or the aroma of essential oils can be so augmenting. Fragrances can act as non-rational, sensual markers that circumvent the separating tendency of the ego. When we later re-experience the fragrance, it acts as a subconscious cue that subtly re-invokes the sacred state or the healing presence.

43

Extraordinary capacities evolve when we are deprived of one or more of our senses. I am reminded of an article I read about the contemporary virtuoso percussionist, Evelyn Glennie. Although deaf since childhood, she learned to discern high and low notes by putting her hands on the wall outside the school's music room. While her teacher sounded notes within, she noticed that some made her fingers tingle, others travelled down her wrists, others into her belly, and so on. She hears music by the subtle vibrations of tone and pitch that she feels in her body. While I am not suggesting we abandon our senses to come to our senses, it is important to recognize how little of the potential of our organism we really are using when we rely on basic First Miracle consciousness.

1. Lusseyran, Jacques, *And There Was Light,* Parabola Books, 1987.

# CHAPTER 5

# THE SECOND MIRACLE

*Becoming Referent to Infinity*

The life of Helen Keller will forever remain an inspiring story of the triumph of the human spirit over adversity. However, from a less anthropocentric and sentimental point of view, Helen was simply struggling to fulfill Nature's instinctual imperative. Through her we can more clearly see the miracle that we usually take for granted: The full emergence of human, subject-object consciousness out of the undifferentiated Ground of Being. This is not to diminish the determination and courage of Helen, her parents, and Annie, but what they sought to achieve was already predetermined by Nature.

Like a bird who must build a nest, or a fox who must dig a den, or a female black widow spider who must kill her mate after copulation, human beings must enter subject-object consciousness. We may think of instinct as an inborn tendency to behave in a particular way, such as suckling in mammals. But, in human beings the development of subject-object consciousness, which is the root of the ego and of intellect, is just as much an inborn tendency. We are no more able to refuse it than a bird can refuse to build a nest.

And if the bird fights great winds to fly back with a twig or piece of leaf and struggles to fit it into the nest, is this heroic? It is arguable that what we are compelled toward by instinct can be called heroic, no matter what the forces of adversity we overcome. I say this to try to shift the inflated tendency we human beings have to regard ourselves as special because of the extensive development of our intellects and our unique capacity to witness our own drama. We are special and we are not. We are special as all aspects of Creation are special, but we, too, are creatures. A bird builds a nest or a bear seeks a den for hibernation, each according to its capacity for consciousness. We all too often dismiss such wondrous behaviors by labeling them instinctual. Yet we pass examinations in school, build shopping malls, sky scrapers, rockets, and computers, and most of what we call human society and culture is equally obedient to a subject-object consciousness that arises in us just as instinctually.

Perhaps then, in the name of genuine integrity, we should dismiss referring to much of our modern technological and cultural achievements as especially heroic or dignifying. At what point does the exercising of human intellect to ease discomfort, or to unburden our labors become something substantially more than merely instinctual activity? I realized as a physician that I had become little more than a memorizing robot, until my unhappiness finally led me to begin to ask deeper questions about myself. The truth is, a person can become a doctor, practice medicine, develop investments, hire architects, and contractors to build *the* gorgeous home, raise a family, play golf on Wednesdays, take holidays, go to church, and never really wake up. The same can be said for being a stockbroker, a lawyer, or virtually any modern career. People can build businesses that generate great wealth by exploiting natural resources, or by exploiting our vanity and insecurities, or by creating food empires built on our weakness for sugar, fat, and salt. In doing so they can employ many people, but often the employment amounts to little more than a socially justified imprisonment. Politicians argue cleverly to reduce taxes, feeding on people's fears of not having enough for themselves, and never question what it means that libraries are closed and the quality of many school lunches are practically a death sentence for our children. All this is learned and performed from a level of intelligence that never goes beyond the subject-object sense of me versus you, mine or yours, either-or, material versus spiritual, and so on. Not that this is wrong; it simply isn't wise. Wisdom is the real demonstration of human intelligence that is more than instinctual. Take, for example, John Robbins, the founder of Earthsave Foundation. Walking away from the background of the Baskin and Robbins ice-cream fortune, he commited his life to the question: What is a diet for a healthy world? Wisdom is our recognition of wholeness and of the fundamental relationship that connects us all. If we have a claim to true intelligence and free will, it holds only if there is real insight into ourselves and wisdom in the choices we make within the manifold of the First Miracle. The choice of the First Miracle was Nature's impulse toward consciousness; it was never ours to make.

Now I am not arguing that this consciousness, because of its inherent creation of separation, is essentially bad. On the contrary, I would not have called it the First Miracle if I was not trying to emphasize that this is a holy gift of life. But our present use of intellect with all that it has and can achieve is not an end in itself. Likewise, with all the popular emphasis on personal transformation, we must remember that what we realize or achieve is never an end in itself. It is service to a deeper impulse whereby Nature is becoming conscious of Itself...forever. It is part of an uninterrupted continuum of consciousness that is calling us to a higher destiny that is forever ours to create. Thus Jesus could rightfully exhort that "Greater works than I have done, ye shall do" (John 14:12).

The very capacity of wisdom to see the relativity of the First Miracle implies a larger sphere of consciousness. As this gradually evolves in the human race it is as epochal an event as the dawning of self-awareness. It is this new emergence in its totality that I call the Second Miracle. In its essence, it is a consciousness in which the subject-object separation integrates; self and other are two sides of the same coin. It has been called Cosmic Consciousness, the Tao,

47

the Kingdom of Heaven, and many other names. The crucial thing for us to realize is that it is not so much the achievement of spiritual discipline, but the expression of the spontaneous movement of the Evolutionary Impulse. At its heart lies a far deeper and more subtle intuition of relationship between all things. Now Existence itself in the sense of the whole manifest and unmanifest universe is, metaphorically, the Mother, and God, or Consciousness in the largest sense, is the Father. What is being born is a new human being who is at once a separate self-aware individual and kindred with All. To realize this timeless awareness is to know for oneself what Jesus meant when he said: "Before Abraham was, I am" (John 8:58).

This is the second birth, the birth in spirit in mystical-religious terminology. Thus Jesus said, "My mother bore me, but my true Mother gave me the Life" (Logia 101). From the moment this consciousness began to make its appearance in the last few thousand years, in individuals such as Buddha and Jesus, its impact on human development has been prodigious. The anticipation of this evolutionary shift in the human race is the Second Coming of Christ, or the return of the Maitreya Buddha, the advent of the Messiah. It does not refer to a single individual, but rather to the emergence of a new capacity for consciousness.

The Second Miracle is a metaphor for a fundamental transformation in the root of our sense of self. At the level of the First Miracle, personal identity is always parented by something objectifiable, such as one's body, sensations, emotions, ideas, family, job, nation, religion, belief systems, and on and on. We characterize ourselves by saying: I am hungry, happy, a conservative, married, an architect, mother, American, a Christian…and so on, and we believe it. It is a self that I refer to as *referent to the finite*. Whatever it may be we consider ourselves, from our First Miracle awareness we are always a step removed from our own true experience, our I-amness. We see ourselves reflected primarily in a rational, materialist reality. It is a world of naming, of compartmentalization, and of boundary and control. This is why we can be so powerfully influenced by the commercial media that is continuously feeding us images of who we could be, how our bodies should look, what we need to own in order to fulfill our identity. To this level of our awareness, fantasies, dreams, thoughts, movie, and television images become easily confused with what is real. Over the years I was often astounded to overhear people in places like Yosemite or the Grand Canyon, saying, "Its just like in the movies." The referent for the reality of ourselves and our world has become the secondary images we receive through various media, rather than through the immediacy of our own direct experience. This is possible because First Miracle awareness is already a derivative, already a representation and not the real itself.

In the world of the First Miracle we can never really learn about ourselves directly, for to do so we must cease being observers and submit to immediacy, thereby risking intense ambiguity, paradox, and feeling. But in this level of ourselves we are never happy with ambiguity; moreover we are terrified of deep feeling. Deep feeling stands at the edge of unformed, inchoate consciousness where our finite identities are easily overwhelmed. While a First Miracle person extols the virtue of love, he or she is largely incapable of love. Everyone and everything, including oneself, is an object. The moment the object of our devotion loses its power to capture our fascination, or begins to invoke difficult feelings, it becomes undesirable or just neutral.

With the dawning of the Second Miracle, the root of identity shifts radically. "I" becomes referent to something not predicated on any objective criteria or characteristic whatsoever. Now we are *referent to infinity*. It is as though one is looking at a mirror seeing all that is reflected (the First Miracle) and, at the same time, looking *through* the mirror, intuiting an unnameable Suchness. Yet paradoxically, the intuition is not impersonal, not transcendent or forever removed as it is imagined from the First Miracle point of view. On the contrary, the whole universe is personalized. It is all (more than metaphorically) oneself, all one's flesh and blood, all immediate and alive, yet unfathomable. Mother-Father-Mystery. It is an intelligent universe, alive with feeling, and in it is born love. Words can only suggest this quality or living, felt space. It is the

49

*Holy Spirit,* the *Shekinah,* the *Beloved* of Rumi, the *I myself* of Whitman. It is the mysterious "Other," a felt presence or imbued attention that shifts the locus of perception from separation to continuity. It is the quality that inspires all living poetry. Not so much the words, but their rhythm and flow, the mysterious something suggested, but never named. Few have described the dawning of the new consciousness and what it brought better than Walt Whitman:

> I mind how once we lay such a transparent summer morning,
> How you settled your head athwart my hips and gently
>       turn'd over upon me,
> And parted the shirt from my bosom-bone, and plunged
>       your tongue to my bare-stript heart,
> And reach'd for my beard, and reach'd till you held my feet.
> Swiftly arose and spread around me the peace and
>       knowledge that pass all the argument of the earth,
> And I know that the hand of God is the promise of my own,
> And I know that the spirit of God is the brother of my own,
> And that all the men ever born are also my brothers,
>       and the women my sisters and lovers,
> And that a kelson of the creation is love,
> And limitless are the leaves stiff or drooping in the fields...

Reflected in the objective mirror of existence, who I am is nameable, referent to some action, sensation, concept. The world is local, tangible, "real." Intuiting through the mirror, identity is no longer predicated on any reflection of any kind. Who or what "I am" is no longer merely local, not ultimately isolatable or nameable, not known through any idea, except symbolically. It is more a quality of attention, a quality of listening, like a clear space felt against the background sensation of one's own body, one's breathing. This listening enlarges the aliveness and substantialness of all that we perceive without devolving into a something or a somewhat. It does not generate a sense of separate identity. Awakening into the condition of the Second Miracle, we no longer have any

50

concept by which to purchase identity—"no place to rest our heads." Yet identity, indeed, far more than identity, is there in the subjective essence of everyone and everything, from the "drooping leaves" to the celestial dance of quasars and supernovas. It is recognized precisely because ordinary First Miracle thinking has ceased to filter the larger experience of being. One has not lapsed back into unconsciousness; rather, the egoic structure of First Miracle consciousness has become the servant of a much larger sphere of being. Herein is the conscious rapprochement with the Ground of Being lost when we ate of the tree of the Knowledge of Good and Evil. We had left the Garden, only to return at last capable of recognizing, for the first time, where we have come from.

It has forever been the challenge of those who have experienced the Second Miracle to find a means of describing and perhaps conveying this new consciousness to those who are still experiencing life only through the subject-object state. When Jesus says, "These children who are being suckled are like those who enter the Kingdom," the disciples ask the inevitable question born of First Miracle consciousness: "Shall we then, being children, enter the Kingdom?" For them everything is literal; everything must have a finite referent. In the Gospel According to Thomas, Jesus' answer speaks to the fundamental shift of consciousness that is the Second Miracle. He says: "When you make the two one, and when you make the inner as the outer and the outer as the inner and the above as the below, and when you make the male and the female into a single one...then shall you enter the Kingdom" (Logia 22).

This is to me one of the clearest and most eloquent descriptions of the transcendence of the First Miracle available to the Western psyche. Making the "two one" is the experience of the collapse of the subject and the object into a single, non-dualistic awareness. Self and other become a single one. It is akin to the undifferentiated condition of the little child in whom inner reality and external reality are, relative to adult consciousness, unified as a sensual-perceptual continuum. Now however, there is a crucial difference: The little child has no sense of individual or personal

51

self-awareness, no sense of its own identity or point of view; thus, it cannot recall its experience. In Second Miracle consciousness, the matured ego provides the basis for self-awareness. Now self and the whole field of consciousness are one and the same. Mind and body are one and the same. Our highest spiritual aspirations and the activities of daily life are one and the same. It is a return to a sense of fundamental connection and belonging. It is a whole-bodied enlightenment; our organism becomes saturated in an entirely new aliveness. It is as though we listen with new eyes, new ears, new touch, with new senses entirely…and we listen to new music —the music of a living universe.

Jesus may say, "When you make the inner as the outer," but he is not saying that the subject-object self can generate or create this realization. Through thousands of years of evolution of First Miracle consciousness we can make mental philosophies, religions, X-ray lasers, political systems, virtual-reality technologies, but we cannot make the Second Miracle. Second Miracle consciousness remains forever the ultimate heresy, the reason to poison Socrates, crucify Jesus, kill Meister Eckhart, and ignore or devalue a whole dimension of emerging sensitivity that does not seem to have any apparent practical value. This consciousness is awakened in each person through a radical process of growth. It cannot be bottled or formulated. A First Miracle person has religion; a Second Miracle person is religion. A First Miracle person forever seeks a context in which to make his life sacred, inevitably violating one or another aspect of himself in the search for what is spiritual vis-à-vis what is real. A Second Miracle person cannot imagine where the sacred is not. She is the fount that inspires and evokes religiousness in her First Miracle brethren. We can even ask whether spiritual practices prepare the ground for Second Miracle realization; they can just as easily imprison a First Miracle person in a new objective structure. But I prefer to think as one Zen Master, who said, "Enlightenment is an accident; practice makes us accident-prone." In the end, the Second Miracle simply happens…through Grace…doubtless in the same way that the First Miracle happened, or that spiral galaxies were formed, or that life came to exist in the primordial aliveness of the ancient seas: through a basic imperative in the universe itself. Our human efforts cannot make it happen, but instruction from those who have entered this space helps give us a context for these new experiences when they do begin to emerge.

>——<

To become referent to infinity is an evolutionary shift in the basis for identity and for living at all levels. As metaphors, the notions of First Miracle and Second Miracle consciousness help us to see the basic shift that is taking place. But the actual process is far less categorical than these simple metaphors suggest. There is a continuum of consciousness between these two archetypal states so that there is no person who doesn't have at least the rudiments of Second Miracle consciousness within them. But the essential process that I am calling the Second Miracle is more than a single, fundamental realization or state of unitive consciousness. It is a process of fundamental relationship in which, as our intuition of the infinite deepens, our experience of self and of other is continuously transforming. Intuition, as I have been using the word, is more than having an accurate hunch or sense about something. It is the condition of awareness innate to the Second Miracle, a form of intelligence far more vast than ordinary intellect because it is an intelligence born of immediacy with the moment, an intelligence firmly rooted both in our subjective sense of being and our objective capacity for awareness.

The teaching of fundamental relationship is essentially a teaching that underlies everything. It transforms the place in which we meet ourselves, our feelings, our fears. Moreover, it transforms how we engage each other, how we listen, or, more truly, where we listen from. The implications in every aspect of life are enormous. There is a return to oneself in a way that was forever missing for the basic ego self and this allows us to risk greater realness and openness in all our relationships. Fear is no longer the god it had been; it is still a formidable force, but the Second Miracle is a dawning of true faith in a beingness that ultimately cannot be threatened. Again, because there is no conscious memory of the

53

pre-egoic undifferentiated state, in a psychological sense subject-object consciousness coalesces out of nothing or absence. Therefore, the ego born of the First Miracle is a house built on quicksand; it is forever insecure. No matter how it tries to establish a sense of self that is not threatened, that self is always fundamentally separate, always fundamentally fragile. It is dominated by fear.

Being fragile, the First Miracle ego yearns, indeed, is driven to acquire a sense of home or connection and security. This then, to us as First Miracle people, is our first fundamental project. We do not see ourselves as servants of a larger reality awakening through us. Rather, we are ends in ourselves to which all else must be subjugated, even God. The First Miracle ego tames God by the very way in which it objectifies and personalizes God. Dominated by the First Miracle, a person cannot intuit Life's mystery immediately, cannot perceive a higher order directly. His perception instead conveys a sense of his own insignificance, a need to become harmonized and obedient to attain salvation. On the one side he feels insignificant and helpless before God; he supplicates and begs, grateful for little parcels of joy, then grovels in suffering. On the other side he has no need for God. He, himself, is the royalty of creation, "owner" of planet earth; it is his destiny to utilize and control every thing and every force he encounters here. In his emotional groveling, and in his intellectual arrogance the First Miracle person attempts to come to grips with an underlying feeling of non-being.

Stop. This is you and me. This is all the good men and women we have known and all the bad. This is today, last year, a thousand years ago, and it is tomorrow. This is the story of the child we were and the children we are raising. This is the way we sadly watch their ever-creative and playful imaginations slowly give way to the concrete perceptions of adult(erated) consciousness. It is the way we grow to exercise consciousness as a means of generating control and security rather than as celebration and worship of the wonder of our existence. It is sad and it is our story...in process.

First Miracle consciousness is trapped in a circle that it cannot escape. The poignancy and desolation of this grows ever stronger within us as the intuition of the Second Miracle begins to surface closer and closer to consciousness. The paradox is that the harder we try to come home, to feel safe, to make our world secure, the more we threaten our own security. This is the wound the ego cannot heal. It can only be healed by surrender in faith, which in turn is only possible as our intuition deepens. In this process Man discovers God. But for the young First Miracle ego, the notion of the Ultimate, of God, is still but another thing, another existent somewhere out there just out of reach. This God is not yet the immediacy of Love, but rather a transitional mental object. A transitional object acts as a bridge. For example, a cuddly toy such as a teddy bear or a soft blanket, is used by a child to maintain a sense of contact with its mother in her absence. In the same fashion, First Miracle consciousness utilizes the concept of God to mediate between its necessity for some finite image and the infinite referent that is the actuality of God. In this process the real referent is lost, or temporarily forgotten. Rather than being the universal solvent in which all subject-object dualism dissolves, God becomes another object-of-consciousness. Unfortunately, in the hands of the First Miracle mentality this is no ordinary object-of-consciousness. Co-opted by the ego, defying common sense, compassion, and brotherhood, God is invoked in support of some of humankind's greatest acts of cruelty and insanity. Yet, *this* God has no existence whatsoever, save as an object-of-consciousness imagined by the First Miracle ego. We can fantasize about popcorn, too, and perhaps we should; as an object-of-consciousness, popcorn is infinitely more benign.

For the First Miracle person, God becomes another notion that provides credibility and substantiation, once again, for himself. But as subject-object awareness rests, psychologically, on nothing, so ultimately does the God it imagines. And because nothingness is threatening to the finite-bound ego, this "God" is threatening. God is to be feared, propitiated, obeyed. This is a God that is forever outside, a God that divides people one from another, that creates sects and nations. As the Second Miracle emerges, our intuition of relationship to existence becomes more direct, more

55

connected, more inside of us. Simultaneously God becomes more and more inconceivable, while at the same time the intuition of God creates an atmosphere of connectedness, love, and integration.

The inability of a First Miracle person to understand the infinite referent underlying his finite religious symbols and beliefs is epitomized in the following article reported in the *Australian Times.*

---

### Loos Face Mecca

Thirty Muslim families in Lancashire have asked their local council to turn the toilets in their houses around because they face east toward the holy city of Mecca, according to *The People* newspaper. It said they had to sit sideways so they did not offend Allah.

---

It is easy to laugh at religion taken so literally, but we should not laugh until we can see more clearly how this occurs everywhere in our own lives. For example, when we are in love, we project goodness, strength, creativity, caring, and so much more on our lover. In how many ways do we reposition our own stance in life, where we live, work, and so forth as a result? Then if we fall out of love and become estranged, suddenly our partner is withholding, mean, insecure, selfish, and so on. Now, often quite brutally and agonizingly, we shift our circumstances once again. In fact, changing the loos can be seen as a metaphor for the contortions we perpetrate upon our bodies, our feelings, our environment, because First Miracle consciousness is constantly trying to fit us to some idea or image. We rarely see ourselves or others as real people; we cannot look through the mirror to see Infinity hiding in all of us. This is why our First Miracle selves cannot deeply love; the object of this love remains forever an object, at best and at worst, the projection of aspects of ourselves. Our organisms understand love; it is as natural as two hydrogen atoms embracing an oxygen atom to become water. But with the creation of the young subject–object bound ego, the lover remains forever out of reach and communication inevitably fails until we have located the real love once again—in ourselves and everywhere. Conscious love between humankind and for our universe begins with our Second Miracle selves.

It seems obvious that once the First Miracle self had labeled enough of its world, that eventually it would begin to wonder about who is doing the labeling. Now, suddenly self-awareness turns back in contemplation of itself to discover/create the Self, the archetypal center of being. It is a place ordinary self-awareness can never encompass, but in contemplating this relationship the ego is forever transformed. I believe that, initially, this fundamental shift of attention occurred spontaneously (as it still does). But eventually, as we began to consciously attempt to return to this unique experience, we found our way into the rich dimension of meditation. Simultaneously, with this inner discovery, our outer appreciation of the world was also growing. Here again, the more conscious we became of the external world the more we recognized that there was something larger, ever beyond our perception. In objectifying this mysterious something we discovered/created the gods, and as intuition deepened, realized the One behind all these forces. In this way the notion of God came into conscious existence for us, and in seeking a relationship to this ultimate essence we discovered prayer. At the deepest place these two modes of listening, meditation and prayer, become the same thing; God is within and without.

Prayer and meditation are our First Miracle selves' greatest tools for inviting Second Miracle consciousness. Yet these tools in the hands of our First Miracle egos are just as likely to limit us, and our God, as to connect us to a deeper reality. It is the catch-22 of the First Miracle self. He meditates and prays to become peaceful, to "see" the way through life's challenges. He uses meditation and prayer like a pill for unhappiness, a method for peace of mind—in short, as a way to protect himself. He may get more peaceful and more healthy as some studies of meditators reveal. But when meditation or prayer is just a balm for anxious, frantic minds, people tend to become flattened in their feeling nature, less original and less vital. Because we are protecting ourselves, we simultaneously become protective of our God, (or our meditation community). They become a source of specialness and exclusion rather than the very basis for integration and communion with everyone else. People who meditate and pray in this way enter a circle in which perturbance and discomfort is to be avoided, and prayer and meditation become a path of insulation, somewhat like keeping oneself in a prolonged energetic womb, fearful of coming out to meet the full chaos and challenge of life.

But with maturity, meditation and prayer merge our personal awareness ever deeper into a more universal stream of consciousness. This is like stepping into a fire in which the ego begins to be consumed and this process can release large amounts of energy. This is when prayer and meditation truly become more than tonics for the nervous system or solace for the anguished heart. They begin to invite us ever deeper into our Second Miracle nature. Prayer and meditation at this level are profound instruments that must be used with wisdom and deep respect, both for the higher possibility and for our ordinary self that requires basic boundaries. The beauty is that this deeper practice actually brings about the necessary wisdom if we can only recognize that prayer and meditation are not merely tools to achieve our own ends, but a means of becoming submitted to Life's deeper intelligence and its ends. Crucial to this is the recognition that spiritual maturity is never a matter of escaping from life, but a growing capacity to enter more fully into it.

As we realize how frequently even the most valuable resources for our growth can be co-opted by our egos, we can understand how, perhaps, First Miracle humanity's greatest ignorance can be to pray to God to ameliorate our personal suffering or fulfill ego-driven hopes, for in so doing we often obstruct our deeper growth. In our fear of nothingness and our dream of salvation, God simply accommodates us. After all, as an object-of-consciousness, this God is our own creation becoming either loving or wrathful depending on how we are really engaging ourselves through our prayer. All that is really created in such a relationship is ourselves, not

God, and this is a lot, a great deal indeed. Rightfully, the intuition of God is the beginning of the end of the isolated, self-protective individual ego and never the self-substantiating servant of our egoic desires.

The quality of relationship to Mystery that is deep meditation or prayer is actually an attribute of our Second Miracle nature. Second Miracle consciousness is, without any intent or effort, a continuous state of prayer. In fact, often we don't realize how deeply we are already being informed by this consciousness. In this case when, from habit, we move into formal prayer and meditation, we often are, by the very effort and form, obscuring the inherent prayer that is already our Second Miracle nature.

⊱—⊰

One of the greatest causes of confusion is the lack of understanding about the simultaneous necessity of both separate self-awareness and ego-transcendance. Realization of the Second Miracle does not obviate, or "kill" the First Miracle ego. Indeed, the ego must remain if there is to be self-reflective consciousness and the potential of unique, individual self-expression. Simply because we awaken to the new consciousness is no proof against the endless objectification perpetrated by the First Miracle ego. It is more that the First Miracle is nested within the larger potential of the Second Miracle. To be human is inherently both these kinds of consciousness, but the latter must remain sufficiently latent until ego development has been accomplished. It is as though Nature required human beings to become self-aware, and slowly, over eons, the First Miracle came about. But for this a sacrifice had to be made, the sacrifice of the Ground of Being, the unconscious instinctual union with Reality. The Second Miracle is the conscious return to that union. Nature had to take two steps forward into subject-object consciousness and one step back out of immediacy and belonging.

But the moment this first big step was made it was merely a movement within the deeper mystery and already the Second

59

Miracle, in whatever form it would eventually be realized, began to make its appearance among humankind. Typically, when we seek for it from out of our First Miracle perception, it appears that a great labor must be undertaken to reach the blessing of the Second Miracle. In fact, there is only the slightest veil to be parted, but this is a radical shift of attention. This shift in itself is not a labor at all, but paradoxically the fruit of a deepening intuition born in a moment or a string of moments of simple being. Here is the harbor in which the Great Vessel of Self drops anchor. The Second Miracle dawns. Perhaps the most important work we can do, in the ever-accellerating busyness of our lives, is make space for this.

There has been, and will continue to be, a ceaseless dynamic of interaction between these two different levels of consciousness that is often very paradoxical. The shift does happen in a timeless moment, or a series of such moments, but the incarnation of this shift into the full complexity of life unfolds in time. Each time the more unitive dimension opens, the First Miracle functions as a witness-servant, making the experience conscious. But when this dimension recedes as it inevitably does, to greater or lesser degree, the First Miracle ego co-opts the experience of opening, making it an object of consideration, a precious memory, the source of the teaching…and finite once again. This dilemma is the process of integration, the means by which we discover what this new consciousness is and what it means to our lives. It is this dilemma that is the basis for some of Jesus' most enigmatic remarks when he asks: "On the day when you were one, you became two. But when you have become two, what will you do?" (Logia 11). Or again: "It is impossible for a man to mount two horses and to stretch two bows, and it is impossible for a servant to serve two masters, otherwise he will honor the one and offend the other" (Logia 47). To be two (that is, subject-object) is the First Miracle consciousness. To be one is the Second Miracle. But when the Second Miracle opening has become an experience in the past, subject-object based awareness dominates once again. The one has become two. Attention is not open to infinity; the Second Miracle vision and presence recedes. It is not extinguished, but like a seed sprouting slowly in the dark, begins to grow within the ego, shifting the underlying referent from the finite to the infinite. The First Miracle ego may try to "mount two horses," imagining itself open to infinity, but this pretense has no true authority. It is only gradually, when the ego is yielded into the larger consciousness, that the two work together and become one. This work, in ordinary moments when we think the new consciousness has left, or when we are faced with such darkness that we feel there has never been any light, is the birth of faith.

It is my personal experience and observation that virtually no one, not even those who have realized the deepest unitive consciousness, can sustain the continuity of the initial state of oneness without inevitably distorting the whole personal domain of life. We do not evolve to a greater capacity for consciousness by eliminating one kind of consciousness and replacing it with another. The evolutionary movement is, I feel, toward ever greater complexity. The First Miracle gives us our capacity for self-awareness and a unique point of view, but fundamentally separates us. We become vulnerable to crystallization, and the repetition of patterns that cause us to become neurotic, conformist, isolated, and feeling at a lower energy level. The Second Miracle consciousness opens us to the One that is infinite movement, infinite potentiality and heightened energy. In doing so it can endanger our ego if the ego structure is not fully matured or has been compromised by earlier trauma. But when these two, in their archetypal essences as finite self-existence and infinite Oneness, co-exist in a mature integration we have discovered our true authenticity and take our positions in evolution as God-man and God-woman. This notion has, again and again, been too romanticized, too removed from ordinary life. It is not a final state, but the emergence of individuals who are, at once, truly authentic, highly energetic, and profoundly relational, individuals who have come to rest in their I-amness.

The Second Miracle exists, archetypally, as a pure state of objectless attention in moments that have been variously defined in such terms as satori, samadhi, fundamental realization, and so forth. But this pure state exists more as an extreme that defines a new

61

possibility of relationship within evolution, rather than as a goal for evolution. To realize the Second Miracle as a state of fundamental realization is to become referent to infinity, not to remain forever absorbed in infinity. Eventually, self-awareness must drive a wedge into the fullness of the Second Miracle consciousness and pull us back from the immediacy. This is a natural affirmation of ordinary life, for we are only just beginners in actualizing this new power of consciousness, and just as we can become isolated in the ego, we can open too deeply to the great Current of universal aliveness and energy that our health and mental balance can be threatened.

But also, and perhaps this is really more the essence of it, in keeping with being "that aspect of nature becoming conscious of itself," we inevitably begin to ask questions of the new consciousness. In this sense, the Second Miracle may at first transcend First Miracle consciousness, but later must submit to that consciousness. This is the great spiral of movement between the poles of the two and the one. This is the fundamental tension of spiritual realization and the embodiment of a new consciousness.

The maturing of Second Miracle consciousness is life's greatest adventure and trying to find guidelines along the way is fraught with paradox. For example, Jesus says, "Whoever does not hate his father and mother in my way will not be able to be a disciple to me"(Logia 55). Yet later he states, "And whoever does not love his father and his mother in my way will not be able to be a disciple to me" (Logia 101). This kind of contradiction is typical of the whole process of trying to reconcile First Miracle understanding with the new quality that is the emerging Second Miracle.

In the first case, Jesus may be suggesting that if we continue to let our awareness be (metaphorically) parented by the old consciousness, we cannot discover the new. The way of the new faith, requires new listening, new perception, new insight into our fears, and how we meet them. This learning does not proceed rationally through memorization and repetition the way learning occurs in the First Miracle level. Instead it emerges spontaneously in its own mysterious way. Eventually, the intellectual dynamic as well as the beliefs and ideas that father our mental egos, and the feelings, perceptions, and sensations that mother our sense of bodily existence, must merge into a deeper intuition, a deeper current of aliveness. Paradoxically, it is by using our self-awareness—to recognize the old patterns of consciousness that obstruct our fundamental relationship—that we gradually cease to energize them. This is the sense in which we "hate our father and our mother." It is not a rejection of the First Miracle that is needed, but a kind of fasting, of ceasing to feed the old consciousness. Then we begin to experience the new life.

Some of this can be engaged intentionally through spiritual practices, but the deeper process is actually propelled from within itself. The real challenge is not so much what we try to do to foster the transformation through our own efforts, as it is to be able to recognize what is actually happening to us so that we stop fighting it and begin to listen in a new way. With this recognition we gradually are less and less the victims of our old psychology, less the victims of our old body consciousness. Now we can begin to use our First Miracle capabilities to witness ourselves, to surrender the old behavior and patterns and offer ourselves forward in growing faith. In this sense we will have "loved our mother and father" in the new way of awakening consciousness.

The Second Miracle is, paradoxically, an experience of realization that ends all referents by which to measure or categorize oneself or existence, yet in this very movement begins a whole new self-reference. Acknowledging the element of timing, Jesus said: "The Kingdom is like a mustard-seed, smaller than all seeds. But when it falls on the tilled earth, it produces a large branch and becomes shelter for the birds of heaven." (Logia. 20). In other words, the experience of realization is not the same thing as the consciousness that is realized. The experience is a tiny seed that enters the soil of our beingness and begins something entirely new, but this new awareness must grow in its own time until it becomes the habitat for a new spiritual life. The confusion and danger arises when we are not patient. The urge of the ego is to categorize and make special, to comprehend, to utilize, and control. We do not trust the seed to grow in its own way. Often before we have lived enough, we try to fit our new spiritual insights into the life we imagine they are leading us toward. Historically, the over-valuation of the impersonal vastness of the new consciousness has tended to demean the ordinariness of daily living. Things become spiritual versus worldly, and without really meaning to we can rape our own humanity. What we do with our opening, how we choose to affirm or deny mystery in the midst of daily living, determines the whole course our lives will take. Perhaps more than any other person I am aware of, Walt Whitman understood this dilemma and made friends with it: "I believe in you my soul, the other I am must not abase itself to you...And you must not be abased by the other."

It is important to realize that the Second Miracle is not just a phenomenon of spiritual or religious significance. It is the very process moving in all of human endeavor. Every real breakthrough in mathematics and science is a deepening understanding of fundamental relationship between things that were formerly not perceived as related. Newton mathematically defined the intuition of the principle of causality giving us the ability to determine the orbits of the planets and build rockets to the moon. Einstein's intuition led him to the principle of relativity that unlocked the relationship between time and space, and matter and energy. But each could only develop their insights to the extent of the foundation of scientific and mathematical understandings available in their respective lifetimes. In effect, Newton's realization was necessary for Einstein's. And this is true for all of us. All cultural development, whether moral or scientific, is possible only to the degree that we have evolved our capacity for relationship.

Once awareness has become referent to infinity, God is never distillable from anything and is never reducible to an object in itself. There is no experience that is more or less real, more or less spiritual. It is this recognition of immanence that is the true kingdom. And not just under special spiritually charged circumstances,

64

but in every moment, even or especially, the most mundane. It is this great acceptance and embrace of ordinary life that is the hallmark of the more complete maturation of the Second Miracle.

>——<

To be referent to infinity ends any illusion of ultimate knowing. Whatever knowledge we have is only accurate within very narrow, finite categories of activity. We can know where to store the vacuum cleaner, or how to construct an airplane, or program a computer, but in these instances a specific context has been established to define the parameters of experience. But in most of life there are no such fixed parameters. Where really are the parameters of such infinite dimensions as intimacy, feeling, the human psyche, even our organisms? The moment we stand as we actually are, in a great sea of being open in all directions to the infinite, we enter a realm where finite knowing is never sufficient, and ultimately impossible. It is only the innate abstraction of First Miracle intellect that creates the illusion of knowing. Just because the subject-object self can label a mood or a behavior, make a diagnosis, ascribe cause, or reveal the chemistry of an enzyme or the molecular structure of a gene, does not mean that the deeper essence is really known. Again, Walt Whitman: "Gentleman, to you the first honors always! Your facts are useful, and yet they are not my dwelling. I but enter by them to an area of my dwelling."

To be referent to infinity is to live in a condition of holy ignorance. It is to live in faith as a friend of existence. It is to be present in sacred attention and to dance sometimes fearfully, sometimes easefully at the very edge of the ever unfolding play of life. We can be conscious without understanding. This is the domain of intuition, where feeling, sensation, and thinking are a unified continuum that is not limited to the boundaries of our individual body, not necessarily limited to time as we usually know it. Now it is impossible to speak of knowing in the absolute or finite sense. This ignorance is not a failing, it is a condition of true intelligence. Because awareness is no longer based in separation, it remains profoundly relational. In this sense attention becomes in itself, the act of worship.

><

*The greatest gift we give each other is the quality of our attention.*

At the level of our First Miracle selves our attention robs each perceived object of its innate subjectivity or soul. Our Second Miracle attention restores the sense of soul, that innate essence in all things that is part and parcel of the continuity of existence. To perceive anyone through First Miracle attention is to make her less than what she is. To perceive her through mature Second Miracle attention is to restore her to an unlimited, living potentiality. This has profound significance in every human relationship; Second Miracle attention, without ever intending to, restores wholeness and connection.

The promise of the Second Miracle is not the promise of salvation or certainty for the future that our First Miracle egos seek through ceaseless efforts to define and control. For our First Miracle consciousness suffering is a finite thing with finite causes and we imagine salvation is possible through religion, or meditation, or science, or medicine, or positive thinking…whatever nostrum speaks to the misery and angst of our forever fragile First Miracle selves. It is not that these things can't temporarily alleviate suffering; it is that they cannot save us. There is a deeper dimension of suffering that is acausal, that is, part and parcel of our evolving incarnation. This root suffering our egos cannot heal.

Causality ceases the moment we become referent to infinity; there is no longer a victim and a perpetrator. Whether we can recognize it or not, every moment is a new birth and what is being born is not merely the product of the past, not merely the cause of some earlier effect, but rather part of a ceaseless cosmos of revelation. The universe and human beings are revelation happening. In a particular sense there may be causality—a defective gene may trigger a cancer formation, an enemy army may destroy our home and kill our family—but from the point of view of the Infinite self, there is no definite causal explanation for our suffering or for our joy. Certainly we suffer, but we are not merely victims. We are that which is transformed in the suffering. Nothing is frozen; everything is unfolding, evolving. One can never return to the event or state in which our circumstances were caused because we have already been irreversibly transformed by that event. There is no turning back, ever. In this sense the past never explains the present, never traps or imprisons the present. The present is always infinitely potential, always as fresh and ripe with inception as the very moment of the Big Bang or the birth of life from the archaic seas billions of years ago. The present is ever ready to surprise us with a movement and a possibility we can never really imagine and never fully control. This is precisely our dread—and the good news.

To become referent to infinity is not to have our identity located in any finite notion of ourselves. We are movement and flow. Our careers, our health, our families and possessions may temporarily represent a harbor for our sense of self, but ultimately we are always far more. Whitman says it so beautifully:

> People I meet—the effect upon me of my early life,
>      or the ward and city I live in, or the nation
> The latest news, discoveries, inventions, societies,
>      authors old and new,
> My dinner, dress, associates, looks, work, compliments, dues,
> The real or fancied indifference of some man or woman
>      I love,
> The sickness of one of my folks, or of myself, or ill-doing,
>      or loss, or lack of money, or depressions or exaltations,
> These come to me days and nights and go from me again,
> But they are not the Me myself.

67

> Apart from the pulling and hauling stands what I am,
> Stands amused, complacent, compassionating, idle, unitary...

There can be no real joy until we have understood for ourselves why we are here and have chosen to become obedient to this understanding. For me, and I suspect Walt Whitman would have agreed, we are not only "that aspect of nature becoming conscious of Itself." We are that aspect of Nature learning to worship the mystery of existence. We are that aspect of Nature learning to love Itself. Truly a Second Miracle!

# II

# THE WORK

*And so, for the first time in my life perhaps, I took the lamp and, leaving the zone of everyday occupations and relationships where everything seems clear, I went down into my inmost self, to the deepest abyss whence I feel dimly that my power of action emanates. But as I moved further away from the conventional certainties by which social life is superficially illuminated, I became aware that I was losing contact with myself. At each step of the descent a new person was disclosed within me of whose name I was no longer sure, and who no longer obeyed me. And when I had to stop my exploration because the path faded from beneath my steps, I found a bottomless abyss at my feet, and out of it comes — arising I know not from where — the current which I dare to call MY life.*

—Teilhard de Chardin

# CHAPTER 6

# THE PRIME DIRECTIVES

*Master,*
*which is the great commandment*
*in the law?*

*Jesus said unto him,*
*Thou shalt love the Lord thy God*
*with all thy heart, and with all thy soul,*
*and with all thy mind.*
*This is the first and great commandment.*
*And the second is like unto it,*
*Thou shalt love thy neighbor as thyself.*
*On these two commandments*
*hang all the law and the prophets.*
                    Matthew 22: 36-40

The journey is never as obvious as the commentary about it. Living this awakening is more haphazard and ambiguous: catching glimpses; a yearning feeling; a curious interest in spiritual life as the old structures of our lives change or collapse. Then new associations form, followed by a loss of interest in the old passions. Then intriguing new associations invite us to reconsider, to re-evaluate our lives; there is a loss of interest in the old passions. And why can't we mobilize our old enthusiasms? Now respite from busyness and doing becomes imperative. We seem to need more and more time.

What comes to us through some other medium of cognition

than ordinary thought, comes in its own way. Only rarely is there a Buddha, a Jesus, or a Whitman when there is a sudden major discontinuity, a great realization of the Second Miracle, which is more or less complete in itself. More often the return is slow like the coming of dawn: imperceptible discontinuities, little tastes of wonder, of sensing that we belong, that we are connected. The book that falls from the shelf unexpectedly answers our deep need. The death that we anticipated would devastate us, but something inexplicably comforts us. Something we know not how to name opens our hearts to an unknown peace. The epiphany when completely absorbed in skiing, rock climbing, dancing, playing music, making love—the body's unobstructed intelligence has taken over and for a little while we are more than we ever imagined ourselves to be. Paradoxically, we realize that this is, in fact, who or what we are. And the call becomes stronger.

The meaning of such moments is implicit in the experience far more than what can be told. But it grows stronger, more conscious in us, when in the same nakedness of being we let words birth themselves. Words come that we didn't know we knew, words referent to something we only cautiously name, respectful for how easily the fullness can be compromised in the articulation. But they are words we cannot deny, words that instruct our hearts and minds, words that bear witness to our own transformation. We have entered, as Walt Whitman put it, "the land of budding bibles." We have begun to be instructed by the deeper intelligence to discover our own truths.

A transformation hinted at in timeless moments when difficult, "efforted" skiing becomes effortless, when my will becomes thy will, when seemingly unbearable suffering becomes peace, and "in the twinkling of an eye" we feel at one. Hundreds, maybe thousands of these moments of sudden discontinuity from a smaller self to a larger self in a lifetime, cumulatively equal to perhaps only hours or days out of the endless self-reflective toil and strain. Yet in themselves and, especially when we are joined here by others, they are the key to regeneration, vitality, and health. Breathing between worlds, between dimensions. These moments are doorways to infinity or doorways into the infinity of being.

Did you know that there are infinite infinities? In mathematics, for example, there is the infinity of rational numbers, the infinity of irrational numbers, the infinity of transcendental numbers, and on and on. But according to an esoteric branch of mathematics called Number Theory, some infinities are larger than others! For example, it is said that the infinity of transcendental numbers such as *pi* is larger than the infinity of rational numbers, such as one, two, three.*

An infinity larger then another infinity...separate infinities? How can this be? Infinity, by its nature, is difficult to think about. It is without limit, boundless, not the common misconception of something very, very small, or very, very large. Infinity is not circumscribed, not a thing, not a place. To speak of infinity is to acknowledge a discontinuity between what can be quantified versus something beyond measure or comprehension. We can quantify doing. We can set goals, measure results, and reward ourselves for achievement. But, for example, how do we quantify being? Does this suggest that there are different infinities of being? Jesus told the disciples: If they ask you: "What is the sign of your Father in you?" say to them, "It is a movement and a rest" (Logia 50). A beautiful description of our deeper beingness, suggesting but not limiting.

It is misleading to try and say anything about infinity, yet the notion of some infinities being larger than others helps us to create an analogy for comparing First and Second Miracle consciousness. Take, for example, the infinity of rational numbers. From this infinity come the building blocks for basic math and algebra and the universe of simple abstractions revealed through calculations we make each day: paying a bill, counting out money, balancing a checkbook, measuring distances, or weighing a baby. In contrast, the infinity of transcendental numbers hides in the flowing river, in every curve in nature, in the elasticity of a willow branch, in the subtleties of quantum electro-dynamics. The discovery of the transcendental numbers gave birth to higher geometry initially taught only in the mystery schools of ancient Greece. It is a statement of

73

how far consciousness has spread within the human collective that these mystery teachings are now standard curricula in virtually every school in the world. The infinity of transcendental numbers allows us to generate an abstract relationship to existence in closer approximation of its vast complexity and fullness, while the infinity of rational numbers allows us to interact effectively, but only very grossly and superficially. Yet it is this superficial level that we consciously employ virtually everyday, while only rarely in our lifetimes do we employ a transcendental number. This is like our usual experience of First and Second Miracle consciousness: cumulatively, over 99 percent of our conscious awareness takes place within the manifold of the First Miracle, yet rare as they are, the moments of Second Miracle consciousness are far more representative of our true nature and the universe in which we exist.

Infinity is a problem; it stops the rational mind, it invites a leap, a discontinuity beyond intellectual thinking. We cannot know the infinite, only where it leads us: into another mode of awareness, something poetic, flowing, never discrete, or finite. I, therefore, at times, treat infinity as something interchangeable with God.

*Thou shalt Love the Lord Thy Infinity with all thy heart and all thy soul and all thy mind...*

How do we love what we can't grasp with thought? How do we direct our deepest affection and the fullness of our intelligence toward something that is not in the quantifiable, finite realm? How do we open our soul, the deepest place of being, toward that which will never reflect us? It is like looking into the mirror and seeing everything and nothing...forever. What is being indicated to us here? It is radically profound if we let it work its alchemy within us.

Just as there are different scales of infinity, so too there are different depths of being. As an illustration, you are driving to the ski slope filled with thoughts, completely unaware that you have a body. All this time your thinking might be suppressing feeling or exciting it. In any case, the thinking is operating autonomously and your sense of self is separate and fragmented, although you aren't aware of it. And your energy level is relatively low. If someone were to suddenly ask you about God you might feel confused. Probably you would respond with the ideas inculcated at church. Whatever you would say, God would not be immediate. Certainly, God would not be you!

Now imagine yourself as you start down a challenging slope, but one that is not beyond your ability. All at once—there is no way to explain it; it is a discontinuity, a happening,—you find that deep body-centered rhythm. Muscles, reflexes, breath, awareness, all click into place together. Thinking collapses into feeling. Doing collapses into being. There is alertness, aliveness, flow… "a movement and a rest." The sense of yourself as a skier on the slope has given way to a sense of continuum with the slope. Your body extends through the skis into the jumps, into the moguls, into the snow, into the ice. And these, in turn, are reciprocal with you: You are the jumps, you are the moguls. This is a high-energy state. You can hear your own voice as if coming from someplace else, yelling with delight. You are delight. It is possible, though it wouldn't come as a thinking process, that you would realize: I am close to God! In fact, for many of us times like this are the closest we ever do feel to God. But God in such a dynamic state of being is not a noun, not any "thing." So just for the sake of shifting our usual thinking about God, let us regard God as a verb. When we are in such a state of flow, at one in ourselves, in a certain sense we are God-ing, or being God-ed. We are letting something more than our separate self live through us.

Now, if at this moment awareness splits off…all of a sudden the self-reflective ego is there objectifying the experience. You think: "Wow, I'm really nailing this!" In that moment, you will likely fall. This is a microcosm of The Fall, the Fall from Grace, the exile from Eden. Just as mysterious, and in its own way, just as miraculous, as entering the God-ing state, it is over…gone. You are back in the First Miracle ego state…ego-ing…fragmented once again into a thinking self, separate from feeling and from body and from snow and mogul. You are exhilarated with residual aliveness from the higher energy state. But it is already a memory. You are coming down.

States of oneness and flow when the body-mind is unified and there is deep connection with the outer reality are, in essence, a category of religious experience, an encounter with the infinity of being. Being-the-skiing is a metaphor for a specific infinity, available in a very particular context, in that moment, with that consecration. It is a step outside of ordinary First Miracle consciousness into a higher energy state. But much of our personality and inner psychology can be set aside in this infinity. We can be masterful skiers, or surfers, or athletes who regularly go beyond our ordinary selves in the context of our excellence and still not know how to be intimate with ourselves in many other contexts. We can be quite incapable of real openness and intimacy with others, unavailable to the Divine in much of the rest of our lives. This kind of infinity, as wonderful as it is, is a smaller infinity, or (within the notion of God as a verb) we are being God-ed by a smaller God. This God-ing is only the beginning, a step toward our Second Miracle possibility. The ego too easily co-opts the experience; this kind of aliveness can become an addiction, a form of high-energy escape that people are driven toward, instead of the beginning of real freedom from the whole limited aspect of ego-ing. We lose ourselves in the wonder of flow, only to make this space the basis for a new identity, a new place to "rest our heads."

In my life, these states of flow during rock climbing, skiing, surfing, lovemaking, and at other times, deeply intrigued me. At first I pursued them for their own sake, because I felt so good while I did them. Gradually, I began to see that the reason they were so energizing was because for a little while my little self collapsed into the fullness of the activity and I felt vast and free. This was why these pursuits were so energizing; for a little while I was not split-off in thinking, I was just a witness to the fullness of experience. Gradually, I began to watch the potential of this process in all my activities and this became the basis for a fundamental shift of attention. In the metaphor of the Second Miracle, we are not talking of a finite state, an ultimate enlightenment, but rather a shift across a continuum between finite and infinite, separate and connected where the center of gravity of consciousness has moved closer to the infinite pole, closer to God. As we approach Second Miracle awareness, more and more of our activities have a natural flow. If the center shifts closer to the finite ego, we lose the flow and live more mechanically, separated from ourselves and everything else.

Being-the-skiing is a metaphor for states of flow we all recognize in one way or another. But we can be God-ing in other ways as well. We can be God-ed by love, rage, hate, joy, any state in which we lose our separate self-awareness, and become total in the infinity of that state. When we are being God-ed by love, the world is whole and wonderful, we move slowly, and every moment feels like a miracle. When we are God-ed by fear, darkness fills our hearts, the world contracts around us, and we become virtually blind to all that is good and whole. This is crazy you think. What is the meaning of God, if God can link us to all we are afraid and ashamed of as well as to what we cherish and hold sacred? Whitman put it this way: "And the unseen is proved by the seen, till that becomes unseen and receives proof in its turn." We are always God-ing, but to see which infinity of God we are living (or is living us) we must look at and into ourselves; we must look at what we are living, and above all we must look in the mirror of how we treat each other. As we begin to see the smaller infinity hiding behind our lives we have become more conscious and our whole way of being changes, becomes more open. We have realized "the unseen proved by the seen." Now, automatically we begin to intuit a deeper level of infinity "proved" by our new openness, "till that becomes unseen and receives its proof in its turn."

I have used the metaphor of being-the-skiing to make the point that there are infinite levels of aliveness, some far more energetic and far more connected to a larger reality than others. The metaphor of God-ing and ego-ing is meant to bring us back to the present Now, to help us see that our egos are not things, but a process of attention. Similarly, God or Infinity is not a thing, but a fundamentally different dynamic of attention. A crucial question then is how to accomplish this essential shift of attention? Can we learn to enter the Second Miracle fullness and realize Infinity in other ways than the intensity of skiing, or suffering, or crisis? Could we realize the infinity of simple moments, let ordinary life compel us as sensually, as totally as it does a little child? Can we begin God-ing, here, now, without intensity and crisis precipitating the discontinuity? YES, unequivocally. It is all a matter of attention.

><

*Thou shall love the Lord thy God...*

Here is the key then of the First Commandment: Where is our attention? The self-reflective ego-ing is not on the act of ski-ing or on the self that is doing the skiing. The whole organism is participating, every cell, the entire cognitive, feeling, sensual self. So just where is the attention? This is what the First Command-ment reminds us of. It is the Prime Directive for recalling our First Miracle awareness to its deeper roots. It says: First and foremost give your awareness passionately, with deepest feeling, with all your genius and intelligence toward That which is beyond any concept, beyond any idea, beyond any feeling, beyond any sensa-tion, even the most sublime experience of energy or presence, something that has no characteristic of any kind. In the instant of doing so, awareness is relativized, all intellectual activity is short-circuited, freeing consciousness from the subject-object ego-ing into a state of unobstructed...I am tempted to write "being," but perhaps there is no word for this place.

There is an intriguing movie called *War Games* in which a super computer is asked by a young computer whiz to play the game Global Thermonuclear War. Unfortunately, the whiz has broken into the military's war computer and the computer's pro-gram does not know this is a game; it begins to initiate a genuine attack sequence for global nuclear war. The only way to stop the

78

computer from perpetrating this nightmare is to teach it that global nuclear war is futile because there can be no winner. But how to give the computer a sense of a no-win situation? Brilliantly, the whiz has the computer run a parallel program playing Tic-Tac-Toe. By playing every move millions of times the computer realizes that if both sides understand the game, no one can win; it is always a tie. The computer then makes the leap of understanding that global nuclear war is also a no-win game, and calls off the attack sequence.

>——<

*Thou shalt love the Lord thy God:*
*Tic-Tac-Toe for the thinking self?*

As we grow in consciousness we begin to appreciate the limits inherent in First Miracle consciousness. We reach beyond our ordinary awareness and see into the immediacy of each moment. This is why "To love the Lord thy God with all thy heart...mind... soul" is so crucial and so paradoxical. It is instructional to begin to challenge the authority of subject-object consciousness by using this same consciousness in an activity that short-circuits it, yet doesn't actually diminish our capacity for consciousness. This activity is to contemplate with passion, determination, and intelligence something that our awareness cannot reduce to any finite object, something it cannot think!

>——<

*Thou shalt love the Lord, thy God...*

This First Commandment isn't an indoctrination into a monotheistic religion; it is a profound guideline for the development of radical intuition, the part of us that is forever listening to the unseen, indeed the unseeable. Ordinary attention looks at our inner state and immediately labels it, in the same way it looks at

79

the object called tree or one's neighbor and stops there. Then, depending on memory and conditioning, this labeled object is acted upon, reacted to, ignored. But when there is radical intuition we look at ourselves, the tree, or our neighbor and see them, while simultaneously intuiting something more.

In the presence of radical intuition the inherent wound of subject-object separation begins to heal. The sense of distance, of otherness, from ourselves, from the trees, or from our "neighbor" collapses, more or less, into a dimension of connection, just as it does in being-the-skiing. Where there is radical intuition, more and more we are God-ed by ordinary life. Attention becomes profoundly relational. The experience of self becomes unbounded; separation and its step-children, distrust and fear, dissolve. Referent to infinity, we begin to perceive that the other is also oneself.

><

*Thou shalt love thy neighbor as thyself...*

The same union that can happen on a ski slope between skier and slope now begins to happen in the most crucial area of all, with each other. Radical intuition of relationship turns ordinary touch into a benediction. Listening becomes a sacrament. When we are being God-ed in relationship, sensuality is highly amplified and our body extends far beyond our skin. We begin to experience energy well beyond the skin boundary. We taste a living presence. Intimacy becomes far more than sexuality. It is breathing presence together and relationship becomes a completely spontaneous flow of connection and discovery. This is what makes jazz so wondrous; it demands exquisite intimacy. Only in this deep surrender to the act of shared creation does the separateness of each performer become a dynamically intimate flow of music, far more complex and alive than anything the musicians could achieve by themselves.

There will always be the First Miracle infinity in which the neighbor is separate, and we (or they) can act kindly or selfishly

80

toward each other. But there is a larger infinity, the Second Miracle, in which we perceive that our neighbor is really another expression of ourselves. Just as the infinity of transcendental numbers contains the infinity of rational numbers, so too the infinity of interpenetrating oneness contains the infinity of separateness. We may only love our neighbor as ourself in brief moments in our lifetime, but this condition is closer to our real relationship than to the thousands of hours spent in the illusion of separation. In my life, committed, intimate relationship is one of the vaster infinities; it includes so much of me, from the highest to the lowest. This is why this level of relationship can be such a profound spiritual path.

The word commandment comes from the root, *manus,* which means hand. This, in turn, becomes handbook, meaning a map or guideline. Depending on where we stand in the continuum between separate ego or infinite being, "To love the Lord thy God... and to love thy neighbor" becomes either a limiting enclosure or a simple affirmation of what already is the case in the deeper part of us. In the former we feel coerced and confined. Often we rebel and refuse to look more deeply at the essence of the commandment. In the latter there is no sense of coercion; we cannot help but love God and one another. This leads to the fundamental paradox of all mystical instruction: What is a simple affirmation of being in the larger infinity can become a life-denying dogma in the smaller infinity. I believe that the Great Commandments are an affirmation of being, an affirmation of what we forever already are and have always been.

As we look to the challenges of our time, we must consider that no problem is solved at its own level. Egos will call for peace or for war. Egos will defend decency or wreak cruelty upon people and nations. Egos will argue for a fair distribution of wealth or for protection of one's private gains regardless of the expense to others. Egos will rationalize the exploitation or the preservation of rain forests and species. But no matter which side we are on, the problems generated by First Miracle consciousness cannot be solved by the ego-ing of First Miracle consciousness.

Life forever conspires to insult our egos. While death is the ultimate insult to the ego, sexual desire and passion do a good job too, as does the challenge of deep intimacy. As the poet Kabir said about love, "Those who seek to be reasonable about it fail." And there is incredible intelligence in this. Our deeper being does not thrive on reason, but on the energy of fully embodied immediacy, on God-ing. It does not thrive on thinking alone or on intellectual concepts barren of such immediacy even when they are noble.

First Miracle consciousness loves passion and immediacy only so long as its ego can co-opt them, only so long as it does not have to fully yield itself, only so long as it can create a new purpose or a new meaning by identifying with its pleasures, its noble ideals, the problem to be overcome, or even its suffering. Indeed, the ego must not be annihilated but it must ultimately be insulted. It must be dethroned and learn humility. It must become the servant instead of the sovereign over human activity. Currently the whole human project threatens to become an immense insult to First Miracle consciousness as the success of the rational-materialist intellect endangers the capacity for the Earth to sustain life. We have a choice to recognize this insult and accept our humiliation, or forever bow to fear and in so doing continue in the illusion that we can fix ourselves.

>———<

*Thou shalt love the Lord thy God…*
*Thou shalt love thy neighbor as thyself…*

Perhaps if ordinary consciousness will accept the challenge to keep the Prime Directives ever in mind—the computer had to play Tic-Tac-Toe millions of times—we human beings can truly submit to becoming co-creative with the larger potential of life.

Co-creation is the most beautiful of notions. To me, it says that when I have been humbled and am no longer so absorbed in my isolated, narcissistic self, I am automatically listening to, and more or less expressing, the larger intelligence of life. To co-create with God, our attention must remain in part forever referent to infinity. We have to let go of what we think this may be and let ourselves flow with life. This is the Taoist notion of not-doing. We are doing, but we are also the one being done. This takes faith; it takes living from our hearts. Our hearts are far more than the sentiment of our yearning egos. Our hearts are the deeper core of our being, our I-amness, where we are dancing with the Infinite, where whatever we create is the living expression of a deeper wholeness. To come from our hearts is exquisitely subtle, yet immensely strong.

Above all, it is profoundly relational. It means we are coming home to ourselves and feel the immanence of God breathing with our breath. We feel ourselves bathed in the goodness of life. We have tolerance and forgiveness for our own delinquency. We delight in the difference of others because in the authenticity of their uniqueness we experience our connection to the Infinite all the more directly. In my life to feel this quiet dawning sense of being held in God's intelligence has satisfied something that even the transcendental state of Union that I have known did not offer. In that experience my ordinary self was practically irrelevant. But now it is my ordinary self that bathes in the extraordinariness of God. I feel at once completely unimportant, and essential and passionately committed all at the same time. I know that I am not doing what I am doing, I am not the source of the teaching. It is being co-created with me...moment by moment.

*A transcendental number in mathematics is any equation or quantity that cannot be expressed by any algebraic expression of a finite number of terms. The modern name for such numbers is "irrational," but I prefer the old usage.*

# CHAPTER 7

# RADICAL
# INTUITION

*Ask, and it shall be given you;*
*seek, and ye shall find;*
*knock and it shall be opened unto you...*
Matthew 7:7

To ask, to seek, to knock, is what we are doing, sometimes intentionally, sometimes not, every moment of every day. Consciousness can be thought of as a question: Who am I? or What are you? or What is that? It is not that we realize we are asking these questions. It is that these questions are implicit in the relationship to existence we call consciousness. The answer is automatically whatever we are conscious of: the dog, our mood, the engineering problem, the chromosomal defect. This dialectic between the subject and the object of consciousness is the fundamental condition that defines our humanness and particularly our First Miracle selves.

But what about the relationship to God? Jung said in his autobiography that the most important question each of us must answer in our lives is our relationship to the Infinite. This relationship, ultimately, defines the heart and soul of who we are as individuals. There is a profound paradox in this: that our capacity for relationship to That which is forever essentially unrealizable, forever prior to any object-of-consciousness, actually makes us more human, more real, more substantial, as though the Infinite where the sunlight against which we are, more and more, clearly silhouetted. This is not, as we have said, the dogmatic and static relationship to God that has alienated so many of us from conventional religion. It is a ceaseless dynamic of attention that keeps presenting us to ourselves, that heightens our self-awareness precisely because we are listening beyond ourselves. I name this quality of attention "radical intuition."

But naming it doesn't make it a thing that we do, so much as it is an aspect of what we are. In this sense we can say that we cultivate radical intuition when we consciously join our attention to the deeper stream of being, as, for example, during meditation. But radical intuition is also more accurately something that we are brought to by life as we live more and more from our depths. It is a very deep listening, but it doesn't make us inflexible or brittle, doesn't exclude us from the fullness of living as some kind of self-consciously driven technique might do. Radical intuition roots us in something beyond our ordinary awareness that frees us to more fully experience life. It is as though we are both in the river of life, fully feeling and experiencing, and on the shore sitting in repose, simply watching. As Jesus said, "If they ask you: 'What is the sign of your Father in you?', say to them: 'It is a movement and a rest' " (Logia 50).

This intuition does not mean that God is impersonal; the immediacy of the sense of relationship with the Transcendental Reality allowed Jesus to speak so personally of the Father. But to have a personal relationship to God does not imply that God is ever waiting to answer our questions, ever waiting to help us solve our ego-centered problems, if only we would sincerely ask. Such a personalized view that assumes God to be a benevolent parent often becomes a way of avoiding a much deeper and more fundamental relationship to existence, a relationship in faith. For our egos to untether from a protective God is frightening, but as our hearts open to this ceaseless relationship in faith, we discover a real sense of personal freedom, self-mastery, and an expanding connection to our world.

The moment we begin to deepen our intuition of Infinity, a radical transformation of ourselves begins to unfold. Emotions, feelings, fantasies, dreams, thoughts, and behaviors that can drive us crazy in their disparity and conflicting directions begin to become integrated as though, all along, all that was needed was a larger vessel, an expanded consciousness. Sometimes this is a happy process; sometimes, at least initially, it is quite disturbing, for to turn to the Infinite is not to be saved in the usual sense of made safe, it is to be saved in the deeper sense of made whole. Jesus said, "Let him who seeks not cease seeking until he finds, and when he finds, he will be troubled...." As our radical intuition deepens much that was unconscious in us comes into view and this can be troubling at first. But if we continue to deepen in our intuition of the Divine, this initial turbulence gives way to a new stability and integration. Then, as Jesus concluded, "And when he has been troubled, he will marvel and he will reign over the All"(Logia 2).

Radical intuition is not merely the activity of the mystic or spiritual seeker; it is a dawning movement in all of us. A mystic speaks of God, depth psychologists such as Jung speak of the archetype of the Self, while a theoretical physicist, a cosmologist, or a student of pure mathematics will speak of hyperspace and higher spatial dimensions. The recent interest in Superstring Theory is an attempt to unify all the basic forces of physics by introducing the geometry of ten-dimensional space. As we seem to live in a three-dimensional universe, for most of us, this sounds fantastic. But the notion of four-and five-dimensional space is a kind of radical intuition of the geometry of space—beyond the three dimensions that our brains only permit us to see—that has already led to discoveries that are profoundly changing our world. The amazing thing is that higher dimensional space helps us unify the physical laws of the universe even though no one can actually visualize these higher dimensions.

86

This is the same phenomena we observe in psychology and spirituality. God, as an object of radical intuition, helps us, through the mysterious alchemy of spirit, to create deep and substantial relationship to the existential issues of our lives. The archetype of the Self introduces the transcendent into psychology which allows us, again with mysterious alchemy, to more effectively integrate the vast multiplicity of inner dynamics of the psyche. Each of these intuitions helps establish a deepening relationship to existence, ourselves, and our world, yet no one can "behold the face of God" directly, or conceive of the Self. Ultimately, whether scientist, psychologist, or mystic, we stand before Mystery. For this reason, for me, a science, medicine, or psychology without God or some notion of the Transcendental Reality is an impossibility. Without radical intuition of higher dimensions there can be no integration of the vast diversity of forces, within and without, that make up the infinite life of ourselves and our universe.

To seek, to ask, to knock, is not so much to receive the answer that we want or that we imagine we need, but to exercise our native capacity for relationship to That which is forever beyond or higher than our ordinary consciousness. And in this movement we transform our understanding of ourselves and our relationship to everything else. The important thing is that we are always answered. And when our attention is truly radical, listening into the very heart of the moment, we are led, apparently willy-nilly, but with remarkable intelligence, into a new and wonderful aliveness. This is one of the great mysteries of life. This is the heart of the ancient tradition of alchemy. We take the basic metal of our ordinary consciousness and transform it into the gold of new awareness and aliveness. Through our radical intuition of the Infinite, moment by moment, we become co-creators with God, we co-author our destiny with Mystery, giving birth to ourselves anew, and in the moment, "reign over the All."

>———<

Spiritual maturation and the evolution of radical intuition are the same process. When we are spiritually young, our faith cannot yet rest on life as it is; it requires signs and what I call confirmational events. The fascinating thing is that Life cooperates with us. At certain key moments in our development, if we need a

87

miracle in order to awaken to faith, we get a miracle. If we need to see demonstrations of spiritual power, such as healings or materializations in order to recognize holiness and spiritual authority, we discover a saint or teacher who has such powers. Often, before we rest in a more direct and radical intuition of Mystery, we may require many confirmational events: experiences of energy, surging kundalini, healings, paranormal phenomena, states of bliss, and so on. It is as if while our intuition is still young, we are given spiritual crutches that help support our awakening spirituality.

I recall some of my first confirmational events. A powerful one took place in the emergency room while I was treating a patient. A voice within me said, "You have nothing to share except love." Suddenly I was suffused with warmth and laying my hands on the man, all his pain vanished. Another time, when I was in my early twenties and feeling really down, I had been mindlessly throwing pebbles at a small stick about ten feet away without ever hitting it. Suddenly I said to myself, "If God is real, I will hit the stick within three more throws." The very next pebble landed directly on the stick. My intellect tried to dismiss it as coincidence, but the feeling of that confirmation remained with me.

The confirmation that we require in order to have faith depends on the depth of our intuition. In trying to convey this idea I use a teaching story:

> A great master lives deep in the forest at the base of the Himalayas. So immense is his power that as he walks through the forest, with a touch or a glance, the trees grow taller and more grand than anywhere else in the world. News of his miraculous gifts spread and seekers travel from all over to receive the blessing of his teaching.
>
> Then word spreads of a great shaman who lives in the remote jungles of South America. Wherever she walks in the gardens of her hermitage, all the ferns grow resplendent and huge. They stand twice the height of a man, the biggest ferns in the world. Attracted by this miracle many people travel to partake of her teaching (some even leaving the Himalayan sage), for surely here is the proof of a great soul.

This story emphasizes that our capacity for intuition of the Divine can be seen in the evidence we require to recognize spiritual reality and authority. Big trees or big ferns are a metaphor for the extraordinary that attracts the spiritually younger seeker. But what do we really imagine spiritual power to be? In commenting on this story, I point out that if the trees grow so abnormally large, the ferns and other forest plants will be deprived of light and will become weakened. Similarly, if the ferns grow so large, they will draw an excess of nutrients and water from the soil and the trees will suffer. What really is spiritual power? How do we recognize Life's deeper intelligence? What if someone walked through the forest and everything was nourished appropriately according to its relationship to everything else? In this case nothing might appear extraordinary. Would we recognize any power? Could we be attracted to this power if we could not see overt evidence of its existence? The answer really depends on where we are looking, and this is essentially the question of radical intuition. That which blesses all things is beyond the ability for us to perceive without a deeper intuition. This intuition is itself a relationship that grows spontaneously in us as, more and more, we greet all of life as a lover greeting the beloved.

The story and commentary also suggests the laws of contrast, balance, and harmony that dominate us at different stages of our maturation. Initially, we require contrast in order to become conscious of something. But contrast, in the case of spiritual or psychological development, automatically necessitates a kind of exaggeration or over-emphasis of certain capacities of consciousness over others, so that they stand out and attract our attention. Automatically, this is achieved by the supression or ignoring of other parts of ourselves. This is usually the path we take in the beginning of our spiritual journey. We are attracted by power, especially tools and techniques that allow us to make rapid progress, for example, with our negative thinking, or with our fears. As we develop self-confidence and can achieve our own aims, and can wield certain powers for ourselves, we have the sense that we are growing, that something is working.

In my own work, I saw how important it was for people to

89

have a powerful experience of energy. For them, and for me as well
at first, the power of the energy somehow confirmed the value of
the work. Over time this changed for me. My own life began to
be governed by the law of balance and I was called to the interpersonal work that I had not yet done. The law of balance requires
that we work on what was left behind. This is typically shadow
work, work on unconscious patterns that are difficult to face, not
the exhilaration of the early triumphs and discoveries. And while
we are making progress, it is not apparent in the way our earlier
steps had been, because this is not expansion work, but in-filling
work. It is preparing us for a deeper movement from within which
we do not, as yet, see. I found this time particularly disturbing,
because it was not psychologically flattering work, and because
the sense of "spiritual" progress became much slower, much less
apparent. I felt that I was betraying my vaster self, that I had lost all
contact with God. I became quite ill for awhile. But this caused
me to begin to listen more deeply into myself and into life.
"Why," I asked myself, "do I think that I am not growing, when it
was not anything that I did that had awakened me in the first
place?" Gradually, I began to intuit something deeper living
through my life, making these difficult demands. Before, I sensed
the radiance in spaces of expansion and heightened energy, but
gradually, through the very humbling of the balance work, I began
to accept how little I really knew.

This changed how I worked a great deal. More and more
I simply became the observer of the process of wholeness that I
could feel awakening in myself and in the people I was working
with. More and more I began to integrate the energy work with
psychological work, body work, and meditation because I realized
that spiritual maturity is not the demonstration of heightened
energy and expanded states, but of something much simpler, a
simple intimacy with ourselves in each moment. If we meet ourselves deeply we discover the Divine in simple things and we
become truly relational. As this was deepening in me, my intuition
of the Divine was also deepening. Less and less, I felt I was the
cause of what happened in the work. I was calling people toward

something that was already calling to them from within. The intuition now had grown to perceive the Divine in everyone. I stopped trying to make anything happen in my work—it is a little slower in my personal life—and realized that I was but the servant of something far more intelligent that was living through me and through all of us. The result is that the whole of my life has a different sense and a profoundly different emphasis. Often I feel that I am being cradled in the Divine and it is not the result of anything extraordinary, but fills me, usually, when I have made a tiny step toward greater honesty in my life.

I tell my story so that we can see that radical intuition evolves naturally as we deepen in ourselves. Then gradually the law of harmony begins to assert itself. Harmony requires that every aspect of ourselves grows in natural proportion and intimacy to all the rest of us. Now, there can be almost no obvious signposts at all by which to evaluate spiritual growth, because our growth is inextricably united with the growth of everyone and everything else. At this level, the work, if we can call it that, is to live ordinary lives with our hearts ever open to the Infinite.

Rather than recognizing the Divine in all people, we at first rely on the saint, the gifted healer, the spiritual master as an intermediary, a kind of transitional object through which our spiritual intuition begins to recognize a higher dimension. Through these will come the sense of psychic richness and dynamism and the beginning intuition of That which is present in everything. This initial phase is often quite magical. We feel we have finally discovered the truth, finally come home. Often there is a great deal of ego inflation and we feel that we have discovered the *only* truth, that we know the *true* way.

But this trip toward the heavens is, by necessity, short lived. Ultimately, the Transcendental Reality does not rest on any experience, any manifestation of miraculous evidence. As we mature spiritually, these supports are taken away and we will, in various ways, pass through what St. John of the Cross refers to as the Dark Night of the Soul. This is the time when the immanence of God that we have known indirectly through our beliefs, our spiritual practices, our faith in our guru, and which has sufficed to under-gird our faith is withdrawn. Now we feel abandoned, all too human, deeply lost and ashamed of our sudden collapse and weakness. We try to resurrect our self-image in many ways undertaking purifications, offering ourselves with renewed passion to our work and our practices, but ultimately all our motivation and the hope of a triumphant return to a greater life simply disappears and we must make our way in emptiness and spiritual darkness. We reach for God through prayer, through contemplation and nothing happens. All that is left is the most unadorned sense of being. It is less than ordinary; it is a sense of abysmal failure and self-denunciation. It is inexplicable sorrow burning in our chests. We are alone, or so it seems. We have come upon the wound the ego cannot heal. Without realizing it we have placed ourselves in the hands of God. Our younger self, our smaller mind, all of a sudden meets the elder self. Now, for the first time we may begin to understand and respect the real miracle of faith; for it rests, truly, on nothing, and yet we are met in a fullness beyond our imagining.

We can never be reminded too often that when we say God or Father or Holy Mother, we are utilizing thoughts that are themselves transitional objects. The first stage of prayer involves turning our attention toward the Infinite via some transitional object. We "speak" or commune with God, Jesus, The Father, Mother Mary, Krishna, even notions like the Tao, or Buddha Nature act for us in this way. But radical intuition emerges precisely as the power of these objects is withdrawn, precisely as we must begin to discover a new depth of faith. It is a wound that can never be healed by any activity of our egos.

Some years ago, a Benedictine abbot who had spent forty years of his life as a contemplative visited me for a few days. He was facing a difficult, life-changing decision: whether to remain in the monastery or to leave. When he held his question in prayer, he said he never got an answer. In fact, he said that throughout the whole of his religious life he had never heard God speak to him. For many, many years this had deeply troubled him and had been a cause of great despair. And then he added, chuckling, "At least now, it is a benevolent silence."

Benevolent silence…a quality of listening, of attending to Mystery, of being simply open and available. Benevolent silence is an answer, a profound answer. Not the answer that the ego desires; not a concrete solution to a real problem; not the temporary support of assurance and rightness that bestows confidence and security. To me it seemed that he had lived deeply enough that his faith could no longer rest on any false premise.

When we are still dealing with God as a transitional object, we unconsciously require God to behave as an object; we expect a personalized response. And as was said, the wonder of it is that the psyche is so generous that for awhile this is precisely what we receive; God obediently behaves like an object. She or he will speak, will give guidance, and so on. But as our intuition deepens we will lose this solace. Usually there are a few good shocks when our guidance turns out to be completely wrong. I, for one, do not want a God that is guiding me; I want one in whom I can submit utterly. It is not a relationship *in order* to reach some condition; it is simply relationship. This relationship has less to do with the choices we make, but rather with the quality of our beingness as we live out such choices. This is not turning to God for the answer to our problems, but turning our attention to the Infinite that grounds our life in the deepest sense of connection and belonging.

Jesus said, "Those who seek to save their lives will lose it." When, on occasion, we wake anxiously in the middle of the night, before we have time to really engage this feeling nakedly, we reflexively defend and resist it. We try to "save our lives." The resistance takes the form of thinking, which almost instantly becomes trying to explain the anxiety, planning to remedy whatever problem is perceived, deciding to speak to the therapist, or perhaps take a meditation retreat. The instant there is any distance from the immediacy of our feeling, any one of infinite universes of response/reaction comes into existence and with them is born a particular self-image and all that will grow around it.

This is the essence of karma; it grows in proportion to our distance from our I-amness. Every moment of conscious existence is really just a relationship, and all relationships are reciprocal. Depending upon what level of our self enters this relationship, relatively real infinities of activity, feeling, and thought emerge that, in turn, define and condition our self-image. Take, for example, sorrow. If we meet sorrow as an enemy from a conditioned level of ourself that has labeled sorrow as negative, almost immediately the sorrow will transform into shame and we begin to withdraw from life and may perceive people as judging us. On the other hand, if we open to sorrow from our deeper being, it often becomes compassion. Here the karma is completely different; our heart opens to others and we feel kindred; we find ourselves trusted and appreciated.

It is paradoxical that radical intuition of the Divine is actually just a more immediate and naked relationship to what is. When we awaken to the feeling of fright or anxiety, instead of self-protection, we can yield ourselves to the feeling. The reflex of the ego is to save itself, but radical intuition is like a deep countercurrent that is saying, "Here, take me, I give myself to you." Immediately the anxiety becomes a doorway and we enter a completely new state of being.

I recently had knee problems and found that I couldn't keep up with a group of men whom I was leading on a wilderness retreat into the mountains. I love hiking and climbing and enjoy feeling vigorous and able to explore rugged natural settings. But suddenly I was unable to be my strong, competent, outdoor self. A voice inside ran a litany of despair about aging, weakness, setting an example, keeping up, becoming irrelevant and replaceable if I could no longer lead. For awhile I found myself resisting these thoughts and becoming tense and bitter. Then all at once, in the quiet of meditation I saw the gift: Let the whole notion of being a strong, capable leader die. Let these dark thoughts do their work; let them do exactly what they were saying. In a moment of radical intuition of infinite beingness this whole image of myself became unimportant. I let it die. Referent to Infinity "I" am not this self-concept or any self-concept, attractive or unattractive. Instantly there was the spaciousness of Being once again. Perhaps it was only coincidence that my knee immediately began to get better, but I doubt it.

When our sense of self is predominantly referent to some level of ego-based identity, then there is the (very real) potential of ego annihilation and we cannot abandon ourselves. We reflexively avoid the deeper relationship and "seek to save our lives." But the result is that we become submerged in an infinite world of reactions, rationalizations, and defenses in which the deeper self is temporarily lost. When the referent for self has become Infinity, there is really no need to resist. We may not know what will emerge, but something is always born out of the relationship. And it is the essence of faith that there is inherent trust that what will be born is a renewed connection to our I-amness. Nothing that we can experience, whether positive or negative in feeling or mental content, tells us what or who we are in our deepest essence. By letting our relative self die, we actually are participating in a ceaseless cycle of rebirth. Each new relative self-concept becomes the next doorway or springboard into a process of ceaseless emergence that is the present moment. This is the essence of the enlightenment that is faith.

# CHAPTER 8

# WORDS THAT SHINE BOTH WAYS

There is an old childhood rhyme that goes, "Sticks and stones can break your bones, but names can never hurt you." The implication is that words, if we refuse to let them bother us, can do no harm. But the real danger of words is not whether they are employed to do harm, but in the nature of the consciousness that does the naming.

One day, as I was sitting on the balcony of a room just above the sand, about sixty feet back from a calm ocean, a large bird glided past, its wing tips gracefully skimming inches above the water surface. Abruptly it dropped a foot, splashing almost clumsily into the water and began to thrust its long beak down, hunting for food. Not only was the beak long, but a sack hung from beneath it. It was a pelican.

P-e-l-i-c-a-n. A word. A name.

The name tells us so much. It makes us conscious of the unique thingness of this creature. Now the pelican stands out from the background of unconsciousness and takes its place as a conscious object that can be analyzed and evaluated. We can describe the mating cycle, the migratory pattern, and place the pelican within a larger context of existence. But in giving us a sense of familiarity and knowing, paradoxically, it also stops another process. That same morning I heard a child's enthralled cry. "Daddy, daddy, look! Look at the wonderful bird. Daddy, Daddy, it's so close to the water. Ewwww!" Here is wonder and delight, not just thingness. The price we pay for words is the risk of exile in First Miracle consciousness. This is the great gamble being played out by creation on our planet right now.

There is an old adage: familiarity breeds contempt. The word contempt means "to cut, divide, or decide." In other words, what we become familiar with, we tend to *cut* away from its wholeness. We *divide* it from a larger field of connection, thereby inadvertently disconnecting it from its blood supply. We *decide* its nature, forgetting that, in the deepest sense, this is at best only an approximation.

The very act of naming does this. When we say, "my wife," or "my house," "my dog," and so on, we make them other. They become things devoid of their is-ness, their mystery, and begin to die. Inexorably, we fall—no, not "fall"—we slip almost imperceptibly out of love. And slowly from childhood to adulthood we gain the world through the *symbol,* through words...and lose our souls. Paradoxically, words bless us and curse us. They bless our intellect and curse our immediate, sensual connection to the world within and without. The word is a symbol; it represents the object. But it is never the thing in itself.

We must come to better understand how language makes us conscious at one level and unconscious in another way. The poet, Rilke, railed against the arrogance that says, "my house" or "my wife." Obviously, in casual usage all of us speak in this way, but subconsciously we reinforce the objectification of the other. In divorcing each thing, in itself, from its unique subjectivity, it loses its God-essence. For it is God, in the infinite sense, that is the Indwelling Mystery, the unlimited potentiality for participation, change, and evolution that is the essence of our universe and everything in it. Take Infinity out of the listening and naming self and all that we perceive becomes forever frozen, forever without the possibility of change and growth. This is why turning our attention toward God as the infinite referent that can never be objectified is the Prime Directive. We must learn to counterbalance the ego's endless tendency to objectify, especially in our attention to what we say and how we use words.

If we unconsciously let our God become an object-of-consciousness, everything else becomes an object: our wife, our neighbor, the trees, the Earth's minerals, and so forth. What happens then is plain for us to see. When we are referent to infinity, God is present in/as all objects. Now "my wife" is a mystery irreducible from her God-essence that cannot belong to me; she can never become someone I ultimately can define or "know." In this sense our relationship paradoxically brings us closer in essence and makes us individually more alone. Relationships at this level are infinitely renewing; this level of ourselves does not fall out of love. The intensity of feelings and sensations commonly equated with love by the First Miracle mentality begins by respecting the God-essence in another—"falling in love" is itself a brief window on infinity—but the inevitable objectification of the other eventually trespasses on this essence. In our Second Miracle natures this respect is ever-rediscovered. Even the very sensations and feelings characteristic of love, as well as sexual intimacy, become infinitized, doorways of discovery rather than finite, familiar ends in themselves. And these doorways do not open to their fullest mystery merely because we can name them; they open only when each moment is approached with attention, deep respect, and genuine unknowing.

In our bodies, our feelings, our whole organism, the rich sensual dimensionality of love must be rediscovered anew over and over again. Infinity guards Her secrets, demanding absolutely everything. As T. S. Eliot wrote:

> To pursue the intersection of the timeless with time is the occupation of the saint. No, no occupation either, but a lifetime's death in love, ardor, self-sacrifice, and self-surrender.

Barring this compelling urgency to submit ourselves to love when we have reduced a person to labels, even positive labels, love is already doomed. And so are we. No matter how exalted or defamed, an object in itself is always barren. And in this way of seeing we have become barren within ourselves. We may believe we know ourself and the other person, but this very familiarity is itself a form of contempt. To live in such assurance is to live a shadow of real life. Then we are the dead, as Jesus says, who must bury their dead.

>—<

All knowledge depends on how it is acquired. There are two fundamentally different kinds of knowledge: the knowledge that comes through words and the knowledge that comes through the immediacy of being. Word-mediated knowledge is essentially intellectual. Franklin Merrell-Wolff, a teacher of mine, referred to this as knowledge-of-objects. It is what we learn from others, in school or at work, from books and through our own intellectual observations. This kind of learning gives us a false sense of safety because in acquiring such knowledge the ego is never challenged to open beyond itself. It remains sovereign in its isolation. The fundamental limitation of basing our self-concept in this kind of knowledge is that it doesn't connect us to our deeper nature; it is only half of wisdom. When we are stressed this pseudo-self will betray us and we regress and revert to the survival imperatives of the basic organism. Then intellect simply becomes the disciple of fear and we are alternately aggressive or helpless. Knowledge-of-objects lives in our heads but not in our hearts.

In contrast, direct knowing that comes from the immediacy of being unites head and heart and more. It is what we realize when subject collapses into object and we are one with our experience. This kind of knowing is not abstract, not second hand. It is the most natural thing for a child, but fades as the ego takes full purchase of our perception. To the degree that any of us "know" in this way we have spiritual authority, at least in relationship to

99

ourselves. But this is also the authority of a true teacher and the basis of an authentic teaching. This is the knowledge that Whitman speaks of so eloquently when he says, "And I know that the hand of God is the elder hand of my own."

Knowledge that is oneself: This is the key. For an ice skater it is how she knows how to do a triple lutz; for a golfer it is the way the whole body understands the swing. We know it when, or because, we are it. It is the place where technical understanding becomes true skill, becomes art. This is how the mystic knows God, or the prophet sees, or the healer comprehends the pattern generating an illness. We can suggest the place, but we cannot fully explain it. This kind of knowledge cannot be given directly to others. Only the conditions for receptivity can be invited and this means, fundamentally, coming home to ourselves. We need to slow down, to soften in our bodies, to feel our breathing, to drift in music, to sing and dance, to be playful, to stop doing so much and learn to listen with our hearts. It helps to meditate, to develop a vigilant, but relaxed, alertness so that we can begin to recognize when we are connected to our depths and when we are split-off in thinking or drowning in emotion and lost to ourselves.

Once we truly have the deeper connection we cannot lose it, though we often imagine that we do. It is a way of seeing that is itself knowing, and it leads us, it uses us, rather than the other way around as with knowledge-of-objects. The only time it fails us is when we abandon ourselves, when we succumb to fear. But this is how it teaches us to come home.

Whereas our egos remain safe in ordinary, outer learning, knowledge that is in our very being is reached through a much more demanding process. The ego itself has to become, for awhile, merged into a larger flow, a fuller aliveness. It can be a vulnerable time; the ego may initially have difficulty integrating this level of experience; it cannot readily translate the new through the old being. We need, as Jesus said, new wineskins for new wine. Integration is like the mustard seed that must grow in its own time. Unfortunately our egos do not know patience. We have had a powerful, mysterious, sometimes deeply disturbing and confusing experience; it must be named, explained, organized, used.

This is where spiritual emergence sometimes ends up appearing like psychopathology, and it is easily mislabeled by the modern, rational/materialistic medical and psychological models. Equally, we ourselves mislabel it, fearing sometimes for our sanity, or falsely identifying with components of the experience and going through a process of inflation. We think ourselves special, defend the experience against critical wisdom and can tend to become absolutist and dogmatic. Wise discernment about this potential is crucial, but we usually have to learn the hard way. There are many teachers to impart intellectual knowledge, but this delicate time of spiritual awakening is when we need someone who has passed through these spaces and contains them within him or herself. Such a teacher can center the opening person simply through his presence and has the experience to give clear perspective: "No, you're not crazy: but let's take a look at the roots of your fear and confusion." Or, equally valuable at times, "So you've had a big experience, you're enlightened...So? Let's get back to daily life." A good deal more might be said, such as taking care of one's obligations as best as possible, spending more time in nature, getting exercise, cutting back or stopping meditation—the boundaries are open enough at these times. Egos that have had a taste of vastness often don't like this kind of feedback, but it is usually precisely what is needed.

Sometimes I feel that rather than integrating experiences of immediacy so that they truly empower our I-amness, the integration is deflected when it is projected onto metaphysical objects. Here I am referring to angels, past lives, higher selves, notions of karmic debt, and even various supernatural entities. A whole metaphysical landscape is created to explain the new energies and experiences. I have personally had many experiences that are beyond ordinary explanations, so that I am willing to keep an open mind about the existence of angels, demons, and a lot more. Yet, for me, it is not the reality of these that is the issue, but the humanity of the person. For me, the litmus test of spiritual maturity is our capacity for conscious relationship. Much of the New Age scene represents a multitude of forms of egoic specialness and glamor, sophisticated (and not so sophisticated) defenses against real social and interpersonal responsibility, against the deep humbling that life must inevitably deal to us. It is easier to hide behind a metaphysical fantasy world than to engage the challenge of full psychological maturity and deep humility.

To me the resolution of this dilemma comes from living fully and with attention. The inflated or threatened ego wants to exclude those aspects of life that insult its sovereignty and the best mirror for this is ordinary life. What is too unimportant for us? What do we disdain and refuse to engage? When do we say yes when we mean maybe or no? When are we deceitful rather than face the discomfort of honest confrontation? The integration of higher energies that cannot be made by our egos and intellects is made naturally in our bodies and lives by not turning away from the alchemy of what Walt Whitman called "life's fierce enigmas." We don't have to look far for these; life is primed with them. What, for example, is one's own authentic relationship to suffering, death, aging? How do we resolve enigmas like being truthful and still respecting the sensitivity of others? What about individual authenticity and belonging to a group or community? How do we reconcile the good of the one with the good of the many, or fulfill long-term commitments, such as marriage and parenting, and not betray our need for spontaneity? As we live these dilemmas, they lead us to the edge where faith begins and we acquire the knowledge of our own essence. Then, that which is revealed to us in times of deeper communion with Reality, finds its way into our lives in the very humility and simplicity of our living. Life in truth is the fire, our false egoic stances, layer upon layer of them, are the straw that must be burned.

For this to happen we must risk to live from our hearts, to choose to challenge our sense of safety by bringing the deepest consciousness into all our relationships. This, I feel, is the definitive yoga of modern life. Angels, demons, extraterrestrials, channeling, karma, and spiritual guides not withstanding, all of these can be seen as objectifying a force outside ourselves. We become the anointed or the victims of these forces. But what of real spiritual substance? It can only come by living deeply. Ultimately, this is not something we talk about, but something we radiate. Above all, it is knowledge of one's own I-amness. Independent of any image or self-concept, this is a connection to oneself that cannot be taken away by changes of circumstance or hardship. This is knowledge that will never betray us.

This is more than just a journey of the mind, it involves a transformation of one's whole being. The whole organism, not just the ego, must be prepared or, in a certain sense, trained, to withstand the energetic shock of moving between different realities beyond the usual infinity of First Miracle consciousness. Rather than avoiding the stresses that threaten the First Miracle psyche, the work is to use such times to learn to gradually remain more and more available and transparent. It makes no difference what labels First Miracle consciousness will attempt to give to such stresses to rationalize a reaction or a defense. From the point of view of infinity this is just energy shaking up the frozen structure of the First Miracle body-mind. By learning to remain non-defensive and transparent, gradually the current of higher energy enters deeper and deeper into our embodiment.

A life well lived, in my estimation, is one that brings us to a greater capacity for consciousness and specifically a greater capacity for relationship. If we want to look at life as a school, then we are being trained or prepared, every moment of every day, to embody the Second Miracle. Developing the First Miracle capacity for ego awareness is fundamental to the child and youth, but the work of an adult is to once again become available to the Ground. It is a journey not merely of the mind, but of the whole incarnate being, for our organism in its totality is far more capable of integrating the higher energies than is the thinking self.

⊱—⊰

To return to immediacy and have words, to return to the point where finite words and infinite being once again converge. To be neither absorbed in an unbounded sensuality like an infant, nor exiled in an intellectual abstraction. To know one's connection to life and abiding aliveness. This is intelligence. This is when the words we use become relational, become infused, become poetry, or parables, or metaphors. This is how Whitman wrote, how Jesus spoke. This is how anyone speaks who tells a story and it is everyone's story at the same time.

>———<

*"In the beginning was the Word,*
*and the Word was with God and the*
*Word was God...."*

One day as I walked in the hills I became aware of the sun and realized the timeless space of being in which it was first named. Not just a word, but a revelation. I could literally feel the awe that must have accompanied the first words as they emerged out from the Ground of Being. Sun...Yes...only over time have words gradually slipped away and lost their rootedness in the larger intelligence. Instead of doorways on mystery, they become ends in themselves.

Sometimes we can see this movement if we look into the origin of certain words. Take, for example, the modern word *abundance*. The contemporary meaning of abundance is "great plenty, an overflowing quantity, strictly applicable to quantity only." Yet in an earlier Latin root, *abundare,* the word means, "to flow as the river flows." Here we see how the earlier sense of the word had its root in nature, closer to the Ground of Being. A river brings water, a source of life. For most early societies, the river's flow meant life. But a river is also a source of mystery and contemplation. Rivers flow slow and deep, fast and wild; they meander; they flood and destroy, even as they replenish the soil of the valleys. To flow as a river flows suggests so much more than wealth or plenty. It suggests fluidity, strength and softness, patience, and power and, above all, movement. True abundance is an inner movement that keeps us from "resting our heads" in a static identity. But abundance in contemporary usage often implies a degree of immunity to change; if we are abundantly wealthy there is no anxiety about recession and so forth. I refer to this as the peace of the ego. But there is another peace, the "peace that passeth understanding," and this peace does not require wealth, though it does require abundare. In a word, *abundare* offers a spiritual quality and less of the materialistic essence of the modern usage.

To declare that "the Word was God" acknowledges the unnameable root of language and intelligence. The Word emerges from the unnameable and the earliest words clothed themselves in the ample metaphors of nature. Truly, to employ words is to invoke the most holy. The Word shines both ways, into infinity and into life.

When we are open to infinity, the voice of another reverberates within our deeper being, communicating far more than the literal meaning of the words. In fact, the influence of words, of voice, must never be underestimated. Jacques Lusseyran, who became blind at age eight, observed:

> The human voice forces its way into us…To hear it properly we must allow it to vibrate in our heads and chests, in our throats as if, for the moment, it really belonged to us.…What voices taught me they taught me almost at once.…There was a moral music. Our appetites, our humors, our secret vices, even our best-guarded thoughts translate into the sounds of our voices, into tones, inflections or rhythms.…I am afraid, for if the time should ever come when greedy and unscrupulous men mastered the art of the human voice… modulate it at will, all that is left of liberty would be lost.[1]

To the enlightened ear, words are kinesthetic, dancing over the skin, penetrating flesh, vibrating, caressing, or abrasive. The words convey the true soul of the person, the quality of her aliveness distinct from the literal meaning of the words. To hear a person speak simply, with real honesty, from her heart becomes a drink, a nectar, a sensual gift. It is wondrous nourishment. God is in such words, and in the naked listening, undressed before Infinity, the universe is knit together, "timeless with time." To the inner ear, the

105

voice never lies. The voice tone of a person suffering the ego-dissolving nearness of Infinity will communicate availability and openness despite the anguished lamentation of the ego expressed in her words. Similarly, the upbeat words of a person secure in her ego-dynamic, rather than communicating the joy she proclaims to feel, will send the message of isolation and self-protection. To anyone open to the deeper moral resonance of this voice, it is the unlived life that will be felt.

The Word is sensual. But first we have to learn to undress, to become naked before a deeper reality. "Take off your clothing without being ashamed...and put them under your feet as the little children and tread on them, then shall you behold the Son of the Living One and you shall not fear" (Logia 37). Moment by moment, we clothe ourselves in psychological structures that predetermine what we will let ourselves experience or perceive. Imagine the image of Adam and God reaching toward each other as depicted by Michaelangelo on the ceiling of the Sistine Chapel. This is "the intersection of the timeless with time," the place where material, finite, timebound, subject-object reality is simultaneously timeless, spaceless, non-local...words simply fail to describe this. Beingness is only present when we stop clothing ourselves in expectations or goals of any kind. This means approaching relationship without the need to be understood or to understand the other. It means approaching relationship without the unconscious need to be liked or to like the other. It is not that we won't be liked, won't be understood. It is that they are no longer prerequisites for our availability. Ultimately, to be naked means that we no longer subconsciously impose the necessity to be safe or to make the other safe. In essence we have to let ourselves and our God become unconditional. We don't even hope that love will happen, for to place that expectation is to be already the prisoner of fear. And the wonder of this psychological nakedness is that now our relationships are illumined by the Great Lover...and love flourishes. They are infused by the Great Intelligence...and understanding flows from new unknown depths.

Thus naked, we are suffused with a sense of belonging and know the true basis for security, our own I-amness.

Unless we live our words as doors, unless they shine both ways, referent to the finite, to the thing-in-itself and to the infinite beyond representation, every word spoken or thought becomes an act of repression. This is how words become deadly, why sticks and stones can never do more harm. It means everything about where we are in ourselves as we speak them. A chemistry lecture can be a boring recitation of memorized facts, or a living, reverberating revelation of the mystery of our world. The former is at best a story about life, while the latter is a story that is living.

The greatest disease of humankind is not cancer, or heart disease, or warfare. It is lazy socializing and mindless talking. It is using words that do not shine both ways, that imprison us in our ideas, just as we imprison others in the images by which we characterize them. Irate words, strident words, intelligent words, righteous words, well-meaning words, heartfelt words, billions spoken every minute of every day, some opening us to the well-spring of connection and relationship that imbues us with living presence, others that distance us and separate us and dissipate the limited lifeforce we have. And when we unwittingly dissipate our lifeforce, when our energy level decreases through the very act of our communication we become vulnerable to the greatest degrees of soulless objectification and separating illusion inherent in First Miracle consciousness. The Second Miracle is a higher energy state precisely because it is a state of continuous relationship. The Word is a doorway onto a universe. "In the beginning was the Word" *and* the consecration, the "in my name" from which those words flow. If we are not ultimately gathered in the name of something we cannot finally reduce to anything, to any object-of-consciousness, our words will reduce us, deaden us, steal our sensuality, and deny us the richness of belonging.

When Jesus says, "gathered in my name," he means the spirit he calls us to; we stand before irreducible mystery, we stand before the uncreated source from which all else arises. Standing thus our

107

attention links finite to infinite, timelessness with time. Words come alive and we come alive with them. As Rilke put it:

> What we choose to fight is so tiny!
> What fights with us is so great!
> If only we would let ourselves be dominated
> as things do by some immense storm,
> we would become strong too, and not need names.
>
> When we win it's with small things,
> and the triumph makes us small.
> What is extraordinary and eternal
> does not want to be bent by us.
>   ("*The Man Watching,*" translated by Robert Bly)

As a former physician I have come to feel that the potential for healing and health (or, said in another way, the probability of being reorganized in wholeness) increases exponentially as we cease to stop at the words we use, or those used by others, to define our dis-ease. A heart is not merely a *heart*. A *liver* is but a glimmering of the incredible organ. *Fear, anxiety, depression, weakness,* whatever symptom we name, each is an infinity in itself. They are beginnings, not ends, doorways into a universe of creativity and discovery, not barricades. Look through these words as though looking into a two-way mirror. The objects are so bright in the mirror; they captivate our First Miracle attention. Labels like multiple sclerosis, chronic fatigue syndrome, Lou Gehrig's disease, and all the other labels, ad infinitum, seem to make us real to ourselves. Yet we are not fully alive until we can look through them…no matter how obscure or dim it may seem.

To listen deeper and deeper into the present moment. To listen at the doorway of our senses and through them. To contemplate at the doorway of our thoughts and visions and beyond them. To stay at the threshold of each feeling and remain wordless, unnaming. To look into existence as it is arising and registering right now in our awareness and to look through and beyond the words that we use to describe it. Ever in movement, ever rooted in something unchanging, each of us is a cosmos. We could exhaust every word ever created and every word that will ever be created and still not fathom the end of even a single one of us. When we speak then, understanding this, this is the Word.

1. Lusseyran, Jacques, *And There Was Light,* Parabola Books, 1987.

# CHAPTER 9

# THE PRODİGAL SON REVİSİTED

The parable of the Prodigal Son tells the story of a young man who leaves the wealth and security of his father's home and sets out to be his own master. Over time he squanders his inheritance, becomes demoralized and, in abject misery and defeat, returns to his father, who welcomes him with open arms. The parable is a restatement by Jesus of the Garden of Eden myth. He is showing that the original exile is repeated over and over again in every person; we are all "prodigal sons" and "daughters." It was the genius of Jesus' teaching that he returns the prodigal to his place in the universe. He describes how human beings are once again reconciled and welcomed back to the larger sphere of being.

The Prodigal Son is another name for First Miracle man. By its very nature, subject-object consciousness cannot partake of the Father/Mother's wealth of immediacy and belonging. In becoming self-aware, the prodigal son must live out of his own energy, out of his own separate existence. To remain in his father's house is to be forever submerged in a universal consciousness. This is tantamount to unconsciousness or the instinctual potential of the so-called lower creatures.

It is a misreading of the parable to think that the prodigal son is actually a willful or recalcitrant sinner. The rebellion and exile of the First Miracle is, as we've said, predetermined by Nature. Whether the prodigal's subsequent actions are good or bad from the point of view of the morality of First Miracle man is irrelevant. This is not a story about reward or punishment. In either case, good son/daughter or bad son/daughter, each prodigal is equally exiled, and whatever the so-called sins, whatever exaggerations each has created to make heaven or hell in his life, each will forever be welcomed by the Second Miracle state when finally the ego is ready to submit to the new potential.

The subject-object ego has been likened by ancient mystics to a cup of water submerged in the ocean. The ocean is a metaphor for the universal consciousness or Self that both fills and surrounds the cup. But the ego recognizes only that aspect of the water that is within the cup, and considers this its self. The prodigal self must go off to drink of life, filling every moment with extravagant objectification, forever separated from immediate participation with the larger Self. Gradually the prodigal discovers, as we all eventually do, that life within the cup is ultimately barren until it is co-existent with the larger life. Attempting to fulfill himself, he finds himself consistently demeaned in his own nature as creature and perversely destructive to the Earth he inhabits. Exhausted and humiliated, contemporary descriptions are depressed, alienated, burned out, soul weary, chronic fatigue, and so on, inevitably he begins the return home to his deeper nature. The beauty of Jesus' story, which he understood from his own life, is that it does not matter how far one may have strayed, when we eventually collapse toward the core of our being we are always welcomed.

It is this potential for profound reconciliation of self with Self, no matter how deep the wounds or traumas, that is the basis for much of my own work in healing. Rather than focus on illness or trauma, I focus on the condition of coming home. Even a few minutes of the experience of belonging begins to restore the possibility of health and well being.

Home. We all long for it. We all long to belong, to rest in the immediacy of now, realized in the simplicity and fullness of being. And it is never a question of being acceptable or worthy; we are always welcomed home. Whether through the door of badness or goodness, immediacy cares not. Saint and sinner alike are welcome. The prodigal may have lived a hard, ugly, cruel existence, or a kind, loving, beautiful one. In either case, as long as he remains in First Miracle consciousness he is exiled. But when he is ready to lay down his ego-driven will, the wholeness of being always awaits.

I have often wondered at the mysterious process that initiates the conscious journey toward the Second Miracle within any specific individual. Clearly, it doesn't happen one way, but many. There is obviously the possibility of initiation by entering a path of spiritual discipline. Probably just as important is the spontaneous emergence of the new consciousness. Here, individuals who don't regard themselves as spiritual suddenly find themselves experiencing a whole new dimension. Classic examples of more or less instantaneous conversion are St. Paul on the road to Damascus or Walt Whitman's opening that is so eloquently described in "Song of Myself." But I believe the process can happen in smaller steps that are less dramatic although perhaps not as radical and deep. Whatever the circumstances, I suspect that the transformational impulse that is driving the unfoldment of the universe is the real cause, and all our seeking and work is a response to its inner promptings. Perhaps, as my friend Aster Barnwell says, it is the prodigal's task to exhaust himself in his seeking, in his ego-driven ardor, thereby, almost by default, becoming available to the next potential.

112 One clear essential is that the ego be mature and strong to be able to become transparent to the vastness of the Second Miracle awareness and not lose the integrity of self-awareness. As we have already noted, anything that compromises the integrity of early ego development, such as sexual or physical abuse, major traumas,

poor parenting, and so forth, may severly hinder the future capacity for the evolutionary shift. A fragile ego structure feels the expansion or dissolution of usual boundaries like a balloon with weak spots; it senses that it will rupture and fragment. In such instances self-awareness can become so disturbed as to threaten the basis for personal identity. The so-called borderline personality, a clinical catch-all category for large numbers of people who have varying degrees of difficulty maintaining ego boundaries, is particularly vulnerable to this. In these instances we can say that the prodigal has trouble returning home because he has never fully left home, never fully matured the First Miracle state. It is crucial then that First Miracle development be set upon a sure foundation.

Paradoxically, there is a certain borderline quality to most introspective and creative people, be they spiritual seekers or not, that is not truly a detriment. This fragility can enhance the prodigal return because of the suffering it causes. A suffering person is not complacent, cannot readily "rest his head," and over time is strengthened by meeting the suffering. Here the individuals are driven by an existential quality of suffering due to their availability to the universal energy of the Ground. On the one side they are struggling to define their own egoic identities. On the other they are being expanded by the universal energy. Often this is the story of genius and of individuals with strong artistic natures. They can seem neurotic and feel that way to themselves. And while there can be neurotic elements to their personalities, the deeper force behind their suffering and their intensity is that they stand nearer to the fire than the average individual. The story of these lives is typically the story of late social maturing because of a need to find themselves and express the force they feel within themselves. I believe their deeper intuition demands more substantial relationships that are discovered in a more organic, less conditioned, timing.

Any notion of killing the ego, or ego death on the spiritual journey is a profound misunderstanding. Obviously, egotism is a form of self-involvement that if amplified by enlargement of consciousness could be very destructive. But a strong and healthy ego is essential to any further growth. Indeed, it takes a strong ego to

113

have the pride and force of character that give one's life fullness. Even if an individual seems totally invested in security, accumulating wealth, creating power—all the worldly activities of prodigal man, if she lives these impulses fully, that very fulfillment calls forth greater energy which can begin to invite the next level. In fact, if there is any liability, it is mediocrity. Mediocrity speaks to a lack of energy, and it requires energy to bring the subject-object self to its knees so that it can at last partake of the great refreshment that lies beyond its own cup.

There is a conspiracy in our culture to protect egos. Too many of us are content to live passively, experiencing life vicariously through television, rarely exercising more than a modest capacity for consciousness. Students are bored because they aren't challenged sufficiently by school. Teachers with high standards who require hard work and who give difficult homework or honest low grades are often criticized for potentially demoralizing their students. They can be undermined and even lose their jobs because parents are all too ready to protect their own egos by ensuring their children will not be faced with failure or made to feel unhappy. And these are the good teachers. Where is the outcry against mediocre educators who live out their tenure, teaching the same curriculum year after year, while hiding their own frustration or outright disinterest? How can we live another day placing our children in the hands of institutions peopled by anything less than the very best of us?

The conspiracy to protect the ego has led to the crippling of leadership. The outraged ego, sometimes organized in private-interest groups, is flattered and bowed to, instead of seen for what it all too often is, a self-protective stance in mediocrity. Physicist Andre Sakharov was a truly great voice against mediocrity in the Soviet Union. Once he was asked why he was so negative and pessimistic about his country. He replied that he was neither negative nor a pessimist. On the contrary, he felt that he was a true optimist because as a scientist he had been trained to make objective observations, to tell things exactly as he saw them. He expressed his optimism in the soul of his fellow countrymen by being willing to tell them the truth. He refused to protect egos from the very wounding that calls the prodigal home.

Today, political arguments and social controversy rarely call us to the crucial bedrock upon which any society must be built—the moral fiber of its people. Here morality isn't simply biblical values, but the very capacity for consciousness within a people. Arguments such as that between pro-choice verses pro-life in the abortion debate—now almost a war—are most significant in that they keep one of life's ancient fierce enigmas alive and unresolved within the collective soul. To resolve such an issue on either side is to suspend a tension necessary for our growth in consciousness. Looking at how people take sides in these issues, I often feel that some people are literally sacrificed, not to something that they strongly believe, but simply to unconsciously sustain evolutionary tension in society. Each side resolves the issue by choosing a concrete position, thereby "resting their heads" and unwittingly coming into mediocrity. The deeper issue is not which side you are on, but whether you can encompass the tension of both sides within yourself.

For example, to automatically say yes or no to birth control misses the deeper issue. In using birth control or not, are we making a choice toward mediocrity? Population growth is perhaps the greatest immediate threat to humanity at this time. But it is not simply a question of numbers; it is a question of what we do to evoke the highest potential of consciousness within ourselves. Just following religious dogma and refusing birth control does not demand our fullest attention and lowers our energy. Using birth control to make sex more casual and thereby decreasing our attention, can also mean a lessening of energy. In all of these issues, simple answers protect the ego. Sustaining the tension of attention within oneself opens the soul to a greater potential in consciousness.

Today, mediocrity permeates the reporting and analysis of complex social issues. The notion of political correctness, which began as an affirmation of fundamental human rights issues, has degenerated into a capitulation to egos. Rather than ennobling

115

our fellow human beings by recognizing and expecting them to express their divine capabilities, we make sure that we honor the popular labels. Mediocrity permeates the medical system's fear of admitting ignorance and refusing to demand each patient to face the full scope of life's insults and misery in a way that can call forth dignity and strength. It permeates the legal system's encouraging abusive lawsuits in hopes of winning fantastic financial settlements to compensate suffering. It is the nature of First Miracle people to look at cause and effect in the crudest terms and, therefore, to seek to place blame. In so doing we eschew the difficulty of life's paradoxes, the fierce enigmas that are the very crucible that prepares the soul for its higher journey.

If God were the heavenly authority he is often imagined to be, he might be saying something like this:

"I gave them bodies but, except for a few, the majority never even experience the exquisite sensations that are possible to them. They procreate in brief spasms of tension release and consider this the bounty of life rather than the most basic reflex that stands at the threshold of magnificent universes. They take their senses for granted and use their bodies like pack animals to haul their sacrosanct personalities from one moment to the next. Even those who truly stretch their physical limits seem content to do so over and over again in the same old sports. And what of their minds! I gave them wonderful minds, but most are content to think what their forebears thought. They don't question enough; above all they don't question themselves. They use the same old labels for their feelings, their emotions, their opinions. When are they going to make a commitment to discover the miracle that I made them?"

Now if God were the CEO of a major Detroit automobile company, he might, in acknowledgment of the poor performance of his creation, decide to discontinue the model. Alas, this may well be what happens to Homo sapiens. Certainly, when too many people accept mediocrity, I fear only great suffering will rouse them to anything more and bring them once again to their Father's house. And many will be lost.

This is why what I call the courtship of lifeforce is the practical heart of the spiritual journey. The courtship of lifeforce is attending to the Prime Directive as it manifests within our whole organism moment by moment. It is resting into life, opening toward whatever is the path of greatest aliveness regardless of the challenge to the ego. So what if we may not succeed? So what if we will be misunderstood? These anxieties are energy that propels us toward the Second Miracle if we do not close down around them.

At the level of the body, the courtship of lifeforce is the ongoing sensitivity to the inner stream of sensation and vital energy. Do I need exercise or some form of active meditation to keep my energy moving and open now? Is it time to rest and let myself slow down? Psychologically, it is a careful appreciation of the tension between openness and availability to others and the need for silence and solitude. It is axiomatic of a psychology of consciousness that one's experience of being depends on how our energy is flowing moment by moment. *Energy not used becomes morbid.* And as long as the energy remains in our thinking, it is always more or less morbid. As we begin to understand the responsibility of consciousness, the courtship of lifeforce becomes the basic discipline by which we honor our sacred potential. We are no longer the victims of our life; there is no one to blame...ever. Our perceptions, moods, thinking, physical well-being, mental clarity, and overall state of being depend on letting life flow through us.

Cultivating openness to a larger consciousness is the great adventure. There is no formula that is good for everyone; the essence of the process is listening to and obeying subtle hints from within the organism. Implicit in calling this *courtship* is that there is delight, not a forced discipline. Here is the hunger of the soul for the nourishment of the spirit. By whatever name or means, it is this courtship that distinguishes the lives of all artists, mystics, and seekers after truth. It is this courtship that is part and parcel of any effort for healing and maximizing health.

We don't have to believe in God or have even the slightest inclination toward spirituality. But what we cannot do is undermine or diminish the lifeforce through abuse of cigarettes, alcohol, drugs or any form of self-deadening, including workaholism. Busyness is often the opiate of the fearful. Such activity dissipates our aliveness and weakens our ability to sustain higher energies. Just the cessation of such behavior automatically ensures an increase in energy and an increase in opportunities to grow in consciousness. If a person is sufficiently self-destructive to actually succeed in destroying his organism's capacity to sustain lifeforce, the result is a diminished capacity for consciousness. Under such circumstances he may well forfeit the potential to actualize the Second Miracle.

This, I believe, is what Jesus meant by saying, "Whoever blasphemes against the Father, it shall be forgiven him. Whoever blasphemes against the Son, it shall be forgiven him. But whoever blasphemes against the Holy Spirit, it shall not be forgiven him, either on earth or in heaven" (Logia 44). First Miracle consciousness, by its very nature, is blasphemy against the Father. But this is simply throwing stones at a creation of its own mind. It has no effect on reality: Therefore, such blasphemy in no way diminishes the evolutionary potential for the Second Miracle—it is forgiven. Likewise, to deny the authority of those teachers who have realized the Second Miracle is merely an activity of pride, fear, and thinking. This, too, has no real power to exclude any prodigal from the re-embrace of the Father. But the Holy Spirit is that indwelling capacity for consciousness in all sentient creatures. Actions, such as destroying one's mind and body with alcohol and drugs that irreparably disrupt the very capacity for consciousness within the organism, cannot be forgiven. This has nothing to do with punishment. If the capacity for the First Miracle has been compromised, conscious embodiment of the Second Miracle becomes impossible. When there is no continuity of consciousness, what is bound in heaven cannot be bound on Earth, and vice versa. On the other hand, illness and disease, at least initially, do not foreclose the potential for higher consciousness. Indeed, illness is often the servant of the evolutionary possibility, working as an embarrassment to the ego. Thus, it can even accelerate our availability to the Second Miracle.

There are certain experiences and times in life when we are innately more available to the possibility of realizing the Second Miracle, times in which the prodigal is naturally welcomed home. These are times in which life itself initiates us into the Second Miracle. One such time is labor, giving birth to new life.

I had intuited the awakening potential of labor long ago, but I did not fully appreciate the richness of the experience until my marriage to Ariel. Her initiation into the Second Miracle came about through her third pregnancy. This journey began with her yearning to trust herself, to allow her own native knowing to guide her. She had come to feel that in her previous pregnancies she had unquestioningly trusted the doctors and given away her own authority. She had not lived these experiences from her deepest intuition.

This is the life of the prodigal self. Without realizing that there is any other way, the prodigal self allows her preparation to be directed by the medical guidelines and social norms that surround her. In short, my wife, like most women, pursued her pregnancies rationally and conscientiously. While her first two births were wondrous experiences, she gradually sensed that something unlived and important inside of her had been betrayed. This intuition grew to become a deep ache that called to her to have a third child.

This time she obeyed her own instincts, her own native, bodily intelligence. She began to inquire even more deeply into everything she could find about childbirth, pregnancy, nutrition. She found an obstetrician who believed in a woman's capacity for conscious birthing. A new level of intuition was beginning to break through from her deeper psyche. The pregnancy and birth became a rite of passage. In the metaphor of the prodigal daughter, she was beginning the return to her Father/Mother's house.

But it was the actual process of labor undertaken naturally, with support but no medical interference, even without the intrusiveness of a particular breathing technique, that ultimately was the awakening event. Here, in the intensity of labor with no external distractions and a deep inner sense of having prepared herself, she trusted her own body's intelligence to guide the labor. On all fours, everything disappeared but the demands of her body and the birth. It became a state of complete belonging, a state of agony, illumination, and grace. She felt opened to mystery and united with her baby in a way that remains to this day, the epiphany of her life. It is a story that I enjoy listening to whenever she finds herself drawn to recount it. Her voice fills with poetic wonder as she relives the mystical sense of oneness that suffused her. Listening to my wife, I can sense the transformation of her being that was born then, and knowing Andreas, her son, it is one of my most personal prayers that every woman and every child could be born in such a state of Grace.

Andreas was born and immediately, with cord still attached, was handed to his mother. He nuzzled and found her breast and began nursing while soft family voices, voices full of the wonder of the birth, murmured around him. He was completely alert, not at all traumatized or exhausted. For the first hours Andreas lay awake blinking and looking all around, completely peaceful. Mother and infant son beheld each other, breathed each other, drifting in a state of mystical communion, nursing, touching, watching. Whereas my opening to the Current came with the experience of the black butterfly, Ariel met the Current in the hours and days following the birth of Andreas.* He was literally initiated into this world suffused with the psychophysical Current that permeated his mother as she rested in the radiance of Second Miracle consciousness. From that day forward, her life began to be guided by a sense of integrity that had its roots in her body and a far deeper intuition of wholeness.

Because we want to think of the prodigal self as the recalcitrant sinner whose redemption comes as an act of religious conversion, it becomes too easy to miss the deeper significance of this

120

story. Ariel's first pregnancies were the acts of the prodigal self. Intellect, posed as good judgement and the norm of the society, defined the sphere of possibility for her experience. It was not that she was prodigal in any willful sense, only that she had her babies having already wandered far from the roots of her own deeper nature. As a result, while these experiences were wonderful, there was something intangible missing, something unlived.

The third pregnancy, in contrast, was the act of the prodigal who has, at last, returned to her Mother's house. By returning to her own native intelligence, the pregnancy was an experience of joining with the universe, of being returned to a condition of prior wholeness. The numinous inner light of consciousness suffused her and has transformed the quality of her life ever since. It is my observation, though only time will bear it out, that passing through life's first primal trauma bathed in such light has given Andreas the gift of a fundamental sense of well being that will, I suspect, enable him to live inherently more available to a larger reality. Moreover, Ariel feels that initial depth of contact between her and Andreas graced her with a deeper capacity for mothering. There is a special quality of honoring and natural easefulness that flows between them that is always present no matter what tensions arise in parenting. I believe that if labor brings a woman to a taste of Second Miracle consciousness, it also instructs her capacity for mothering and parenting, giving her a deep bodily focus, a touch-stone of rich inner feeling that guides her.

It is such bodily well being and maturity of the feeling nature that is, I feel, the rock upon which we build the church of mature spirituality. Without this, our spiritual philosophies and psychologies, no matter how profound, end up employed in the service of our fear and pain rather than the celebration and embrace of our I-amness. How could we ever have believed that the foundation was the mind alone and have denigrated the whole organism so profoundly? This distortion has led to centuries of disembodying spirituality rather than movement into richer incarnation.

The recognition of our own prodigal nature is not just at

121

those moments of darkness and contrition when we pray to be re-stored to well being and peace. Our prodigal nature has created the very world in which we now live. Our prodigal nature begat the whole infinite play of possibility we call the modern world. It is our institutions, our healthcare systems, our governments, our armies, our pillaging of the Earth. It is the way in which we imagine we can solve the problems of environmental deterioration that plague us. Our prodigal nature is all that we set out to do with our thinking, all that we undertake from the infinity of self-concepts, before we have actually experienced in our bodies and hearts a sense of immediacy and participation with life that makes oneself, each other, and this magnificent planet, holy ground. Yet no matter how far we have diverged, if we have diverged, from a path of participation as creature in creation, our Second Miracle nature is already forever waiting. We are already forever forgiven. Already whole. The Earth will be forever changed, we may not even survive, but the potential to participate as one with our world, itself the manifestation of an unspeakable intelligence, has never been denied us and never will. This is the story of the prodigal children that we are.

>——<

It is one of the great mysteries of the process of spiritual growth that it is often the apparent self-destructiveness of the prodigal self that is necessary to initiate, and even enable, the journey home. Like a teenager who soils the nest, creating crisis and rebellion to gather the momentum to break from the childhood home and head out into the larger world, the ego-based self-concept needs to undermine itself to be able to submit to a higher potential. This is destructiveness in the service of a higher evolutionary imperative. This is self-destructiveness that weakens the subject–object ego more than it actually interrupts the capacity for consciousness.

Usually, the prodigal self will not make the return journey until thoroughly miserable, thoroughly disillusioned. Why risk anything new when life seems to be working, even if just barely?

Until recently, this avoidance of risk, this protection of egos, has been the attitude of the developed nations toward their over-consumptive economic activities. We pretended that it is all right, even as more and more of the Third World fell into poverty and misery and the environment steadily deteriorated.

Even when miserable, the ego resists becoming the servant to a new and very different quality of consciousness. An analogy can be made with the survivors of the Uruguay rugby team whose plane crashed in the Andes in 1972. Even when rescue was impossible and death assured, the two men chosen from the group of survivors to make the journey for help, clashed. One wanted to turn back to the familiar crash site rather than risk the unknown terrors of crossing the treacherous mountains. The other chose the unknown and was willing to die walking. His perseverance saved them all.

Is a large part of humanity uncertain and afraid of risking a new approach to our lives and world? Is it that our prodigal nature, which for so long seemed to be leading us to autonomy and freedom, has just not made us sufficiently miserable yet? Is it possible then that our headlong (pun intended) collective rush toward greater technology and consumerism, with the resulting environmental and social self-destruction is a global prodigal nest-soiling; the prelude to the homecoming with the Earth community? Will the misery of a dying, polluted Earth be enough? Or like the reluctant Uruguay rugby player, will we prefer the rotten husk of the Earth and the broken, xenophobic societies to a new but uncertain life as a cooperative member of the global community?

How are we to regard our own destructiveness? Is this not often the very route of return of the prodigal? The old adage that states "pride precedeth a fall" adroitly sums up the dilemma. Realization of the Second Miracle implies a strongly developed self sense. If this is not the case, submission to the Second Miracle would result in a dissolution of self-awareness and loss of consciousness rather than expansion into a larger consciousness. Pride is an attribute of a strong ego, a means by which First Miracle humanity actualizes itself and fulfills its own ego-driven ideals

123

with greater excellence. But pride blinds us to the full impact of our actions until, suddenly, what we have not let ourselves see comes back at us wounding the very root of our prideful self-sense.

In the beautiful ecology of psyche, often this wound is self-inflicted. As an individual example, the life of Malcolm X comes to mind. He rose from the streets of the black ghetto to become a powerful and important voice for black outrage and pride. Given the atmosphere of terrible racial oppression and denigration in his early life, criminal activity was a means of asserting individuality and self-autonomy. While I am not defending criminal behavior, in certain social climates such behavior may be healthier for an individual from the point of view of establishing a strong ego, than to fall back on conformity and submission to a social norm that is unjust. For Malcolm X, his powerful lifeforce and pride found self-expression through violence and crime. Eventually this became the source of the wound that would begin a new movement in his consciousness. I am referring to his self-destructive rebellion in prison that resulted in him being placed into solitary confinement. Here, finally, he fell into deep psychic chaos, where, for awhile, his own will and personal pride could no longer sustain him; he was forced to submit. This submission, a crack in the First Miracle armor, became the door to a new life that came in the form of a spiritual conversion. Under the guidance of a Black Muslim mentor, he undertook a stringent self-discipline in the service of a new self-image: the dedication of himself to the cause of the Black Man in America.

But this whole transformation, including becoming a celebrated evangelist for the Black Muslims, was all within the capacity of the First Miracle ego. As a criminal he was referent to his own prideful self-indulgence and misguided rebellion; now he was referent to the stringent identity of a Black Muslim and most especially to Elijah Muhammed, his guru and master. First he had no need for God; now he was a zealot with very concrete notions about God which extended into his whole worldview. Women were objects to serve men and their families. Children were objects to be cultivated like farms. White people were demonic objects and black people were the chosen.

Racism in any form always implies an exaggeration of the object pole of First Miracle consciousness. And while the racist is unaware of it, he too is an object to himself, a state in which there can ultimately be no sense of personal sacredness and true inner peace. It was not until Malcolm received the wound of recognizing the clay feet of his teacher that his prodigal pride began to crumble and he was forced back upon himself in an entirely new way. He undertook a pilgrimage to Mecca. But Mecca is an outer symbol for an inner truth; he had begun the quest into his own infinite subjectivity. He began to see himself mirrored in all people and all life. Thus began the opening of his spiritual heart, the dawning of the Second Miracle. It was his realization of a new tolerance at the end of his life that marks, in my opinion, his true greatness and the hope his life offers for all people of every race.

For me, the life of Malcolm X says that when we try to look only at the outer appearance of a life, we can easily misjudge the deeper psychic forces at work there. Even self-destructive and anti-social behavior can be in the service of a deeper truth at times, the truth of the unfoldment of the soul. If Malcolm X's prodigal pride had not finally brought him to disaster he might never have become available to a deeper life. But at the same time, without that pride and passionate lifeforce, he might never have escaped the degradation of his earlier life. Like so many millions of others he might have simply disappeared into a life of mediocrity and self-abasement.

The transformational impulse, the deep call of evolution within our beingness, requires psychic energy. While I am not in any way condoning violence, true inner peace is not the fruit of any kind of mediocrity and self-repression. On the contrary, it is the fruit of realization of a larger condition of belonging. Whatever errors occur along the way, when the prodigal son finally submits—and the impulse to submit can look, at first, like self-destruction—a new consciousness is always waiting to receive

125

him. Perhaps the question for us all now is, has our collective First Miracle pride reached such a peak that we are perched at an imminent fall? In the next few decades, will we have wounded ourselves deeply enough to begin our return?

*In 1977 a black butterfly landed on the middle of my forehead and I suddenly entered a state of satori and was changed forever. I write about this kind of experience extensively in *The I That Is We* and *The Black Butterfly,* also published by Celestial Arts.

# CHAPTER 10

# THE FOUR PILLARS
# OF THE
# SPIRITUAL JOURNEY

O ver the years, I have come to understand that there are four areas, or foundations, that my own work focuses upon. It wasn't that I had intended it this way; rather, it evolved naturally out of the demands for a broad and balanced approach to my own, and other people's, spiritual emergence. It seems to me that these areas are universal to any comprehensive path of consciousness exploration, indeed, that they weave together and, in a certain sense, are indivisible. They are, one: **meditation and prayer** (and also devotional practices and contemplation), two: **symbolic reality** (myths, fairy tales, teaching stories, films, imagery and, most especially, dreams), three: **body consciousness** (including various forms of yoga, stretching, body work, dance, and all sports at the point where we live the activity as opposed to doing it), and four: **energy awareness** (which includes healing work, attention and presence exercises, energy-sharing practices such as Sacred Meditation,* and so on). Each of these areas by themselves is a profound path, even a life-art form, and in truth, none can be followed deeply without crossing over into the others. Each has been the subject of countless books and discourses throughout human history. Whatever the differing belief systems, spiritual practice throughout the world stands in varying degrees on these pillars. In this chapter my intention is to very briefly look at each of them from the aspect of consciousness they principally address and how I have learned to integrate these in my own work.[1]

## Meditation and Prayer

Meditation and prayer, are ancient and profound arts that involve relationship with our deepest nature. As a practice, meditation encourages more and more subtle observation of the movement of thought, sensation, and feeling. As we grow in the ability to become detached observers (sometimes I like to say that we learn to laugh at ourselves in the sense of no longer being hooked by things that arise in our awareness) many things begin to evolve. For one thing, we are less threatened by our thoughts, less likely to be caught in belly-mind, the circle of thinking that feeds emotion that, in turn, feeds more thinking, and on and on. In this way we do gradually develop equanimity. Simultaneously, and even more important, as we become less trapped in uncentered mental and emotional activity, we begin to develop radical intuition. Gradually, we become so attuned to even the most subtle planes of consciousness, that we begin to experience the immediacy of That which is forever prior to any identifiable object of consciousness. This is when meditation becomes a truly spiritual path.

Meditation and prayer encourage our vulnerability to a larger reality. Vulnerability is not suffering; it is true strength, even though it implies a certain risk and even discomfort when we stand at the edge of vastness, at the edge of the new and unknown. The paradox of faith is that the deeper our faith, the greater our vulnerability, yet the more we are able to rest in that vulnerability. Meditation and prayer are means of shifting the referent from the finite object-of-consciousness to the infinite. The subtle difference between prayer and meditation is that, while meditation cultivates a way of detached listening, prayer is a more active dialogue with mystery. Above all, prayer approaches the infinite through feeling. It is the devotional quality of prayer that reaches toward the infinite like a lover listening for the beloved. It is the feeling with which we speak to God, that in turn is the feeling quality with which we embrace our fullest selves. Just as music can lead us into experiences that are impossible to describe in words, feeling allows us to appreciate a far greater interconnection with reality than is possible through thought alone. The whole devotional aspect of prayer is a reaching toward God through feeling, through our despair, our outrage, our hope, and in the deepest places, through our love. By making ourselves vulnerable to God, we begin, as with meditation, to become responsive to a larger intelligence. When we truly know this as love, we know ourselves as whole.

The art of freeing attention from identification with the objects of consciousness at more and more subtle levels is the principle gift of meditation. There are many techniques or forms for beginning to evolve this art. Some, like Zazen, involve body posture, breath, and open-eyed attention. This kind of meditation tends to quickly jump to a relatively impersonal state of attention and, in my opinion, is not the best for developing subtle insight into personal psychological patterning. It is almost as if we jump over or skip a necessary stage of intimacy with the shitty side of our personal psyche, and this does not necessarily prepare us to meet our shit when, in the course of ordinary living, it inevitably comes up.

Other meditation forms, like Vipassana, use the sensation of the breath in the body to anchor the attention and then encourage a soft, receptive openness to anything that arises. This kind of meditation is excellent when we are fairly calm, but does not have sufficient intensity—unless prolonged for long periods, or we practice it in group intensives where there is a lot of collective support—to be utilized by someone who is in intense crisis. Similarly, Transcendental Meditation, which involves tethering the attention to a repeated inner word called a mantra, is excellent for developing deep relaxation and inner mental stillness. But here again, if a person is in intense feeling, he will not be able to force the mind to follow the mantra. This is true for most meditation practices when done alone; there has to be a certain degree of equanimity just to begin. But if we do discipline ourselves to regularly meditate, gradually there is a quality of centeredness that evolves, which allows us a far greater capacity to become aware of, but not drown, in the endless stuff of the mind.

I have explored several different meditative traditions, but tend to flow between them in accordance with my inner state rather than adhering to one specific form. For example, an excellent contemplation that returns the attention to awareness of one's psychoemotional state of being is the question, "Who am I?" This is, afterall, the premier question every person must answer deeply with her life, and each answer is a doorway into an infinity of living everything from heaven to hell. By asking the question, our attention looks at exactly how we are feeling and what we are thinking. For example, right now I might answer, "I am aware of being absorbed in the act of writing, but I hear the bird chirping outside." Answering this question can center us in simple acknowledgement of where we are right now. I often suggest that before trying to work out interpersonal issues at work, or in a marriage, we sit down and just repeat this question ten times and follow each answer deeper and deeper. If, for example, having posed the question, "Who am I?" your first answer is, "I am afraid of rejection," the second time you ask the question you might say, "Who am I that is afraid of rejection?" Now the answer gets more subtle, goes deeper. Perhaps the answer now becomes, "The part of me that feels unsafe." Now the question might become, "Who am I that feels unsafe?" and the answer might be, "A person who has lost touch with his deeper self."

Thus the contemplation of this question can lead us deeper and deeper in a process of insight. Invariably, I have found that when I hit the answer that, all of sudden, reverberates in my body and instantly calms the emotional state (or the judging state, the desiring state, and so on), I have attained to a deep relationship to myself. This is now the time to do the interpersonal work, or to begin to sink into a deeper state of meditation that is simply receptive and no longer directing the attention in any specific way. The

130

question drops away and becomes the condition of attention itself. Now, quite spontaneously, we can use any of the other more subtle meditation techniques, or simply remain attentive. If there is intense crisis, then any of these meditation techniques will be inadequate to compete with the force of emotion that has possessed the person's attention. In this case I have found that bio-energetic exercises, such as standing for thirty minutes with one's arms straight out from the shoulders, will call so much inner fire and willpower that we can then have authority over the rampant mind. Now it can become possible to begin an insight process with the question, Who am I? and even enter into deeper meditation.

I do not believe that attaining to such a profound level of objectless attention, as certain yogis do who remain absorbed in this way for most of their lives, is the goal of evolution, or a necessity for the development of most individuals. But the capacity to observe the subtle movements of thought and sensation is crucial to learning to listen to our connection to life. Then we can feel when we are closing down and disconnected from the fundamental relationship to ourselves, the Infinite, and, of course, to each other.

In the last analysis, meditation and prayer reflect our relationship to Mystery. To meditate in hopes of becoming enlightened is to just be caught in the wheel of desire. To touch meditation more subtly is to learn to listen without expectation. Even if in prayer we imagine that we are talking to God, we are also talking to ourselves at a depth we usually don't regard as ourselves. We must do more of this. I often tell people, "You have to learn to talk to yourself, as though you were talking to the wisest being you could imagine." But wisdom is the key, and wisdom must be learned. Sometimes in a sweatlodge or during other rituals where prayers are spoken, I feel that part of my responsibility is to silently protect people from their prayers. Some people, unwisely, pray for too much. They pray for something that is wonderful at one level, but very dangerous or even impossible at another level of themselves. I'm not sure we are ready to have our immune systems act unconditionally loving, or deplore violence when facing an invading bacteria or virus.

131

Sometimes a person prays to be so purified that only their deepest essence remains. But if such a prayer were answered it might be a horrendously cruel process for the simple self and the basic organism to bear.

The old adage, "Be careful what you pray for," is very wise. It is crucial that we learn to talk to our deepest selves, for in so doing we learn to have an intimate sense of relationship to God. But we must not forget the paradox that, ultimately, God is beyond all referents, and that prayer, or inner dialogue at this level, is really a conversation with ourselves. If we want a kind God, we must begin with being wisely compassionate about our own evolutionary potential.

## Symbolic Reality

If I have one caution about meditation, it is that meditative practice must be the servant of our deepest intelligence. It must be grounded into ordinary living. That is, rather than meditate to escape life's irritations, or attain some notion of self-transcendance, the gift of meditation is to be more self-aware so that we stop energizing the part of us that resists life. Our egos can be amazingly subtle, amazingly tricky; our spiritual practice can become the root of a pseudo-identity and this is not our deepest essence.

I have met several advanced meditators, where this was exactly the problem. One man, a Western Buddhist monk for nearly twenty years, and a meditation teacher himself, was gradually being led into severe illness by his identification with his practice. With the blessings of his master, he had begun a one year solitary meditation retreat. Two months into the retreat he was getting sicker and sicker and the people who were delivering food to him asked if I would speak to him. When he came he described his practice: an hour of sitting in full lotus utilizing very exacting inner attention techniques, followed by thirty minutes to an hour of walking. This cycle was repeated throughout the day from early morning to night. Every day. As his body revolted with intensifying abdominal cramps, he at first tried to ignore it and dedicated himself with even greater determination to his practice. But soon he couldn't sit, and only when he was resting would the pain diminish. I could see that his practice was being directed by his ego, specifically a masculine notion of attainment and self-transcendance. I asked simply, "Do you know what Existence wants of you?" He responded, "No." I asked if he thought his master knew? He answered that he doubted that anyone knew the ultimate answer to this question for themselves or anyone else. "Well then," I asked, "why are you forcing yourself? Doesn't such determination presume, somehow, that you do know where you are going and what you should achieve?"

As we discussed the spiritual ambition and perhaps, insecurity, that was underlying his efforts, a light dawned in him and he related a simple dream. In the dream he had seen Rada, the feminine consort to the Buddha. She was sprawled casually, almost sloppily (his word) on a sumptuous couch or bed. Looking at the dream it seemed obvious that her whole demeanor suggested a very different orientation to spiritual practice. He took the gift of this insight. For the rest of the year he socialized, learned to rock climb, meditated only when called to from within. After a few months he asked his master to be released from his seventeen years of celibacy. Within a year he was getting married and was even a step-father. No, this story is not mine, though it is similar in many ways. But it is true, and it shows us that we need more than meditation practice; we need to listen to the deeper intelligence that speaks to us through symbolism and especially in our dreams.

The narcissistic ego is like a black hole calling everything to itself, in essence forever avoiding fundamental relationship. But dreams, spontaneous imagery, myths, and teaching stories help us to stand outside the event horizon of our egos and see the patterns within our ego-driven behavior. It is through dreams, more than almost any other means, that we begin to really see and trust a far larger intelligence that is living through each of us.

133

Much of life, more than we can imagine, is beyond our capacity to consciously perceive or engage. All of what we call reality is really a representation and, in this sense, can be said to be symbolic. One of the great shocks to me was when I realized just how deeply this goes. Watching my own life, and carefully observing the lives of thousands of people, hearing their dreams, seeing into their hidden fantasy lives, I came to realize that often we cannot distinguish between the outer and inner symbolism. They are superimposed upon each other so that we can think we are living a reality, but it is more a creation of our own imaginings. This projection of our inner symbolic reality onto the outer world can deeply threaten our capacity to meet life directly and genuinely. One way we can begin to see into the labyrinth is through becoming students of our dreams. Through dreams and imagery, forces, dynamics, patterns, and structures that are otherwise beyond our conscious perception—because we are so embedded in them— are presented to us. If we can decipher the meaning of the symbols, or the story, in the dream or imagery, we become conscious of what was formerly unconscious in us.

Working with dreams is a subtle art that is far more than interpreting the symbols of the dream by simply giving them other names. In fact, even though certain symbols may be universal or come from an archetypal stream of consciousness as Jung pointed out, in reality every symbol can have many interpretations from one person to another. One of the crucial insights is that the person or thing that is represented in a dream may not have anything to do with that person or thing in outer life.

For example, a woman I know fell deeply in love with a man I'll call Frank. After a short but deeply felt affair, Frank broke it off, which plunged her into misery. Over time it became very clear that he had no intentions of ever re-engaging the relationship. But in her dreams, Frank continued to be an important figure. She often dreamt that he ignored her and she was filled with anguish. At other times she dreamt that he was calling to her and she was filled with hope and joy. She was so obsessed with Frank that her fantasies about him blocked her from enjoying other male companionship. Her problem was that she was confusing the Frank in her dreams, who was an inner symbol, with the outer Frank who would never be a real-life companion. I pointed this out to her. Then she began to see that Frank had become the symbol for her inner beloved. When she dreamt that Frank was attentive and affectionate, her waking state was filled with happiness and energy—she was connected to the beloved within herself. When in her dream Frank ignored her, her waking mood was of emptiness and depression—she had lost her connection to the inner beloved. In fact, when she was finally allowing herself to open to a new companion, John, that was precisely when she'd dream that Frank was calling to her. Then she would become confused and withhold herself from John, re-energizing her hopes for Frank. But as she realized that the dream Frank was a symbol for her own loving energy, this confusion stopped. It was her very opening to new love with John that was being reiterated to her in her dreams about Frank's return and affection. This is why interpreting symbols is such an art; we have to learn to listen with our whole being and in the context of our whole lives, not just with our intellects, which have a very limited way of perceiving and organizing reality. The range of what dreams can be referring to can be quite vast. Obviously this is only one example of how a symbol can represent an energy or dynamic and not the object itself. It would be impossible for me to fully discuss the depth and nuance of dreamwork here, but some crucial suggestions and insights can be helpful.

First of all, listen to the dream as deeply relaxed into your body as possible. This kind of listening is, for me, almost a state of emptiness in which the usual associative mental processes are set aside and I just rest into my whole being. Imagine that the dream is a tapestry, or a stained-glass window. Pull back from the specific images and take the whole dream in at once, if possible. Feel where the attention is drawn, what I call the center of gravity of the dream. There can be more than one center of gravity. Then notice if there is any pattern in the way the action of the dream organizes around each center of gravity. The dream with Rada is, obviously, very simple. Just feeling the image says it all. The feminine spirituality is not so driven, not so excluding, not so divided between what is spiritual and what is not. Formlessness is also a form, easefullness is also as rigorous as focused attention.

Another way to approach a dream is to try to give it a name.

Dreams are often stories whose meaning is in the story itself. The significance of the individual symbols may not be interpretable except as necessary elements in presenting the story. For example, at the end of one of my ten-day retreats, a male participant, a lawyer, had this dream: He is standing outside his family's home in the country. It is a sunny and beautiful day. Suddenly he sees armed enemy soldiers coming around a distant hill. Immediately he tells his family to go inside the house. But even as he is closing the door, it bursts open. The soldiers rush in and machine-gun everyone. He awakens in great anxiety. He interpreted this dream to mean that there was a lot of anger in him that he didn't know about. He felt ashamed of the violence in the dream, ashamed that he couldn't protect his family. Other people in the group started making up other interpretations that amounted to telling stories by reframing the various symbols: The soldiers were his masculine side, and this was overwhelming his feminine side, and so on. Sometimes there is value in this level of interpretation, but too often this is just the intellect assembling one of its endless abstractions, in effect avoiding relationship to something immediate and consciously lived.

To me, the dream was very obvious and direct. After a ten-day retreat that had expanded him greatly, it was a story that said quite simply: My usual defenses aren't working. The dream was preparing him to go home. It was making him conscious of his vulnerability. While the dream wasn't telling him what to do, by becoming aware of how open he was he could take appropriate measures, such as moving slowly, staying in his body, not defending himself against the feeling of vulnerability. The level of intelligence that I have seen revealed in dreams has, as much as anything in my life, caused me to trust the incredible wisdom in each of us. Equally, it has brought the immanence of God home to me over and over again. Listening to the dreams, mine and others, understanding only a fraction of them, nevertheless has brought me ever deeper in faith.

If the dream's story is not obvious, I have found it helpful to ask the question, which Jung often asked, "What is this dream compensating?" In other words, if you hadn't had this dream what would you not be aware of? What the dream makes us aware of— a feeling, the sense of confusion, anxiety, joy, well-being, connectedness, or disconnection—any of these can be very important to us as we step back into our outer life. I often wish that before any major government decisions, such as cutting off funds for childcare or going to war, that every politician would have a horrifying nightmare, something like the dreams in *A Christmas Carol,* that eventually open Scrooge's heart. After a nightmare, if we don't immediately harden our hearts and reassemble our facade, for a little while we are mortal, shaken, and simple things matter. And it is usually in simple things: the moment we pause to hear another, to empathize, to be grateful for a smile, that we come to remember what really matters. A nightmare, if we let it, can shake us loose from our usual egoistic grip; it can open our hearts. And so can many dreams. They can show us that we are not alone when that is what we feel in everyday life. They can show us that we are not as strong as we pretend. They can expose our lies, both those that make us smaller than we are and those that make us too big, too important. Dreams are important because they reframe or replay our waking consciousness in a way that can help us see the patterns that we live in, but which remain invisible to us until we see them presented in a contrasting form.

And this is why the last step of any dream work, for me, is to sense the dream so deeply that we have actually become conscious of something new—a pattern, a way of defending ourself, a need we have been ignoring, or denying—in such a way that we now have the ability to live more consciously. By being presented with a dream in which he sees himself as so vulnerable, the lawyer was being invited to meet this vulnerability in new ways. Instead of closing down at the first sign of threat, he could identify his feeling, "Ah, this is my dream, I'm feeling too open, too vulnerable. I think I'll take a few deep breaths and sink into my body. I'll walk a little slower and rest closer to my I-amness." Without the dream he might have panicked, his responses might have led to greater tension, or a cycle of defense and attack. The dream opened a door to new possibility simply by making him aware of himself in a way that had not, until the dream, actually been conscious to him.

The reason I work with dreams as part of nearly all of my seminars is that I do not feel clear enough to see another person's essence in the full complexity of their life process. Just sensing their energy, or watching them in the various situations and exercises that are part of the seminar, can give hints of what they are working on, or where they might need some suggestions. But their own dreams are undeniable statements of their being. The dreams can come from so many levels; that's the brilliance of them, but they are not under the control of the basic ego. They reveal the ego and patterns that support or obstruct the expression of essence. They reveal far more than just ego dynamics; they can indicate potentialities that instruct us about the deeper forces of the psyche. But even here I don't presume to interpret another person's dream. Especially, when a dream is presented as part of a group process, I ask that each participant, including myself, comment on the dream as though it were his own by beginning one's remarks saying, "In my dream…" Dreams, like myths, fairy tales, stories, movies, or reading tarot cards, invite our own projections. In this way one person's dream becomes the mirror for many peoples' psychic orientation. We hear one dream, but together we speak of many dreams. And as the individual who shared the dream listens to mine or other people's sense of the dream, he may suddenly resonate to some of these interpretations and feel himself connected to the dream in a more direct way. Now the dream is no longer an intellectual construction, but a direct connection to himself in a way that reorients his awareness of himself. This to me suggests that we have begun the return process of moving from the story and the symbol back to the feeling and deeper energy of the dream.

138     A technique that can help this essential return is—assuming the story was not obvious and we haven't been able to sense what the dream is helping to make conscious—taking each key symbol and by sinking into body consciousness, let it translate itself into a feeling or some dynamic that we can recognize in our energy. For

example, we cannot readily recognize concepts such as the feminine, the masculine, the inner child, or the higher self, in our bodies. But a child in a dream might be a quality of feeling, or a very open state of being. A rat in a dream might be fear. A husband or wife that appears in a dream may not have anything to do with the person we are married to. But he or she could be the animating energy of a particular quality of our personality, or of an important aspect of our life such as the "husband" of our body consciousness, the "wife" of our emotional life. A woman I know dreamt that she was riding bareback on a stallion. Her husband was walking on the ground next to the horse, firmly holding the reins. She interpreted the dream to mean that she and her husband had a good relationship. But there was little conviction or energy in this interpretation; it didn't help her in her life. As the seminar progressed she realized that her "husband" was her intellect and that it was tremendously inhibiting her vital aliveness. This interpretation was like a shock of revelation. She literally took off her granny glasses, let down her hair, and abandoned herself into the dancing. Just before the end of the seminar, she had another dream. Now, she was riding bareback on a stallion. Her husband was on a separate horse and they were galloping across a pasture, leaping fences. Obviously, she had freed the energy from her intellect into her body, but her mind was there for her to celebrate with, without repressing her aliveness.

If we can take each symbol and feel into the part of ourselves represented by the symbol, we begin to approach a point where sometimes the dream can be restated as a dynamic of consciousness in our whole organism, as the woman above had done. I have found that this becomes easier if we have also done a good deal of meditation and have learned to watch the shift of subtle states of consciousness. It becomes easier still if we have developed a deep connection to our body consciousness so that we have a profound and subtle connection to our sensations and feelings. When this level of sensitivity and intelligence about ourselves combines with the dream we can discover profound insight. The dream can give us a story or picture that takes something that had been operating subconsciously and brings it into conscious awareness. Obviously the possibilities are infinite, but the crucial thing is to bring the awareness back to the level of feeling that connects us to our sense of organism that we live from all the time. If the dream helps us to become more conscious in the immediacy of now, it has brought us closer to ourselves and closer to mystery in our conscious lives. Our capacity for consciousness has increased. This is growing, this is evolving.

The creative process of meeting the dream is, to me, just as important, or even more important, than whether we ever actually understand the dream. In a closed universe there may be one correct interpretation of a dream. But in an open universe, as ours is, just the relationship of our attention to the dream is a process of inception that can give birth to all kinds of understandings. Even if all we experience is perplexity, so that the ego wants to dismiss the dream as meaningless, the truth is we could use a lot more perplexity at the level of our egos. The world is far more mysterious and complex than ego-based awareness ever lets us realize. Ultimately, we may never know whether the interpretation is right or not; what really matters is what we give birth to, that the dream has opened us to a creative relationship to ourselves. Psyche is mysterious. She does not ask us to be right, only that we be reverent, that we not ignore her, and not deny her intelligence.

## Body Consciousness and Energy Awareness

Too often the insight born in meditation or through our dreams becomes just another mental universe if it is not grounded into the immediacy of our ability to feel more fully, to evolve the capacity for sensual intuition of a larger reality. As we learn to sense into ourselves, into our sensations, our feelings, our emotions, the space of our body, and by listening simultaneouly toward the Infinite, we begin to expand and refine the vocabulary of our conscious self-awareness. The Infinite is like the horizon: We can never reach it. But as we take a step toward the Infinite in ourselves we become more incarnated. To do this requires working directly with body consciousness. The deeper impulse of spirituality, of evolution itself, is not to think about God, but to approach God directly in our own flesh. Our human organism is information evolving. We are the intelligence of the universe incarnating. And incarnation is never complete; we are a mystery beyond any reductionist contemplation. Consider the millions of chemical and electrical interactions taking place right now in our thousands of billions of cells. We realize immediately that an infinitesimal amount of this is under conscious control. A dancing, singing, speaking, playing, loving, or hating human is just the merest tip of an inexpressibly vast iceberg, just the tiniest mirror of that vast submerged beingness.

If we close our eyes and just let our attention rest deeper into our organism, we perceive a space that is mostly without characteristic, a vague sense of something we might call fatigue, irritability, restlessness, flowing energy, calmness, tightness, and so on; it is constantly changing, unless of course, we are locked into some powerful emotion or severe pain. (Even this is changing, but it is very difficult for us to sustain the kind of attention that can recognize these changes.) The degree to which we have words for our experience in this space, is the degree we have become conscious of ourselves. Seen in this way, how many names do you have for this subtle space of self? For some people to name even fifty would be a great deal. An individual who has named many hundreds is much more self-aware and more incarnated. She will have considerably greater inner authority. She has come closer to God in herself. To a person with a much smaller repetoire of inner being, such an individual would seem like a God, just as Jesus did, or the saints do to the average person. It is not that naming itself is what is important, it is the movement toward the Infinite, toward the Beloved, within ourselves. This is the heart and soul of deepening body consciousness.

Now, if—still with eyes closed and listening very intently, yet easefully, in this space of ourselves—we move our attention to what seems to be outside of us, we discover that this boundary is very difficult to isolate. To our deeper attention, the inner and the outer are a continuum. For the surfer, the inner continuum is as much defined by the wave that is being ridden as by anything that

141

can be said to be only inner. Our conscious experience is the reflection in which we recognize not only our relationship to ourselves, but our relationship to a far larger beingness. This level of consciousness is not just of our mentality, it is of our whole organism as it exists embedded in a limitless universe. Body consciousness is not merely consciousness *of* ourselves as isolated creatures, it is conscious *as* ourselves. Body consciousness, as I use the term, describes the experience of consciousness *as* the body, as a whole indivisible organism, rather than consciousness *of* the body. Consciousness *of* the body is relationship to our physical and feeling self as an object to be dissected, analyzed, used, trained, manipulated, and fixed. Consciousness *as* the body is the fundamental environment for relationship to existence.

Again and again, as we have seen, the First Miracle ego co-opts our relationship to ourself. Often, yoga practice, sports, exercise, almost anything we do with our bodies, become activities in which the body is merely a machine directed and disciplined for some desired end. We can spend a lifetime using our bodies in this way and never really learn to listen to life through our whole organism, never learn to hear the intelligence of the universe in our very cells.

Everything in our world is changing. Every atom of our body is replaced in a few months or slightly longer. All our ideas about ourselves and our world will be almost completely different in a few decades. Whether in our families, or in our businesses, all that any of us have to anchor ourselves amid all this change is what we feel, what we sense immediately in our bodies. In essence all we have is our attention, our capacity to listen. This, above all, is what we are. Yet, most people cannot feel themselves very deeply. Rather than allow themselves to grow in the capacity to listen within themselves, they are deeply threatened by it and attempt to anesthetize themselves. They may have to grow ill from cigarettes, alcohol, or poor diet before even beginning to notice that they have a body. If they are lucky the suffering helps them to awaken. If not, many can pass through life and never know the miracle of deepening embodiment. Seen in this way, the various things that

142

many of us do to ourselves in the name of spiritual practice, or just cultural rebellion, from self-mortification, to long fasts, to hyper-ventilation, to using psychedelic drugs is, for better or worse, an attempt to create contrast within the ocean of our beingness in order to grow more conscious of ourselves.

I realized long ago that it is futile to pursue spiritual develop-ment without working directly with the totality of our beingness. I approach this in my work in many ways: through chanting, singing, extemporaneous speaking, breath-work, fasting, stretch-ing, and various energy-sensing exercises. I use a wide variety of music for dancing, listening and various movement processes, and all of these combine at times in rituals. Also, the aesthetics of the teaching environment and the quality and presentation of the meals contribute to a deepening experience of embodiment. In practice, the work is to gradually perturb the old body-ego patterning so that it opens to a new and larger patterning. This means balancing intensity with deep relaxation and varying the exercises frequently enough so that the ego cannot readily organize the experiences into a familiar context. Nearly all of the special meditations and inductions call each person into more direct relationship to his own deeper sensuality and feeling nature. Many of the exercises are finely crafted interactive meditations in partnership with others, so that the other person becomes a mirror in which one risks to see oneself more nakedly, with less self-protection. It is the induction of the exercises that is crucial. It is my own openness to Infinity that acts as a matrix for keeping the activities from becoming a means to an end, rather than an end in themselves. Again and again the guidance is to be referent to Mystery, to remain present, to allow, and thereby submit oneself—with and through one's whole organism—to the immediacy of the moment. It is a process of invoking a more refined yet balanced sensitivity in one's whole being. A new awareness grows in which we are the servant of the organism's intelligence. By allowing ourselves to be moved, be sung, be spoken and, above all, to listen to oneself at ever-deepening levels, we begin to discover this intelligence. In the spontaneity and creativity of these activities, the consciousness of the whole

143

organism is once again released into its natural capacity to feel into the boundless universe.

Such spontaneous self-expression is only rarely the kind of wild catharsis that is popular in certain schools of consciousness exploration. The relationship that I invite is a new intelligence within each person that tends to release emotions from their usual frame of reference so that rather than regression into emotions we have already named (and blamed for our predicament) there is a general discovery of a new capacity to feel. The heart of the work then becomes learning to be one's own teacher, learning how to submit to and trust feelings, to not be afraid to feel whatever comes. Through this, without any specific goal or state that one is trying to attain, there is a deepening immanence of Consciousness. The key is not that we generate pleasant states of consciousness, but that attention rests ever more naturally in the sense of organism—consciousness *as* the body.

To work with body consciousness is to work with the whole of one's personality and being. The personality is not simply a mental phenomenon, it is a body phenomenon as well. We can think of this as body-personality or body-ego. This is ego-ing that expresses itself in the voice timbre, in the quality of our laughter, in our breathing, in the flexibility of our joints, the pliancy of tendons, the armoring of muscles. Body ego-ing hides in our movement, in our posture, in our capacity to express in dance or song or play. And it goes even deeper than these more obvious manifestations. The body-ego powerfully influences our basic physiology. It influences our metabolic and hormonal processes, how we dissipate or hold stress and tension, our susceptibility and response to illness, even the aging process itself.

It is easy to imagine the investiture of body-ego if we consider how a child begins to imitate the physical mannerisms of his parents. Then, gradually and insidiously, every child begins to take on the physical norm of his whole culture. As the ego turns our body into an object, it gradually lays claim to our whole sense of aliveness. Instead of trusting the intelligence of our organism (we lose even the intuition that there is such intelligence) the ego takes its cues from outside. Thus begins the reign of terror in which we submit our bodies to the images of health, vitality, and youth that forever bombard us via the popular media. Here is the root of binge eating, bulimia, and brutal dieting and exercise regimes, not to mention untold emotional misery. We become victims of a superficial perception and lose our capacity to listen to the universe in its larger, more inchoate, mysterious depths. But it is such somatic listening that is the organic basis of the deep feeling-intuition of our I-amness. Without rooting I-amness in the deepest dimension of feeling, all of what we are discussing only exists as concepts without somatic immediacy and the individual is seduced and swept along with every fear and changing fad. The ego is the disciple of fear and will submit our bodies to whatever indignity gives a temporary sense of belonging and safety.

What we call personality refers to distinctive patterns and qualities of mental activity, emotional expression, behavior, and so forth, but obviously it is meaningless to separate this from the whole sense of body consciousness. For example, researcher Joan Borysenko describes a case of a multiple personality in a young man who is diabetic in one personality and not in another. In the personality in which he is diabetic he has all the advanced physiologic changes common to severe diabetes, such as retinal degeneration and partial blindness. But when he shifts to a different personality structure not only does his blood sugar return to normal, but these other "physical" changes also rapidly return to normal. Ordinarily our notion of personality more or less discounts our organism. Such a case suggests that personality, behaviour, and health are a continuum inseparable from our body consciousness, our incarnation. Crucially, this evidence suggests that we are not frozen in one level of incarnation, that as our body consciousness shifts, so does everything else.

145

All spiritual or consciousness work is about attention. The power of our attention—really our level of energy—is our capacity for consciousness, our capacity to sustain the fundamental relationship to ourselves, each other, and the Infinite. What separates a

Christ, or a Buddha, or a mystic, or saint, or a great thinker, artist, or business person from the average individual is the power of their attention. It is the depth to which they have become intimate with Mystery, simultaneously incarnating ever more deeply in themselves, and discovering the inseparable relationship with everyone and everything else. Attention, in this sense, is the most precious commodity of all, and it can be cultivated. This is the essence of energy work; really, it is the essence of spiritual work.

Both body consciousness and energy awareness go hand in hand in that, to make attention something more than an abstract notion, we must first learn to feel it or in some manner to sense it. Then we can begin to notice how shifts of attention alter our awareness of ourselves and of our world. All the various forms of energy work have one thing in common: the splitting of attention. This is paradoxical, as attention is a continuum, not something that can be separated. Yet, like light existing as both wave and particle, depending on how we regard it, our attention can be described as having an infinite and finite dimension. The splitting of attention is, in essence, linking radical intuition of the Infinite with sensation. The most common, easily accessible and universal of human sensations is that of the breath. By linking a corner of our attention to the sensation of our breathing, we remain present in ourselves. I compare the attention to the breath to that of a musician's attention to the conductor's baton. Too much attention to the baton (the breathing) and we lose the notes we are playing and the sense of the rest of the orchestra (the full experience of being, within and without). Not enough attention to the breathing and we're off in our heads, or our emotions, or wherever, but we are not attuned to the larger music of the here and now.

Once the attention is anchored subtly in ourselves through the breath, we can begin to explore the splitting of attention. This is hard to describe, and to bring people into this space I usually talk them through a process of induction, using my voice and my familiarity with this space to call them toward it. Imagine, on the in-breath opening to the Infinite—God, Christ, the Universal Source, the White Light—there are any number of transitional concepts that, like the Prime Directives, shift our intuition to a larger sense of being. On the out-breath become aware of your whole body, your hands, and the immediate space around you. On the out-breath merge the attention into the Infinite that is ever-present in the immediacy of your own organism. But because attention does not discriminate between inner and outer, we can extend our attention out beyond our skin boundary. On the out-breath we can extend our attention to include someone else, whether near us or at a distance. Reiki, aura balancing, polarity therapy, therapeutic touch, the laying-on of hands—all these are forms in which one side of our attention is open to the Transcendental Reality while we rest our full attention on another person. In this way we heighten our vibrational state and with practice—and, most essentially, if we have lived deeply and become naturally refined by life's deep challenges and opportunities—we can activate what to ordinary consciousness can feel like extraordinary energy.

And this energy can powerfully affect us and those with whom we share it. Yet, I often ask the question, "Why have we experienced so much, but learned so little?" Energy awareness has been part of the human scene probably from earliest times. Every indigenous culture has their own way of describing it, their own practices for activating it. In more modern times, German physician Franz Mesmer revitalized the awareness of this vital process. Energy awareness teaches us that merely by shifting our attention toward the Infinite, we change our sense of connection. It shows us that we are all linked in a continuum of consciousness. Shift our attention and our whole sense of ourselves is changed, and with it the basis from which our relationships take place. This is why I say, over and over again, "The greatest gift we give each other is the quality of our attention."

But even with millenia of such experiences, we still some-how refuse to see that the connection is there whether we shift our attention or not. The shift of attention that produces the awareness of the energy field is analogous to moving our hands quickly through still air in order to feel the air. Still, our egos co-opt the context; the experience of energy becomes an end in itself, and the rituals and beliefs by which we invoke it becomes a new basis for personal identity and egoic specialness.

There is a deeper step that is needed. We must free the whole exercise of shifting attention and generating heightened energy, from the whole notion of energy field dynamics that give rise to the split between healer and healee, therapist and client, guru and disciple, and so on. In the deepest place attention does not rest upon nor require the sense of the activation or movement of energy. I have called this step Sacred Attention. Here we become more silent in ourselves, more attuned to the real center, our I-amness that is emptiness. This is where energy awareness and working with energy becomes deep meditation, deep prayer. Here we are naturally invited into a level of relationship to Mystery in which even the sense of energy is no longer truly a means of perceiving the deeper level of our connection to ourselves, God, or anyone else. Ultimately, we are asked to meet each other in faith. Whether in harmony or conflict, beyond any emotion, feeling, sensation, or any beliefs whatsoever of our connection, in the midst of the most ordinary living, we are already One in the arms of the Beloved. This Divine ordinariness is, to me, sanity. This is true authenticity. And when we meet each other here, we are truly well met, we have the sense of being seen, of coming home.

1. I have written extensively about energy, group energy, and the phenomena of transformation as we become open to states beyond ordinary ego-consciousness. Rather than recapitulate that material here, the reader can find these discussions in: *The Black Butterfly,* and *The I That Is We.* I have also discussed how to heighten energy in order to prepare for surgery, or for self-empowerment during other crisis times in *Surgery, Self-healing, and Spirit.* Many of the meditations, and energy exercises that I use for inducting energy awareness are available on audio cassette.

148

*Sacred meditation is the term I use for a ritual of sharing loving energy.*

# CHAPTER II

# ÎNCARNATÎON
# AND HEALÎNG
# EARLY CHÎLDHOOD
# WOUNDS

When I was a little boy I grew up near the ocean. In the summers, I spent a great deal of time playing on the beach, building sand castles and trying to defend them from the waves with elaborate walls. By the afternoon, I would get drowsy and lay down to nap. Dozing in and out of sleep, I would open my eyes like slits against the glare. There, just below my eyes, was an endless tumble of tiny grains of sand and bits of wood and shell. The beach seemed white from a distance, but up close there were so many colors.

Lying like this with the warmth of the sand and sun bathing me, I discovered a game. I would take my finger and slowly move it beneath the sand. Inches from my eyes, the sand looked like boulders undulating in an earthquake as thousands of them gave way before my mighty finger. Finally, I became fascinated with trying to use my finger to move a single grain of sand. When this failed I would use a small twig. Bringing the twig inches from my eyes, I would concentrate with all my might to keep my hand still. The slightest tremble sent dozens of grains tumbling. Sometimes an unguarded breath would puff a tiny cloud of sand into my eyes, or a slight gasp would have me choking on grit. Try as I might, I never succeeded in moving only a single grain of sand.

Years later, as I searched to find imagery to convey the sense of maturing consciousness as a process of incarnation, rather than as a philosophy, this memory of childhood play returned as an allegory about the world of Stoneman and Sandman.

Imagine a person who is made of small stones. He appears human in every way, but inside he is packed with thousands of stones the size of marbles. If he is touched by some experience with sufficient force so that the stones within him move, then he perceives some degree of relationship between himself and whatever has touched him. As he initiates interactions, he perceives his own impact according to how his stones are affected. If only a few stones move the contact is almost imperceptible, perhaps less meaningful. If many move it is stronger, more intense and hence more significant. If too many move and the organization of his stoneness is perturbed more than he can accommodate, he may regard this as suffering.

In this allegory, the stones are metaphorical units of consciousness; the amount of energy it takes to move the stones is a Stoneperson's threshold of awareness. Specifically, it his capacity for fundamental relationship to himself, others (the world), and God. Stoneness is his incarnation, the degree to which Consciousness has taken root in flesh and blood. It is stoneness that determines his sentience, his intelligence, his perception of meaning, and his values. Crucially, it is stoneness that determines his whole moral nature, for our moral nature is nothing less than our capacity for relationship.

Now consider another person whose being is made up of small pebbles, or yet another comprised of millions of grains of the finest beach sand. Each refinement of the units of consciousness implies a greater capacity for relationship to life. It takes so little energy to move a minute grain of sand relative to moving even a small stone. Thus, a Sandperson's capacity for consciousness, her threshold for perceiving relationship with life, is far more sensitive.

This refinement means relationship to people and the world around naturally has a greater feeling of connection. Sandperson's whole way of being presumes a degree of belonging and connectedness where Stoneperson's might not understand any relationship at all.

Intellect has been evolving for hundreds of thousands of years. In terms of a Stoneperson's or a Sandperson's capacity to work with ideas and abstractions, that is, for either to be a doctor, a lawyer, a politician, an engineer, and so forth, both can be very bright, very capable. But the foundation of connectedness upon which the intellect rests is substantially different. Sandpeople are more intelligent because they innately have a greater capacity for relationship to themselves and life.

It is in the domain of feeling that the true difference begins to be apparent. Sandpeople have a far greater repertoire of feeling, a far greater capacity to allow and express feeling. Stonepeople require greater intensity to perceive relationships within themselves, with others, or to the world. Thus, for a Stoneperson, feelings and subsequent emotional communications are cruder; there is a greater potential for violence in their expression. No judgment is implied here, only a statement that the evolution of consciousness is, significantly, an evolution of the capacity for feeling. It is this deepening and refining of feeling that begins to grow in us as the dawning of intuition.

All people feel passion, fear, anger, rage, joy, love, and so on. But the richness and intelligence we recognize through our feeling depends on our depth of incarnation. Emotion itself is feeling that has been somewhat tamed by naming; it is feeling that has been rationalized enough that we can talk about it. But sentient existence is far more than just the feelings we have been able to name at this point in our evolution. It is about a never-ending, ever-evolving capacity for sentience and feeling. We trick ourselves into thinking that the world and the universe is confined within the boundaries of our perception, that it can be tamed and captured by concepts and ideas. More accurately, we swim in a dimension of information that is the living intelligence of the

151

universe. It is the continually wakening capacity to recognize and consciously engage this intelligence that is the very process of incarnation. The mind is not just the body's organ of perception; our organism in its totality is Reality taking conscious form.

As we incarnate more deeply we become available to this larger relationship to the universe. Despite our tremendous pride in our intellects, the evolution of consciousness is not so much a process of thinking as it is a capacity for consciousness in totality, and central to this is our capacity for feeling. Thinking sees, feeling knows. Thinking is confounded by complexity, whereas feeling can incorporate and is already the synthesis of enormous complexity. If you think about yourself and your life you will get lost in paradox and contradiction. You'll drive yourself nuts. But if you listen to your feeling you will come to know yourself profoundly, although trying to say what you know may not be easy. Stonepeople have a more brittle, one-dimensional, and personalized capacity for feeling. They are less able to recognize that others have similar feelings; therefore they are less likely to feel remorse, forgiveness, compassion. As we incarnate into sandness, the growing sensitivity is greater intuition into the feelings of others. Here, then, is the difference in the moral nature of Stonepeople and Sandpeople. It is a difference in the capacity to feel and the ability to recognize feeling as a continuum in which all of us live. From this intuition naturally is born compassion, caring, and forgiveness, as well as a growing sense of the sacred. It is not that Stonepeople are more immoral or less spiritual; it is just that their moral nature and spirituality is less evolved, less incarnated.

It is meaningless to speak of any level of human behavior without considering the dimension of incarnation. The human organism is an organ of relationship, an expression of the ceaseless relationship that is the living intelligence of the universe. That Stonepeople cannot perceive this as fully as Sandpeople, and live in a world of rationalism and materialism, is not an issue for argument, it is simply a (relative) failure of feeling. This is the crisis of our time. And it cannot be adequately addressed philosophically, politically, or psychologically if we remain only at the level of dialogue, of thinking. It is not, and will never be, a question simply of our thinking, because thinking is the servant of our capacity for consciousness, not the source. It is a question of incarnation. The challenge of any spiritual teaching, of any enlightened education is the challenge of engaging the whole body in recognition of its relationship to life. The work is to transform our stoneness to sandness to powderness...forever.

As incarnation deepens we begin to live more consciously in our bodies. A Sandperson naturally tends to listen to life through his or her organism and less via mental dictates. Through this feeling-intuition we awaken to the sense of energy, a level of attention that we can feel and thus attune to. Through awareness of energy, relationships are understood more directly, people are less likely to become mere objects. The subject-object split becomes less dominant. The metaphor of stoneness to sandness is a metaphor for the evolution from First to Second Miracle consciousness as it is rooted in our embodiment. In terms of human activity, this movement is lived as a deepening capacity for intimacy with every level of life. In terms of human relationships, spirituality is not about transcending or rising above the dilemmas of life. On the contrary, spiritual maturity is our capacity to remain consciously present and relational at ever deepening, more complex and subtle levels of feeling with life. All of life is, in a certain sense, ordinary when we cease splitting one part from another and elevating one aspect over another. But this ordinariness becomes more and more imbued with meaning as we refine in our incarnation. Because the immanence of God is more directly available through the feeling nature and intuition of Sandpeople, we can say that living has become the play of divine ordinariness. For this reason, as we deepen in our incarnation we tend to resist less and less of life because it is all divine.

Obviously this extends into the whole sensual play of life. Sexuality has been, and will continue to be, one of the crucial issues, because Life demands it of us while simultaneously making it among the most unforgiving mirrors in which to view our consciousness of ourselves and each other. But, again, it is meaningless to discuss sexual issues without asking of the level of incarnation. The totality of our capacity for relationship—the recognition of oneself in and through the mirror of the other, the resulting openness or withholding, integrity of behavior, caring and kindness, the quality of shared attention, the responsiveness of our organism to sensation, the unboundedness of our feeling nature, the capacity to meet and merge energetically—emerges from the depth of our incarnation. As we incarnate more deeply, the split between love, sexuality, and spirituality diminishes. Sexuality is spiritual experience, a focal point for conscious relationship, a mirror for our inner and outer psychology. It is, to me, meaningless to discuss spirituality and not look directly at what this means in terms of our deepening capacity for sensual intimacy in our own bodies, as well as our capacity for intimacy with others. If spirituality is not the immediacy of our intimacy with our world, if it is not moment by moment felt intercourse with Life, then what could it possibly be?

This leads us to the obvious and essential question: How do we evolve ourselves at the level of incarnation? What is an incarnational spirituality? To me this is the heart and soul of what we are discussing in this book. It is what we all are doing—or Life is doing through us—more or less consciously. Often I am asked: Can early childhood trauma be healed? Can we overcome injury in the formulative phases of ego development or are we forever doomed to be limited by these wounds? Certain schools of psychoanalysis, particularly the Freudians, believe that early injury irreversibly predetermines personality dynamics; we must simply learn to adapt to them and live as best we can.

I agree that we have to adapt, but this is not the whole story. The possibility for wholeness is not automatically precluded by our early-life traumas because of the mystery of our prodigal return. As the ego submits into Second Miracle consciousness we can be reorganized in a new harmonic of wholeness. I have had some experience that these areas can be thoroughly redeemed in the sense that a much fuller potential as conscious people can be realized. But this is more than a psychological process; it is an incarnational one and fundamentally spiritual. As a psychological process it involves developing insight into one's fears and compensatory behaviors. Most importantly, this means letting go of a victim-perpetrator stance and deciding to accept what life has delt us, thereby becoming a disciple of one's own experience. This is essential and difficult work, but the hardest work, the part that is often not engaged in the psychoanalytic approach is the incarnational work. As an incarnational process it requires meeting these memories and feelings directly and consciously in the body, not mediated by thinking or analysis, so that the process becomes an incarnational event.

Incarnational event is the term I use to describe a process of meeting deep, deep feeling that is usually experienced as suffering. It is the way in which this feeling process is met and experienced: We are taken by it, literally led by feeling, into the most archaic depths of our being, to the edge of what would seem to be ego-annihilation. In this process of coming to meet the unspeakable, we burn in the refining fire of the Infinite. Through this event a whole new person emerges who is far less governed by these early forces. It is an incarnational movement in ourselves like the transformation from Stoneman to Sandman.

A full discussion of this process is beyond my intent for this book, but the challenge is whether, as adults, we are able to regress to the more unobstructed level of feeling, a condition similar to the more undifferentiated awareness of the child—the condition in which the original injury resides in our bodily and deep psychic memory. These are feelings from a time when we could not defend against them, when they seemed to be the totality of ourselves and existence, when there was no aware ego to contextualize them, and we could not understand what was happening to us. This is a time when faith was not conscious. This is what we must re-experience and often many times. We must be led by these awful spaces to the threshold of Infinity again and again until faith does become conscious.

These traumatic states of sensation, states that occurred either through childhood illness, through parental neglect or abuse, or just from the confusion and pain inherent in the child's collision with the requirements of egoic development, stand as a threshold beyond which the individual cannot evolve. Every time the individual begins to open to new possibility, this movement stops wherever there is feeling and sensation that the individual is unable to bear. Under the best of circumstances, even with a perfect, loving childhood, regression to a condition that can allow a new patterning of consciousness is inherently difficult. The quality of feeling, even where there was no major wounding, still is so non-rational, so oceanic in its nature, that it is, at least initially, over-whelming, even terrifying to the rational ego. If the ego structure is already compromised by early wounding, the somatic and cognitive memory may be too threatening. This becomes the boundary or limit of our self-awareness, the limit of our enlightenment. It is, in actuality, the limit of our faith.

If psychoanalytic work cannot reach to this area it is because the dialogical form of the one to one, therapist–client relationship, rarely engages the level of energy that is necessary. It takes a form that invokes much higher levels of energy—usually, a longer re-treat form and group dynamic, and rarely just once, but more as part of commitment to a full teaching. I don't mean in any way to diminish the value of mature psychotherapy; therapy has played an invaluable part in my life. It is one of the great intellectual and spiritual impulses of our time and very valuable as a preparation and adjunct to the work I am proposing here. However, for the issue we are discussing, the limitation of conventional psychotherapy as a practice is that it rarely works directly with energy or body consciousness and tends to stay conceptual, in a word, too tame. Also, some psychotherapy denies its spiritual roots. This deprives people of a crucial inner connection to spirit and a foundation for greater faith that is ultimately necessary to risk really entering the energy of these profoundly disturbing feeling spaces.

156

I believe that to truly re-pattern the ego in health takes a process of work such as I described in the Four Pillars chapter, where meditative insight, psychological understanding, energetic opening and, most important, body consciousness, are all cultivated as part of a deeply felt spiritual practice and way of life. If the early memories are to be re-encountered in their immediacy, this must occur at a similar state of undifferentiated openess as when the original trauma occured. To do this requires a great deal of energy. This requires a teacher with a deep understanding of the energetic processes that relax the boundaries of the mental and body-ego structures. It means the guide already directly embodies the higher, more integrated states and understands how to invoke them, how to stabilize them, and most of all, how to hold this process in faith.

The difference between the early injury and the redemptive movement is the presence of an aware ego. If there is too much unconsciousness in the ego dynamics, then basic ego level work must be undertaken first. It is here that psychotherapy makes its most crucial contribution. As our egos become more aware—and now meditation becomes an essential practice—we become capable of sustaining the capacity to witness as we descend into the primal feelings. The ego may feel deeply threatened, but as long as awareness does not split away and continues to witness all the feelings and images that arise—which means that there can be an intense sense of suffering because we are not defending or escaping from these feelings—gradually we begin to intuit the larger Self beyond this wall of anguish and terror. Slowly, the power of the suffering to confine our self-awareness is relaxed. This is actually a learning process that has to do with attention and trust. To undertake such work requires that we have made an irrevocable commitment to consciousness. I believe it is the commitment we make to wholeness that calls forth what ever we need, including a teacher to guide us.

I have found that body consciousness work is crucial to this kind of healing work. Of the many practices, one of the key means for learning to navigate through deep feeling is breathwork. There are many forms of breathwork that vary from intense hyperventilation to very soft continuous breathing. I prefer the softer forms because I feel they teach us how to learn to navigate with ever deeper attention into the subtle spaces, whereas the more intense forms tend to blind us with the power of the experiences they induce. However, each form has its place. Intensity tends to override the controlling ego and to break up stubborn psychic structures, while softness tends to take us deeper into vastness once we are more open. It is the linking of breathing and attention that is ultimately the key to learning how to be present in deeper and deeper levels of sensation, imagery, and feelings that can span heaven and hell. In any case, we are talking about a very deep and difficult work in which Grace plays a central part.

The paradox of all that we have been discussing is that, at least in my own work, what makes it possible to undertake such deep healing in an original way is by not looking for it in the first place. I don't mean not looking for the specific early wounds; I mean not even looking to heal oneself. One might argue that this is nearly impossible, that it is the very nature of the First Miracle consciousness to protect itself, and to therefore, anticipate danger and attempt by whatever means to alleviate it. Yet, while the ego may define the wound, it is not capable of healing it. The very means it attempts only creates a reality of rationalization and distancing from feeling. This is what disturbs me about so much of popular media-driven psychology; there is a tendency to label every form of suffering without really knowing how, or wanting to really enter into, the deep feeling in an authentically transformative way. Sadly, this often results in a disheartening name and blame game, a victim-perpetrator mentality that is burning through our culture like a prairie fire. Deciding where the problem resides is already overly objectifying the suffering, and it is an over-objectification of the individual herself. To be referent to Infinity is to realize that there is no self; there is only a process of evolving and deepening relationship to Existence. Therefore, all fundamental healing is always a spiritual process that involves our relationship to God, and specifically an incarnational event far more than a rational, intellectual one. The work requires the relaxation of psychological defenses at the level of their bodily roots. If we work responsibly at the level of fundamental body consciousness, in an environment of deep love and faith, we can redefine the basis of psychosomatic identity once again in wholeness. It is upon this basic cellular feeling of well-being, of belonging, of being loved, that is prior to any level of the ego-ing self, that we unfold our spiritual journey. This is the true rock upon which we build our church—our spiritual body.

Central to such work is deep reverence for the sacredness of ourselves as personalities, as bodies...in all ways. The exploration of energy and body consciousness enters profoundly into extremely sensitive areas of the psyche; therefore, it is essential to trust the deeper wisdom of psyche, to move slowly, intuiting the underlying consecration in wholeness. In this way people can gradually be returned to a sense of organism open to Infinity, simply and vibrantly alive.

# PART

# III

# THE LIFE

*Where does the wind come from Nicodemus?*
*Rabbi, I do not know, nor can I tell where it will go.*

## PUT YOURSELF INTO THE
## PATH OF THE WIND, *Nicodemus.*
*You will know the thrill of being born along by something*
*greater than yourself.*
*You are proud of your position, your security,*
*but you will perish in the stagnant air.*

## PUT YOURSELF INTO THE
## PATH OF THE WIND, *Nicodemus.*
*Bright leaves will dance before you. You will find yourself in places that*
*you never dreamed of seeing. You will be forced into places you have*
*dreaded, and find them like a coming home.*
*You will have a power that you never had before, Nicodemus.*
*You will be a New Man.*

## PUT YOURSELF INTO THE PATH OF THE WIND.

— Myra Scovel

CHAPTER 12

# HEALING AND INFINITY

W here do we set the limits of what's possible in healing when we understand that human beings and the universe of consciousness is an open system? A system referent to infinity can never be reduced to any finite conceptual abstraction: "This is what you have....This is what you are....This is what you do." Open systems are dynamic, capable of undergoing metamorphic changes, of growing and reorganizing in ways we can never anticipate. The medicine of First Miracle humanity tends to reduce the body to a static, closed system and within specific limits, usually of a simple biochemical or mechanical nature, can be quite helpful. But the moment we enter the full complexity of most human ailments there is no simple mechanism. Everything is in relationship and influencing everything else.

Consciousness is relationship. Modern medicine, or any form of medicine, is merely one of the potentially infinite dynamics of relationship with the phenomena of living and dying. When we become ill—and no more nor less so than when we are well—all we really know is relationship. The statements, "I feel tired," or "I feel sick," are labels that provide a basis for self-consciousness. The diagnosis, "You have cancer," gives a specific name to a nebulous complex of feelings, sensations and symptoms that hadn't fully crystallized as a conscious pattern of awareness. The diagnosis itself is a new conscious relationship to oneself. The more important question is, is this the end of our relationship or the beginning? Do we now "know" what we are dealing with, and what we should do, or like Alice in Wonderland, are these descriptions holes into ourselves which, if we are willing to fall into them, start the beginning of an unimaginable adventure?

Self-healing is, first and foremost, our capacity for relationship to ourselves. It is this fundamental relationship that is a microcosm of our broader relationship to/with/as existence. Go deep enough into oneself and you arrive at the threshold of infinity. At the threshold of infinity we vibrate with the intelligence of the infinite One. Here the probability for wholeness becomes greater and greater. This is why the journey of consciousness and self-healing are so inexorably tied together.

To dramatize this, let me tell the true story of Rachel. I first met her in 1986 when she came to one of my seminars. She was gravely ill with pancreatic cancer that had spread to her liver and infiltrated her aorta. She had received radiation treatment with little response. There was nothing but pain control left to her as treatment and her doctors expected her to be dead in a few weeks, although she had already survived beyond their original expectation. But Rachel was a strong, stubborn person who wouldn't give up. When her sixteen-year-old son gave her my book, *The Black Butterfly*, she read it and decided to make the long and painful journey to attend a conference. In her condition, this was an act of real courage.

As an aside, it is interesting that her son had gone to a bookstore looking for something to help him in his struggle with his mother's illness. The bookstore owner suggested *The Black Butterfly*. There is a connectedness in events that transcends mere temporal relationship. If we imagine ourselves as closed systems living within a closed system, then her son's search, the bookstore owner's suggestion, Rachel's resonance with the book, and her decision to attend my seminar, were merely a series of coincidental events. But if we are open systems then we begin to recognize an inter-connectedness in these events. Rachel, her son, the bookstore owner, myself, like all of us, were/are always and already partici-pating with a larger intelligence.

Rachel arrived pale and jaundiced. She was very weak and often in great pain. As the seminar progressed, I was always acutely sensitive to her suffering. When someone is in such crisis and demonstrates so much courage, I know that I am in the presence of mystery and this calls my attention into a deeper listening. But a person in Rachel's physical condition always represents a dilemma. Her fragile health genuinely demanded extra care and caution that were inimical to encouraging her into activities requiring self-surrender. There was the real possibility that she might die while she was with us, not to mention that some of the more challenging activities could increase her pain. How much was I to encourage her to participate while at the same time accepting her limits and protecting her? A key part of my work is to go beyond the limits of the First Miracle ego, not only psychologically, but with the whole body, thereby inviting a new patterning of ener-gies. This can be stressful. Although it is a positive stress, with Rachel I was often apprehensive about what was possible for her. I wanted her to take responsibility for everything she chose to do, while at the same time not discourage her from risking.

One night, as the group was lying down in the dark listening to music, I saw Rachel crawling out of the room. I followed her into the adjoining room and saw that she was in a cold sweat, racked with pain. She said she was going back to her bedroom to take more medication until the pain passed. For myself, I was just present, listening toward infinity. Perhaps she took my silence as criticism because she asked whether I thought she should do something else. In that moment, quite without thinking, I said gently, "What difference does it make if you suffer alone in your room or in the company of these people?" She just stared at me for awhile and then got up and went back inside.

When she returned to the room, the music had ended and the group was sitting quietly in a circle. Everyone was sensitive to Rachel's ordeal, so they were waiting attentively. I gave her my chair to make her as comfortable as possible and sat quietly next to her. Several minutes passed in silence. As we sat, I gently placed my hand across her back just as an expression of compassion. Almost immediately she moaned and said my hand was like a fire burning into her, intensifying the pain. For a moment I pulled my hand away in concern, but I knew that I was not consciously doing anything except being present. I asked if it was all right if I left my hand there and she agreed. Over the years I have felt energy and heat of all kinds coming from my hands when I do energy sharing, but in this instance I was aware that whatever she was feeling was taking place outside the range of my own energetic perception. There was nothing to do but trust.

Soon, I began to hear a very high-pitched sound and mentioned this to her. She said that she too was hearing something. I suggested she try to tone it, but she said it was too high-pitched. At this point, a man across the room remarked that one of the women had made extraordinarily high-pitched tones during a singing exercise earlier in the seminar. He suggested that she try to make the sounds for Rachel. Rachel agreed and the woman began to tone. The sounds were astonishingly high-pitched and loud. Suddenly I felt something abruptly release in Rachel; it was as though her whole energy field instantaneously changed. Simultaneously, she took a deep breath and in amazement said that her pain had vanished. Very soon, her color was improved; she was almost glowing.

The singer stopped her sounds and Rachel sat very still breathing slowly and deeply. I could sense her attention; she had spontaneously fallen into a space of silence and presence that I readily recognized. In this state the breath links to a deeper attention that permeates the body and seems to circulate energy or presence within and beyond the physical form. The mind becomes still and a soft sensation moves like a tide coinciding with the breath. Because, Rachel's cancer had metastasized to her liver and had begun growing into her aorta, every deeper breath had caused her pain for months; she did not dare to breathe deeply. Now she was feeling herself take one slow deep breath after another. For the first time, she said, she saw into the space of her pancreas and her liver. During her illness, whenever she had tried to sense into her body, these areas were dark. Now it was as though she was inside her organs and could breathe into them. This was a miracle to her.

In the days that followed, Rachel had no pain and her jaundice faded. She danced and sang, sat upright in meditation, ate full meals without getting ill, and did not need medication. On the final night's celebration, she danced the cancan, legs swinging high. I thought for a moment of the largest artery of the body infiltrated by a tumor and potentially ready to burst at any second, but she seemed fearless and filled with vitality.

A month later, Rachel returned for a visit. She did not look well. She had remained vital and pain-free for about two weeks, and then the pain and jaundice began returning and she had to resume taking pain medication. Nevertheless, on this visit she brought her fiancé. Despite her grave illness, they had decided to go forward with their marriage plans. The wedding was scheduled for the following week. I found this choice remarkable, but inwardly I wondered at the wisdom of this decision. As they were leaving he asked me if there was anything more he could do for her. An image came into my mind and I said, "Build her a swing on the back porch and give her lots of time alone."

More than a year passed and I hadn't heard from Rachel. I didn't know if she was alive or dead, until one afternoon when she telephoned and proceeded to tell me a most incredible story: Upon returning home from her last visit, her condition rapidly worsened. She was constantly in pain and using so much medication that her speech was slurred. Her fiancé had to hold her upright at the ceremony and she was barely able to say the words. Then to her shock, in the middle of the ceremony, she had a deep insight. It was that she needed to be alone. She spoke about this with her new husband and asked for his help.

167

A few days after their wedding, Rachel entered seclusion in her own bedroom. Her husband agreed to watch their combined children. He would make sure that a simple vegetable broth would be left outside her door. She left firm instructions that no one was to disturb her no matter what they heard. If she screamed or cried, they were to just leave her alone. She had no sense of how long she would do this, imagining it would be for a few days. Astonished, I listened as she told me that she then remained in her room alone for more than seven months!

In the first days, the loss of external stimulation caused her to fall even deeper into pain and depression. But she kept falling. She slept a lot, wrote in her journal, sang spontaneously as she had learned to do during the seminar. She used many of the exercises that we had done together in the conference. As she felt stronger she whirled like a dervish and danced to her own songs. But she was not following any formula; she was just following the moment. At one point she blindfolded herself for several weeks. Soon her senses of hearing and smell came forth with new aliveness. Morning was announced by the aroma of fresh coffee wafting through her windows. Sounds had a whole new power. Her sense of space changed and with it the locus of her attention; she settled even deeper into the immediacy of herself. During the whole time of her solitude, her dreams became very vivid. She would contemplate the feeling in them and try to give life to the dreams. One in particular, a recurrent dream of falling, led her to begin exploring the sensation of falling. First she flopped backwards from a sitting position onto the bed. Later she began to take full falls. She even jumped off of a chest of drawers onto the mattress. She was trying to develop the bodily feeling of utter surrender. Gradually she became silent…and breathed.

After about six weeks, she no longer needed any medication for pain. The state of silence and breath that she had spontaneously entered while at the conference had returned. After six months, she knew that she was healed, but when she imagined going to her doctor and being re-examined, she felt herself become anxious. She realized that she was still not fully established in the new patterning, so she continued the solitude. Finally, when she could fantasize seeing the doctors, having the tests, meeting everyone's reactions without fear, she knew she was ready and left her solitude.

After emerging, the new bodily aliveness continued to be her teacher. She would awaken every day at 3:30 a.m. and go for a long walk along the beach. Often she would whirl. At other times she danced. She wrote in her journal, sang, meditated, reflected, and moved moment by moment with the flow of her inner being. This process often took five or six hours every day and she self-ishly guarded this special time. She had discovered for herself what I refer to as the courtship of the lifeforce energy.

Eventually, friends and acquaintances began to become curi-ous and a few wanted to join her. For a long time she refused; it was her own process. But eventually, if they were willing to get up that early, she let them whirl and dance with her, whatever was her sense for that morning. She told me that one of the first people to join her was her oncologist. He was impressed with her healing and how much she had changed. She was completely free of all signs of cancer. As of 1991, the last time Rachel and I had contact, and four years after coming out of her solitude, this continued to be the case. Oddly, the side effects of the radiation treatment didn't spontaneously resolve themselves. About a year after coming out of solitude, Rachel began to have abdominal pain and feared that the cancer was returning. Once again she went into solitude, this time only briefly to prepare herself for exploratory surgery. There was no cancer, only adhesions and scar tissue from the radiation. This was easily treated and, true to form, her post-operative re-covery time was rapid. As soon as possible, Rachel resumed her personal practice of courtship.

Six months after Rachel had left her long solitude, she visited me for the third time. As she shared her story with a large group of my students, the most impressive aspect was the quality of presence that radiated from her. When I sat near her we would fall into silence immediately.

Ironically, these changes were playing havoc with her mar-riage. After supporting her through such an ordeal and being

169

without her for more than seven months, her family felt neglected. Their joy and gratitude that she was alive and well remained, but Rachel's practice of courtship of the energy seemed unusually self-involved to them. When was she going to be, once again, the woman and mother they remembered? From their point of view, she seemed unpredictable, contradictory, and controlling. She would say yes to something at one moment, but then would often change her decision as her inner state shifted. Also, her emotions could flair with intimidating force. From her point of view she was just obeying the energy. She felt that her life depended on this even though she realized it was not easy for them. Her ongoing challenge would prove to be learning how to live her new aliveness without being insensitive to others. For any of us, this is no simple task.

Rachel's story is living proof of the resources each of us has when we begin to tap the power of our I-amness. All that is asked of us is to turn our attention back to the root of our own immediate experience and thereby, once again, regain access to the Ground of Being. To do so, the first step is to realize that we are not closed systems, but manifestations of consciousness referent to infinity.

The world is divided in many ways around the subject-object polarity. The Eastern psyche's general orientation has been toward the subjective pole. The basic injunction is to "go within." This has given birth to the richness of Eastern mysticism and the many yogic traditions that are, in essence, about self-mastery. In this orientation the notion of energy or lifeforce evolves around relationship to the underlying energy of the universe. This relationship is obscured by the activity of the outer mind, what we have called the First Miracle. If we can see through the outer mind, the relationship to the deeper current of lifeforce can be optimally maintained and balanced, and the organism restores itself to health. This process can be helped by making direct adjustments to the energy flow, as in acupuncture, as well as by the use of herbs and natural remedies. Homeopathic medicine is a relatively recent or recently rediscovered form of energy-based medicine that works directly at the level of body consciousness. It begins with the premise of the wholeness of the organism and focuses on body, mind, and emotions as an indivisible interpenetrating relationship. Homeopathy seeks to amplify our organism's natural self-healing capacity, by challenging it with very diluted doses of substances that invoke an energy response. While modern homeopathy was rediscovered by Samuel Hannehman, a German physician, its roots are from the East.

The Western psyche, in contrast, has generally been oriented to the object pole. This is what I call the mysticism of the object, and, in its purest form, is science or what might be called "other"-mastery. The power of this mysticism is clear in all that we have achieved technologically and in the areas where modern Western medicine is very effective.

But whether we approach this through the object or the subject, eventually we enter a level of consciousness that is both and neither. Thus in the deepest states of self-realization, the mysticism of the subject leads to oneness with the whole manifest universe. Similarly, quantum physics has demonstrated that if we penetrate deeply enough into the mystery of any object, at the sub-atomic level there is no longer any division of the observer and the observed. Science has thus come full circle back to the subject, the self.

Between these too extremes lies the whole range of First Miracle phenomena and a relatively predictable, stable, but also mediocre range of energy and aliveness. But the moment we reach infinity, whether through subject or object is irrelevant, we tap into enormous creative power, the power of the evolving universe itself. This, I believe, is what Rachel's journey demonstrated, and in the next chapter I will discuss more of how each of us can make this journey for ourselves in our own unique way.

171

Today we see an ever increasing degree of autoimmune disease and other illnesses that have to do with heightened reactivity or weakening of the immune system. Clearly, Rachel's fall into a primal experience of Self led to a remarkable strengthening of her immune system. This potential is available to all of us. But we need to revise our understanding of the forces that animate our consciousness as organisms.

The mystical metaphor that human beings are a cup in the ocean to describe the relationship of the ego to the universal energy can be helpful in considering how to understand and respond to diseases of the immune system. I believe—regardless of the secondary chemical and other biological dynamics we may discover—that one basic level of this problem is a battle between the body-ego (the personalized lifeforce within the cup) and the Ground (the universal energy that is the ocean around it). Actually, it is the same energy within and without, but the body-ego does not recognize it that way. In this time of the quickening of the Second Miracle potential that is awakening us all, everyone is beginning to open energetically. We may not, from the point of view of our conscious selves, be aware that this is what is happening. But regardless, the new energy emanating from the Ground, or larger Self, is increasing and it is perceived by the body's personalized energy as other. From the energetic basis of our ordinary body consciousness it is resisted, fought against. This, I believe, is the basis of the increasing autoimmune problems; in essence it is self fighting Self.

Our main problem in healing this conflict is that our First Miracle intelligence is rooted in separation and therefore, perceives all dynamics in terms of self and other. In this paradigm the purpose of the immune system is to fight off, destroy, or neutralize invaders in order to protect the integrity of self against the incursion of foreign forces. However, the immune system, like the brain and all the rest of us, is constantly learning, constantly evolving, constantly transforming itself. In protecting the integrity of self against something perceived as other, a relationship is created in which both self and other are transformed forever. When the immune system synthesizes a molecule, called an antibody, that never existed before in order to neutralize a particular invader, a communication has taken place that becomes part of the body's heritage. Seen in this way the immune system's real purpose, like our universe's, is not separation and destruction but relationship. The immune system is part of how our organism learns to be in ever-growing relationship to the totality of existence. It is part of the bodily intelligence that develops relationship to the new and unknown chemicals, viruses, bacteria, and so on, that will forever challenge the identity of our organism.

Seen in this way it might be more apt to rename it the commune system, since its real task is to create community, or at least some degree of sustainable relationship whenever possible. As a result of the friction with the new and unknown we become more intelligent. Certainly, some immune cells do attack invading organisms and both are killed; this is one level of relationship. But the immune system of today is the community that we have generated over literally billions of years of interaction and relationship. Some of these interactions will forever be hostile, while others will be incorporated into our community. This is what happened millions or billions of years ago when viruses became ribosomes and bacteria became mitochondria, each essential elements of every cell of our body and every other higher creature.

Take our current struggle with the AIDS virus. Here is an organism that mutates so quickly that most human bodies do not know how to adapt to its invasion. But over time we will learn, whether through our intellects by creating some medication or vaccine, or through the depths of our own bodily intelligence. AIDS is a tragedy, but for our immune systems it is also a teacher. We might ask ourselves who would we be as organisms if ten to twenty generations from now the majority of us have learned within our very cellular intelligence a way to not be overwhelmed by the challenge of the AIDS virus? How much will our cells have learned? How much more intelligent, as organisms, will we have become? This is what we have done with countless other assailants that we are not even aware of because they are no longer a threat. Even tuberculosis was once far more infectious than it is today. And while a new strain has reappeared, it is part of the endless

173

dance of relationship in which not only do we learn, but the bacteria and other creatures learn as well.

When we research the immune system with the assumption that its task is attack and exclusion, we miss the essence of its nature, because we have as yet not recognized the essence of our universe. This essence is, as we have said, ceaseless relationship. To support the immune system's intelligence we need to work with our whole organism and increase our capacity to meet and say yes to our own deeper energy. We need to increase the energy of our human community as well, for as Jesus said, "When two or three or more are gathered in my name, there shall I be in their midst." It is this higher energy that brings us together in brotherhood that knows how to imbue us with the intelligence to create community with the constant "other" that will forever be joining or challenging our community of being. Until we know how to create relationship and the potential for community with these entities, we become sick, lose our own bodily integrity, and maybe die. Sickness is itself the means of learning how to have a relationship with these new entities. This is why it is not always good to interfere with sickness. Our bodies, like our mental egos, need discontinuities for the old pattern to be impressed by a new one. Just as being-the-skiing opens us briefly to higher energies in the discontinuity when the ego enters the state of flow, sickness, high fevers, and even coma, for our cellular level of consciousness, may actually be forms of discontinuity in which the old structure weakens enough for a new patterning to begin. Perhaps for this reason medical research has observed that it is not a good idea to overtreat childhood illnesses by suppressing every fever and infection with antipyretics and antibiotics. Children who have been treated too much in this way have a higher incidence of weakened immunity when they become older. One of the great challenges today is that, in our daily life and with increased traveling, we are exposing ourselves to so many new chemicals and allergens. In order to adapt to this stress, we have to access a higher energy that is capable of incorporating more of these forces. In my earlier books

I provided detailed information on ways in which one can access these energies.

I have observed in my seminars and through my work with individuals that, as people become more open and transparent to the universal energy, their allergies and auto-immune phenomena diminish or completely disappear, at least for awhile. I have worked with several asthmatics who required regular usage of broncho-inhalators who discover that they simply did not need them or could significantly diminish the dose. Many with hyper-immune diseases, if they are able to let go into the exploration, find themselves able to eat a wide variety of foods that would formerly have made them very ill. And this happens within days of beginning the work. When the energies of our prodigal bodies merge into the deeper ocean of aliveness, when self is reconciled to Self, this is when we come home to the universal intelligence of our organism. This intelligence knows how to create community in a vastly complex world. This is Health.

# THE THREE KEYS TO THE KINGDOM

*The Art of Self-Healing*

I often say that the first time we are opened to the Second Miracle, it is grace. The second time is hard work, really a life's work. The first time there is no expectation, no past memory to intrude. The new energy takes us. A more permanent return to this state involves our whole life and the integration of all facets of our complex natures. We go self-consciously with our First Miracle awareness intact. There is memory of the original experience and this always interferes, because it shows us every moment that is not the moment of fullness and being we remember. In this way the memory wounds us and often people will simply let it remain a kind of precious dream and not strive for the full embodiment. But, as Rachel's experience in her healing shows, the return, not to the state of the past, but to a new and enduring state, can be made.

I have written extensively in *The Black Butterfly* about what I consider the three fundamental aspects that together form the nexus of the transformational potential. It seems important to review them briefly now against the background of Rachel's experience.

I called these three forces spontaneous creativity, intensity, and unconditional love. In the years since writing that book, I have come to appreciate a refinement of these concepts. Now I still utilize the concept spontaneous creativity, but for intensity I have substituted authority and for unconditional love, I feel strongly that it is more important to speak of grace. Before going any further, it is essential to realize that these are not separate forces. Language coerces us to discuss them sequentially, but we are speaking of different aspects of one inseparable mystery: graced spontaneous creative authorship. I think of it as intuiting into the generative potential of Nature as she lives though us as human beings.

Spontaneous creativity refers to the unique subjectivity that we embody. We each have a unique vantage point that is no one else's. We can express this in virtually infinite ways, but when we are truly spontaneously creative, the expression is a direct connection to our own unique subjectivity, our I-amness. Without trying or even realizing what we are doing, spontaneous creativity is an affirmation of our deepest nature. While all of us are similar in so many ways, nonetheless, each of us is one-of-a-kind, participating uniquely with life moment by moment. No two voices are identical. No two laughs are identical. There is something about our intuition of God and the incomprehensible vastness of the universe, with the great physical laws that we are beginning to understand, that has its counterpart in the profound, unrepeatable subjectivity of each human being and each created thing. Therefore, when our actions are animated in a manner that is spontaneously expressive and honoring of our authentic nature, something is happening that has never happened before and can never be repeated. In this way we literally become the instruments of the Infinite and we are, quite unconsciously, an expression of the intelligence and wholeness of the universe. For Rachel, apparently, it was solitude and the imaginative ways she experimented with herself. For someone else it could be entirely different.

Now, it must be emphasized that just because we achieve the

177

First Miracle, there is no assurance of the capacity for a truly authentic and spontaneous self-expression. The enormity of the power of the collective mentality to forge conformity and mediocrity cannot be overestimated. Human beings automatically achieve the consciousness of the First Miracle, but until we truly think for ourselves and awaken to some degree of the Second Miracle, it is doubtful that we should be called conscious. In fact, most people act as though they were members of a herd, ever looking to each other and the past to define their hopes and fears, their roles in family and society, and ever checking with the consensus values to determine their personal success or failure in these roles. This potentially soul-deadening conformity permeates even how we experience and respond to our own sensations and feelings. Our habituated language and labels can obstruct our capacity to have a spontaneously creative relationship to our own aliveness. The consequences for self-healing are enormous.

When we are ill it is the most natural thing to begin to define symptoms. By giving a label to our suffering, we believe we can perhaps gain control over what is happening. This is fine as long as it marks the initiation into deeper relationship to ourselves and not the end-point. But merely finding a label for our disease and beginning any variety of treatments is little more than the compulsive naming and reacting mechanisms of First Miracle consciousness. Only rarely can this be considered spontaneous creativity. This was the path that Rachel started down, as do nearly all people when faced with illness. She went to the doctors, had the tests, received the diagnosis, and began the recommended treatment. Unfortunately, this is essentially where modern medicine rests its head. In contrast, for our infinite nature, no label and no treatment is the end; it is just a potential beginning of a profoundly radical relationship to being alive.

The sum total of human culture is the artifact of the spontaneous creative authorship of countless human beings, most long gone from this world. What today we accept as the basis for science, technology, law, literature, and art began as a moment in which a human being fell into an original relationship to himself and to That which had already been present but was not yet consciously realized. The very words we use, the attitudes we profess, all that we accept as reality began this way, in Mystery. We stand on the shoulders of countless individuals who lived such moments of radical aliveness, spontaneously expressing their creative authorship and slowly, through grace, revealed the universe's secrets. Yet, instead of worshipping this living fountain as our true heritage, we make false gods of their discoveries and creations. We betray the courage and elegance of their lives by becoming the prisoners of their achievements. Jesus said that we would do greater things, but oh, the agony he would feel to see the coffins we have built, within and without, in his life's name. Our inclination to make false gods from the very things born of our God-ing remains one of humankind's great challenges.

Today, modern medicine is the cumulative result of countless moments of fundamental, spontaneously creative authorship, yet the institution of medicine has become a frozen behemoth. It makes us prisoners of our bodies instead of the incarnation of Mystery. In the domain of the psychological, where we forever stand at the threshold of the unconscious, we are endlessly entranced by the psychological offspring of the great psychologists like Freud and Jung. What these men birthed out of their authorship has become, in some hands, an ever-deepening inquiry into the mystery of the psyche but, in others, a trivializing of the complexity of the soul. Day by day, the list of the different inner selves and archetypes grows until one can only imagine that there is a great mob within us. Like everything else in life, the right tool in the wrong hands leads to wrong results.

There is a fundamental tension between form and formlessness, order and disorder, incarnation and disincarnation. For every person there is a fundamental tension between authenticity of self and belonging to the group. This tension can only be resolved at the expense of our aliveness. To live in and with this tension is what I have called radical aliveness.

Every day is an opportunity to live this. It is hard to begin to imagine, in the context of traditional medicine, the possibility of

179

the spontaneous creativity such as that which occurred that momentous evening when Rachel experienced, for the first time, the transmutation of pain and the birth of the silence. Yet this principle is happening all the time, even in traditional research institutions. For example, new treatment protocols often have better results in the originating laboratory than in other institutions that attempt to repeat and confirm the original results. Is this not the principle of spontaneous creativity influencing the flow of aliveness? While mimesis is a fundamental way in which we learn, repeating something lacks the very originality that, I believe, imbues original and spontaneous actions with a power that transcends any rational analysis of those actions.

Even prayer, which is a time-honored way of invoking the Transcendent, becomes frozen when it becomes institutionalized. And when a person rediscovers prayer as a fundamental act of creative relationship, she does so out of a spontaneous and original personality that is often contradictory to the dogma of her church. Many health-care facilities provide pastoral counseling and prayer intercession as a means of bringing spirit into what is otherwise thought to be a scientifically based enterprise. Yet, the division of some things into science and other things into religion is inimical to wholeness.

The spontaneous and unobstructed way in which Rachel's crisis unfolded with the group that evening is not something I know how to orchestrate, nor do I ever count on such happenings. The art is in leaving room for the possibility. Society, itself, is caught in this dilemma. The increasing incidence of cancer and many other diseases, as well as the escalating ecological crisis is, I believe, the price we pay for the increasing restriction on our ability to live spontaneously from the inside out. We have achieved a degree of security from many of life's ancient plagues but we pay for that predictability. Now we face the plagues from within our increasingly repressed souls.

As I said earlier, I initially used the concept of unconditional love rather than grace. I myself, was, as always, in a process of discovery and my use of the term unconditional love felt right to describe the underlying coherence of the universe. But over time I saw that the notion of unconditional love tended to be co-opted by an egoistic effort to achieve this kind of love. It is a mistake to think that unconditional love is something we can do; it is something that is expressed through us when our hearts are open. We may consecrate ourselves to unconditional love, but any conscious effort to be unconditionally loving is a manipulation that has the underlying consecration of rejection, either of oneself or of the circumstances. I saw that my use of the term was more misleading than helpful. I don't remember how grace, as a concept, entered into my understanding, but one day it simply spoke right to my heart.

As I have already discussed, I think of grace as the intelligence of the whole that tends to reveal itself to each of us when we are living from an open heart. The open human heart is one of Life's true wonders. It is a yes to existence without intent, so that we live at the edge of the infinite without any hidden agenda. Openheartedness and grace were present that night with Rachel and the rest of us when the sounds released her pain. There was heart and grace in her decision to be in solitude and in her determination to remain so until she knew she felt secure in her own I-amness. It is not that grace is only available at some times and not others, or that there is less grace in modern medicine than in what Rachel eventually did. It is that when we are ego-ing, the activity of grace is acting through a smaller infinity and appears less active in our lives. When we are living from an open heart, grace is everywhere.

To expect that we will receive grace when our actions are merely the repetition or imitation of earlier graced actions is again the error of the ego. For example, to try to heal oneself by imitating what Rachel did might well lead to positive results in some cases, but applying solitude like a formula, I fear, would do as much harm as good. This is not an uncommon situation for some monks and nuns who can be emotionally and psychologically crippled by submitting themselves to a discipline that does not emanate from their own spontaneous creative authority. This is also why I have reservations about most self-help methodologies. They are authentic to the person for whom they came forth in spontaneous creative flow, but when they are imitated, where is the creative impulse? If I use laughter as therapy because an expert told me to, this is not my own spontaneous creative authorship. Doing something that does not come from my own I-amness can be an underlying self-rejection, an underlying fear to fall into my own wonderland. True, we are always learning and turning to others for inspiration. This is a good way to begin, but there is less grace in imitation than in that which emerges from one's own spontaneous creative authorship.

I do not want to discourage anyone from going forth to find new ways to understand himself by following others. Yet the challenge of self-healing must not be subverted by any conspiracy to protect our ego. Sooner or later we all must face what I call the Door of Aloneness. It can be the moment of physical death with the ego resisting and denying unto the very end, or it can come long before in radical aliveness. Paradoxically, this isn't about healing but about living. It isn't about isolation but a new community of relationship, collaborative, co-creative, and mutually reverent. We are each the authors of our own lives, and to be one's own author, to exercise authorship over ourselves, is true authority. If it is nothing else, Rachel's story is a call to such self-authorship.

Who can say when Rachel's journey back to herself really began? From conventional medicine, to attending the conference and experiencing her first taste of the deeper aliveness, to her decision to affirm life by marrying, and finally her odyssey in solitude, each step was part of a continuum leading her, like Alice, into the Wonderland of herself. Her first steps with her doctors relied on external authority and other peoples' past creativity. The doctors themselves are nearly always relying on other peoples' past discoveries; this is the basis of the institution of medicine. Attending the conference demanded more of her active participation, yet even this experience still relied heavily on my authority and the context of the group energy. In a sense that first opening was like an appetizer. She could ride on the grace of that experience for a little while, but she could not gain access to that dimension out of her own authority. The full accessing of her spontaneous creativity and authority did not occur until she entered solitude and would not turn away from herself. To do so she had to go against the tide of conventional wisdom, as almost all fundamentally creative movements of the soul must do. Though we do not understand what we are doing as we are living it, true spontaneous creative authorship is a positive relationship to the transcendental reality emerging from one's own nature that does not look back to see if anyone is following, if anyone agrees, or what has been left behind.

Like Rachel, many people obey or disobey their doctors. But rebellion against modern medicine, or anything else, is still using the rejected external authority to leverage one's own position. This is often more life-sustaining than passive obedience, as survival studies have shown, but it is rarely the fullest potential of creativity. Neither obedience nor disobedience is necessarily true authorship. Many people fall in love and marry, yet romance is usually a force that drives us, not one that we ourselves author. This is one reason why romance ignites us for awhile, but like Rachel's temporary healing, romance borrows from mystery; it is not the embodiment of Mystery. When Rachel left behind her doctors, her family, and her romance, this, *for her,* was an act of profound self-love. She risked death and insanity, and the kind of loneliness few ever let themselves know. Very few people ever turn toward themselves with such utter and total dedication as she did. She gave herself no place to escape to, no distractions, and no hope.

This is, I believe, in one way or another, the kind of journey that all of us must make to stand near the fire of our deeper being. Rachel heard "the still, small voice" and obeyed. How many of us have such insight and let it pass by without paying any heed? Of course, Rachel's suffering was extreme and she had nothing to lose. Yet suffering like hers is happening every day to millions of people, the vast majority of whom cannot even imagine the possibility of something so fundamentally creative as to fall into one's self. Here is Whitman's "farther, farther, farther, sail...are they not all the seas of God?" Rachel hoisted the sails of her soul, hauled up

183

the anchor—the security of the known—and entered into the ocean of herself.

Here then is a prescription for all of us, yet it is no prescription in the usual sense. I cannot write, "Take two weeks of solitude...or become a vegan...or sit at your window looking out at the city recalling and forgiving every cruel and insensitive thing you ever did in your life...or, disturbed by a mysterious childhood dream, begin a deep exploration of the Unconscious." Yet each of these examples was a spontaneous creative authorship by an individual who is now regarded as a leader and a hero.

When a person asks, "What can I do to heal myself?" what answer can we give? It is not so much what we say but what depth we speak from. Are we answering from textbook learning, from preconceived notions, from personal beliefs, or are we standing as nakedly as our lives have led us to become, at the threshold of mystery? Are we choosing the peace of the ego or the nakedness of ignorance? And most important of all, can anyone teach another how to listen and honor his or her own beingness? Why are so many called, but so few chosen?

The actual incidence of spontaneous remission is difficult to quantify and probably unknowable. Some medical sources speak of one in ten thousand, while others feel it is much rarer, one in a hundred thousand, or even less. I believe that the incidence is actually much, much higher. My experience has repeatedly shown me that as a person begins to fall toward fundamental relationship, the probability of being reorganized in wholeness increases exponentially. Some years ago an old physician, Evarts Loomis, one of the pioneers of holistic medicine in the United States, said to me that there was no such thing as an incurable disease. He knew that there will always be someone somewhere who will live into her life in such a way as to vibrate, once again, with the Great Intelligence. In this sense, disease is like a question: Who would you be if the energy that is now creating disease could express itself healthfully? While I have not tried to gather statistics, I have met many people through my work who answered this question and regained their health. However, there is no way of knowing in advance or being assured in any way of the result. We must simply take the journey because it is the deepest urge of life that we do so. As Whitman wrote: "Camerado, I confess, I have been urging you onward with me and still urge you, without the least idea whether we shall be victorious, or utterly quelled and defeated." Those who want assurance can choose to stop with the modest but predictable statistical probabilities offered in the current First Miracle approach to healing. For those who feel worthy of more, we can, as Whitman says in "Passage to India," sail farther seas "and risk the ship and all" in the great adventure of consciousness.

When Jesus taught, "When you make the inner and the outer a single one," he added:

> "…and when you make eyes in the place of an eye, and
> a hand in the place of a hand, and a foot in the place of a
> foot, and an image in the place of an image, then shall
> you enter the Kingdom" (Logia 22).

These enigmatic words hold the key to the change in relationship to our own bodies that is the heart of all self-healing. Jesus is saying that we must once again have an unobstructed relationship to our own organism. This is what it means to "make a hand in the place of a hand." Obviously, all of us have hands and feet, but to Second Miracle consciousness a hand is not merely a grasping mechanism with an opposable thumb. One's hand and the self are part of the Great Intelligence. Just as a fragment of a hologram contains the whole image, this "hand" carries the full authority of the Self which is not limited to the body or local space and time.

The first time Rachel entered this level and "made a liver in the place of a liver and a pancreas in the place of a pancreas" was the moment after the high-pitched singing when her energy system shifted. The liver and pancreas that she could not feel were First Miracle objects-of-consciousness, that is, abstractions or concepts that she had learned long before when she was in school. Now her doctors had added some more weighty abstractions like "metastases" and "tumor infiltration" and so forth. Remember, I

185

am not denying the validity of these descriptions from a certain point of view. They are damnably accurate. I am saying that this doesn't help YOU very much. It certainly didn't help Rachel. She had the labels to describe her physiological condition, but she had the expected prognosis of a few months to live as well. If she had stopped there, statistically at least, she would now be long dead. But she didn't stop there. She spontaneously entered into a deeper level of consciousness in which the sense of herself and the existence of her pancreas and liver were not separate; she was immediate with the space these abstractions indicate. She was not merely connected with her internal organs; she was connected with the deeper current of self. In doing this she gained access to a higher authority than First Miracle consciousness; she touched her Second Miracle self.

For Rachel, this awakening during the conference was grace, but she was only a witness. She had no conscious relationship to how this had happened. We could say it was miraculous. And it did not last. Why? Probably because Rachel's dominant energy patterning still emanated from the First Miracle state. It had temporarily submitted to the higher possibility, but like a drug, it had worn off. The second time around, through her long, hard labor in solitude, Rachel made it her own.

True authority rests in tapping our Second Miracle nature, our deeper I-amness. In regard to this Jesus says, "If two make peace with each other in this one house, they shall say to the mountain, 'Be moved,' and it shall be moved" (Logia 48). The "two" are the subject and the object level of consciousness. In the Second Miracle they "make peace" with each other; they "become as a single one" in the house of being. If in this state we say, "I am whole," we are whole. Paradoxically, being already whole, why would there be any necessity to say it? We have misunderstood the statement: "As a man thinks in his heart, so is he." How we "think in our hearts" is the unified awareness of the Second Miracle. It is the self-awareness when "inner and outer, above and below, male and female...are as a single one."

This is not egoic-based thinking. This is not thought directed

186

by ordinary self-reflective consciousness. We cannot mentally affirm a positive thought to achieve the state of "as a man thinks in his heart." Such efforts are inevitably rooted in fear. Further, when the hand, or the liver, or the pancreas, or the brain, and so on, remains a First Miracle object-of-consciousness, the you in this consciousness is fundamentally separate from it and has virtually no authority to influence it. At this level you can say: "Cancer go away," or "I am healthy and free of all disease," or any other affirmation, and it has virtually no power whatsoever over that cancer. What these affirmations do have is the power of displacing outer awareness away from the fear and thus temporarily achieving psychological well-being. Since excessive fear is stressful and may weaken our immune system, such peace of mind is not without some benefit in a healing process. But this is only the peace of the ego. This is a house built on the sand of self-hypnosis and denial and not a church built on the radical energy of "the peace that passeth understanding."

Self-healing is a far more radical adventure than virtually anything advocated by popular psychology or the mental sciences. It means no more labels to rationalize our suffering. It means no longer placing the authority for our wholeness outside ourselves. Now we begin to fall, not only into an entirely new relationship to our life, to all that is free and joyous, but equally into our pain, fear, doubt, confusion, and rage. The sum total of how we create relationship to ourselves, as well as interpersonally, must be challenged and brought into the light of truth. As Plato said: "An unexamined life is a life not worth living." As Jesus said: "If you will know yourselves, then you will be known and you will know that you are the sons [and daughters] of the living Father [Mother]. But if you do not know yourselves, then you are in poverty, and you are poverty" (brackets mine).

Initially, this turning back upon ourselves intensifies the suffering. Here is the crucial moment, the Dark Night of the Soul, the Door of Aloneness. There is no looking backward, no asking for approval from any source but our own essence. We are naked before existence. Now, at last, guided solely by our own light, and with grace ever present, we do not turn away. We breathe into the

187

darkness, we dance the fear, or write poetry out of our misery, or cry, or scream. We may utilize conventional medicine or not. Indeed, there is infinite possibility and no one can tell us what to do. We each must author this ourselves and whether we live or die is no longer relevant. If we are to live, gradually the energy will turn. The lifeforce that had been ebbing away will begin to well up anew. We will discover our courtship of aliveness that gradually integrates this energy into our daily living. But more than we can understand, we will have taken our stand with evolution. Every life offered in the service of That which seeks to awaken within us serves the whole of existence.

And we can't pretend. Chemotherapy and radiation are difficult roads, yet they are usually easier to undertake because they stand on the foundation of First Miracle scientific rationalization. The road to ourselves is even more demanding and stands on no rationalization whatsoever, only on our faith. Here is a labor that offers no guarantees whatsoever of healing, only an increased probability for wholeness. We must pick up the cross of our own subject–object self and begin to use it to turn our awareness back onto the deeper awareness of Self. This is the only true authority any of us have.

When someone says, "I gave my power away," this speaks to the poverty within them. Indeed, losing oneself in another so that we forsake our own essential nature, is one of the common miseries that reveals our poverty and helps propel our prodigal return. Sadly, too many of us conspire with a partner to together live less than our personal potential. Here the poverty can be bearable, but the impulse for the return is postponed. When our attention becomes too absorbed in any object-of-consciousness, whether it be a spouse, wealth, success, fame, fear, and on and on, this is the basic root of how we give our true power away. This is also the basis of how our lifeforce slowly ebbs away until, perhaps as a blessing, illness and suffering try to call us home. We may hope that some outer authority, perhaps a doctor, therapist, priest, psychic reader, or guru will be able to fix us. But until we become the authors of our own attention, "all the King's horses and all the King's men" cannot put us together again.

The real key to self-healing is the way in which we gather our attention and pass through the whole domain of First Miracle reality and enter the state where we make "the inner as the outer, the above as the below, and the male and the female as a single one." The moment Rachel's attention first jumped into the new patterning, the subjective sense of herself collapsed into, and became at-one with, her sensation of pain. We could say that the pain of her illness was enormous unintegrated lifeforce that all at once could be received. Simultaneously, her illness could be received. Instead of it being other it was now self. Simultaneously, since mental activity is almost always produced from a condition of separation in consciousness, all the morbid thoughts of dying, and anger, and fear, and searching for healing ceased as she entered the Second Miracle. Instead of thinking about herself, she became the witness to herself. This is not a condition of thinking, only of unobstructed attention.

The dawning of the Second Miracle is an incarnational movement, a movement of embodiment. The dominion of First Miracle consciousness is greatest when our embodiment is crudest (the metaphor of Stoneman) and gradually accesses the Second Miracle consciousness as our embodiment refines (Sandman). This can best be understood as a dynamic of attention. As attention shifts from the finite referents to increasingly becoming referent to infinity, incarnation deepens. Rachel's process of seclusion and extreme introversion turned her attention away from past and future, away from goals and hope, and back toward its root in the infinity of the present moment. The longer she sustained this immersion in the present, the more the radiance of the Infinite refined her embodiment. At a certain point it is like reaching critical mass in a nuclear reaction, and the process begins to run itself. Gradually and then faster and faster, a tremendous amount of energy is released.

189

Looking from the outside, all we would have seen was Rachel eating very simply, whirling, dancing, blindfolding herself, falling onto her bed, writing, and often drifting for hours, seemingly daydreaming or entranced. But inside, a wellspring had been tapped and her whole organism was suffused and transformed in the Current. In an alchemical sense she was creating the philosopher's stone, although this notion usually connotes more of a psychological achievement than an embodiment. In our incarnational metaphor she was moving from stone to sand and even perhaps to powder. What had occurred first as grace now became embodied in her. She had returned through her own initiative to a level of energy where the deeper current of self forever bridges "inner and outer, above and below, male and female." This is true authority.

I feel it is the energy born of the fundamental relationship, self to other and to Infinity, that is the heart of transformation and self-healing. In anthropology, the term *participation mystique* is used to describe the capacity of aboriginal people to become one with their environment. *Participation mystique* was crucial to their survival because hunters, in particular, had to enter into a state of oneness so that their quarry could be approached. Learning to enter this state involved special initiation and ritual, not dissimilar to what Rachel did. They understood that if the creatures sensed the hunter's presence as a consciousness separate from the general milieu, as my young visitor did when I tried to send love to him, they would become suspicious and seek to escape. The hunter's challenge was to become one with both the creature he was hunting and with nature as a whole, while simultaneously remaining grounded in himself and his personal intent to kill his quarry. Because hunter and quarry had become so fused in consciousness it was natural to honor the quarry as brother or sister in life.

Today's hunters using high-powered rifles do not need *participation mystique,* though they pretend to it. Technology allows us to cheat. Without ever having to relinquish the First Miracle state, we can kill. Today's weapons have obviated the need to master the ancient process of bridging self with other. The generalized loss of this capacity is part and parcel of the growing violence of modern societies. If we cannot bridge self and other, then other can become anything, even something to just snuff out without a second thought. Here we see the antithesis of the healing that extends organically from a fundamental relationship with life.

And this is the same problem with modern medicine's reliance on technology; both physician and patient are losing the ability to bridge between self and other. For the doctor this means that his or her own healing presence becomes more and more diminished and the *participation mystique* (bedside manner or healer's art) with the patient becomes weakened. Then we try to compensate with more technological wizardry for what our organism can do organically when it is referent to infinity and drinks of the Great Intelligence.

This understanding offers a map for the direction healthcare can take in the future. Healthcare must draw not only upon the mysticism of the object, but equally upon the mysticism of the subject. Health care as empirical science is "that aspect of Nature becoming conscious" of the human organism, revealing the laws of Nature that sustain its life. Health care as the mysticism of the subject is spirituality. It is about the process of incarnation in which the energy of attention is, again and again, freed to infinity and back into fundamental resonance with the intelligence of the universe.

Rachel's story encourages us to become the authors of our own destiny, to explore more freely the richness of our own creativity and authority. It is a testimony to the power that flows through each of us when we come home to our deeper self. If her story seems more challenging than you can imagine for yourself, we must remember that we are all just beginners. The Second Miracle is only just dawning now among us. We mustn't be afraid to fall through the door even of failure into the wonderland of ourselves. We must keep going one step at a time. Failure is but a word created by an ego referent to some finite goal. Let failure do its work: Let it empty us, humble us, bring us to our knees so that we can begin to listen and become servants to That which ever seeks to awaken in us.

# CHAPTER 14

# SUFFERING, FAITH, AND DISCIPLESHIP

The alchemy of Consciousness awakening in matter over billions of years, the kindling of Life, the birth of sentience, the increasing subjectivity of creatures as they become more and more conscious, this is the great mystery of Incarnation. It is not as if we are locked at one level of incarnation and cannot escape it. Moment by moment in the consciousness of our relationships, in what we invest with our attention, in our capacity to intuit the Infinite, we invite the potential of moving from stoneness, to sandness, to ever more refined embodiment. Who can say what the limit of our potential really is? This is radical aliveness in which we live spirituality with our whole being. At the heart of such a life is our capacity to allow feeling, and this requires, indeed demands, a fundamental shift in our relationship to suffering.

Webster's Dictionary tells us that the root of the word *suffer* means to bear up, or to carry. From this, suffering has two meanings: the experience of pain and sufferance, the capacity to endure pain. What we must come to understand is that incarnation is the progressive, continual enlightenment of the whole organism. In effect, the question that life puts to each of us moment by moment is: How much Reality can you bear? Here is the paradox of incarnation: The more we embody Consciousness—the more enlightened we become—the greater our capacity to suffer.

We must look beyond the popular reaction against suffering; there are certain spiritual and consciousness raising circles that would expunge the very idea from our thinking. They attest: "Pain is inevitable, suffering is an option." This reaction is not without good reason. Centuries of seeing an agonized Jesus on the cross has tended to overly ennoble suffering. Embracing suffering has become Christ's work, or the work of saints, not the affair of the average person. Further, we have grown in our understanding of human neurosis and psychosis. A great deal of suffering is directly the result of psychological adaptations that initially defend the ego, but later lead to withholding, self-protection, and making ourselves smaller—prescriptions, indeed, for increasing isolation and misery. To a certain degree this kind of suffering can be changed by a shift of perception through self-understanding and especially by an opening of the heart to deeper love. Obviously, the enormity of suffering perpetrated by human beings upon each other is a tragedy not to be minimized. But suffering for which we can attribute a cause or frame a context is not what we are considering here. There is a deeper level of suffering that is not an option. I have referred to it as the wound the ego cannot heal. It is a different dimension of suffering that hides in all the forms of suffering we have just considered. Ultimately, it is not something that can be fixed or changed by any activity of the First Miracle self. Rather, it is the Evolutionary Impulse demanding that we grow in our very capacity for sentience. Whether it is our stones being ground to pebbles, or our sand being refined to pumice, it is the fire in which our whole being is submitted to a larger relationship to Existence. I believe that our capacity to evolve in an incarnational sense rests upon our willingness and ability to enter a spontaneous creative authorship to this dimension of suffering.

Suffering, in this larger sense, is coming into conscious relationship to a dimension of feeling for which we have no context,

193

no vocabulary, no means of rationalizing or containing. Sometimes this is referred to as the Dark Night of the Soul. I have called it the Door of Aloneness. No matter what labels we try to give to ourselves or the feeling, it will not yield to reason. It is the Teacher and it demands nothing short of fundamental relationship. No vehicle of the First Miracle intellect, whether medicine, science, psychology and psychotherapy, exotic religion, or popular spirituality will ever alleviate this suffering. The longer we allow the pretense that they can, the longer we prolong a childish adolescence and delay entering genuine spiritual maturity.

Let's take the common experience of fear. It is the most basic of emotions; we all suffer it. There are perhaps hundreds of nuances of fear: fear of death, fear of embarrassment, rejection, failure, abandonment, annihilation, even the fear of God as the ego is presented with the Infinite, to name but a few. Now, just for a moment, stop and realize that our very capacity to experience these is, itself, miraculous. To merely label the experience "fear" in the inevitable manner of ego-ing demeans the billions of years that it has taken for an organism to be able to evolve such complex feelings. And, more important, such a label often means the end of one's relationship to fear as if, somehow, being able to say, "This is fear" or, "I am afraid" has made the feeling sufficiently conscious. It could be otherwise; it could be the beginning of a relationship. It could be a doorway to another level of being, a new level of incarnation.

What is fear to Stoneman compared to Sandman? If we are less incarnated there is less of a sense of connection to our own depths, more of a sense of the other person as separate, less of a sense of connectedness and belonging to the world in general. Now our response to fear is more oriented to self-protection, whether of our life, or our self-image. We lash out, attack, build walls, close down. We perceive clear contrasts between who are the good guys and who are the bad guys. We lie awake at night trying to figure out how to make ourselves safe, what response will bolster our ego, secure our image, alleviate the danger. We are the victims of the fear instead of disciples of ourselves. Gradually, as our incarnation deepens, fear becomes much more multidimensional. There is a highly complex trembling in the soul, a weaving of interpenetrating issues of responsibility, morality, commitment, compassion, and more. Sandman's fear can have so may levels coming from within as well as from without that he can't really protect himself. Whereas Stoneman may want to reinforce his boundaries and push others away when he is afraid, for Sandman fear may actually be a prayer to open outward, to get larger, to stop avoiding real relationship and intimacy.

Enlightenment usually implies freedom from suffering, but as author Aster Barnwell has framed the paradox, it is also the capacity to suffer.[1] As our incarnation deepens, our capacity for sentience has grown, and with it, our capacity to more fully experience everything from suffering to joy, despair to awe, everything becomes both more intense and sublime. Now pain is far more than physical; it will more and more have a psychological component, reverberating into so many corners of our soul. In this sense we can potentially suffer more, or, said in another way, our *capacity to suffer* has increased. Yet here is the paradox: Our deepening incarnation is also a growing intelligence, a deeper sense of connection with our essence, our I-amness. Many things that we feared when we were spiritually younger no longer disturb us; we no longer invest our sense of self in so many things that life will eventually threaten. Now we can also say our *capacity for suffering* has increased; we are more enlightened.

We need simply look at our own lives to see the evidence of this. What has become of our childhood terror of the dark? Are you as afraid today of peer group judgment as you were as a younger person? One of the most dramatic examples of the transformation of a basic fear is reported in the cases of Near Death Experience (NDE). Afterward the fear of death is almost universally gone. In an NDE, the survivor has entered a direct relationship to a process that formerly could only be imagined and anticipated with dread. As a result of actually living (or dying into) the experience, the dread is gone and much more has been added. The NDE is an example of an incarnational event brought about by "accidentally" (are there any accidents?) becoming referent to infinity at the threshold between life and death. After an NDE, people describe the birth of a new spirituality; their whole personality undergoes profound changes. Often there is a new sense of trust in life and a new sense of vitality.

For example, the few survivors of suicide leaps from the Golden Gate Bridge have been well studied. These survivors almost uniformly begin renewed lives that are filled with hope and joy. In jest, I invite people to "Golden Gate Bridge Seminars," promising them a 100 percent guarantee of fundamental transformation. Then, facetiously, I add the caveat: 100 percent transformation, but only 2 percent survival.

In certain cases the NDE actually fosters the birth of paranormal faculties, such as the capacity for "psychic reading" and communication with the spirit world. However we regard such faculties, it is apparent that the person's new level of incarnation has access to a whole new range of sensory intuition and symbolic experience. A question remains, for me, of how large the infinity is that is entered in this way? I don't doubt the power of a NDE to cause such an opening, but the spiritualism born in this way is not necessarily the wisest; a great deal of basic work at the level of one's personal psychology is necessary, I believe, to interpret the new perceptions maturely, and this is not automatically given when we are plunged so suddenly to the edge of the infinite.

As a human being, acknowledging "I am afraid" can be a valid and important revelation, a step toward greater self-awareness… the first time(s). But what we make conscious—and this is the crucial challenge of all psychotherapy—we are also gradually divided from, even our own sensations and emotions. We rationalize the feeling, analyze it, look for its cause and the immediacy of the feeling is lost; it becomes dead. This is why a diagnosis is a double-edged sword. It gives us a way to rationalize our discomfort. The ego then says, "Now I know what this is…there was something wrong…I wasn't crazy after all." This brings a temporary relief. Simultaneously, this label becomes the rationale for a treatment program or some plan of action. But the doctor's, therapist's (any so-called expert's) label also drives a wedge between our basic consciousness and the immediacy of our experience. We begin to deal with fear by distancing ourselves from it. It is the same with any other labeled symptom or self-description; instead of the immediacy of our own sensations, feelings, images, and thoughts, we gain the peace of the ego that comes through a rational explanation for our experience. We can say, "I suffered sexual abuse" and in just this degree of distancing from the immediacy of the feelings, the discomfort retreats. But this improvement is usually only temporary. It is achieved at the expense of the capacity for fundamental relationship to ourself. There comes a moment when the name for our suffering, (fear or whatever), and the explanation (abuse, abandonment, parental alcoholism, and so on) are no longer helpful. They may have been at first; we may not have been ready to meet this deep wound in our soul. But, now like an NDE, we must die into our feeling prior to its name. We enter the oceanic movement of original feeling. It is an incarnational initiation. It may feel like we may die or go mad, but what can, and often does, happen is we are reborn into a capacity for new feeling, for new life.

I am certain that, as far as self-healing is concerned, a paradox is that the more labels we have for our experience the less likely we are to heal ourselves. In the case of fear, once it is carefully elaborated in whatever is the traditional or current popular explanation, we then can talk endlessly about ourselves, our wounds, our situation. This is what the Gnostics meant by "making the living dead." This is why Jesus said, "In the days when you devoured the dead, you made it alive" (Logia 11). And again: "You have dismissed the Living (One) who is before you and you have spoken about the dead" (Logia 53). Finally, when the disciples saw a Samaritan carrying a lamb on his way to Judea, Jesus said to his disciples, "Why does this man carry the lamb with him?" They answered, "In order that he may kill it and eat it." He said to them, "As long as it is alive, he will not eat it, but only if he has killed it and it has become a corpse" (Logia 60).

Using the lamb as a symbol of Life in all its simple innocence, Jesus is speaking figuratively about one of the most difficult things in the world for ordinary consciousness to grasp. He is saying that real Life, the Living Reality, cannot be taken in (eaten) directly by our usual consciousness. First we have to "kill it"—that is, make the experience an object of consciousness, an abstraction. We have discussed this as the First Miracle and the process of the subject-object separation. Literally, as ego-ing splits awareness off from immediacy, we "make the living dead." As soon as this happens a universe, an infinity, of (relative) consciousness is generated that we can intellectualize about and discuss ad nauseum. Completely unaware of what we are doing, we take this "corpse" and invest it with thinking and emotion, thus evoking further feeling. Now we are suddenly ashamed, or guilty, or indignant, or enraged, and we begin to plot our reaction. It is this very condition, mystically referred to as being asleep or living in a dream, in which we have "made the dead alive."

The catharsis of these "dead" perceptions that we have "made alive" causes a sense of release that can be construed as self-healing. But this is only temporary; we remain the victims of feeling and not the disciples of our infinite capacity for aliveness. It is this process of labeling, rationalizing, distancing from immediate feeling, and then catharsis of self-generated feelings that keeps us from awakening. It has become a mass epidemic that is literally being propelled by the popular psychological movement, by political –analysts, by policy planners. We are asleep drowning in our own dreams. Then Jesus challenges, "When you come into the Light, what will you do with it?" Precisely. Only when we come into Consciousness prior to the subject-object ego-ing can we understand the craziness of what we are constantly doing. And then what? Do we imagine that we can objectify this Light? Referent to Infinity, what can we actually say about ourselves that captures our essence, our true nature? Nothing.

198 The miracle of incarnation is ever before our eyes, but the wonder of it eludes us. Consider the difference in the capacity for love and joy, as well as the capacity for suffering, of human beings versus that of cattle. This became clear to me many years ago during my visits to a friend's ranch. When it was time to wean the

calves, the herd would be driven into a holding pen. There we would separate the calves from their mothers. The cows and calves would bawl in terror, which, for me, was emotionally disturbing to hear. I always was curious about my friend's detachment and admired his skill in separating the animals, using a minimum of violence while avoiding being trampled. Afterward, we herded the cows and calves into different pastures as far apart as possible. Within minutes they resumed grazing again, though they continued to cry out for each other for a few more days. After a few months when they are brought together again, there is little or no recognition by the cow of its calf, or of the calf for its mother.

What if human beings were herded like that? What if mothers were ripped from their children? How long before you or I could settle down to a meal? How long before we would feel relaxed and natural once again? This has happened to indigenous peoples in North America, the Jews and other national and ethnic minorities in Nazi Germany, the Kurds in Iraq, and it continues to happen between us on our planet. This kind of terror and horror is not over in ten minutes, not forgotten even in ten generations. History shows that the consequences of such terrible suffering breeds hatred and revenge that curse generations to come. This kind of suffering, in fact, all human suffering, is never merely physical. It is psychological, spiritual, and existential as well. The wound becomes the basis for identity, creating borders and nationalism. And this momentum from the past does not end until this suffering becomes an incarnational event rather than an ego-ing force. This is personal work, done in deep aloneness where we, at last, become disciples of our suffering instead of its victims. Now the suffering leads us to the very edge of our being, until we are carried into the infinity of ourselves.

The enlightenment of a society can be read in the reaction of the people to suffering in all its forms. Consciously and unconsciously the response to suffering permeates our whole notion of values, morality, ethics, law, art, the very meaning and purpose of life. It is the motive behind much of our inventiveness and the technology that is designed to increase our pleasure or diminish our discomfort. What would the economic and political reality look like were people not afraid to feel, where they have become the disciples of their fears and suffering, rather than victims?

The pursuit of happiness is one of the "inalienable rights" of every person, according to the United States Constitution. But the pursuit of happiness is usually the avoidance of deeper relationship to life more than it is the fruit of genuine spiritual maturity. Happiness, real happiness, rests on the bedrock of I-amness and is the hard-won fruit of a life lived deeply and well, and not a life lived in the "pursuit of happiness." Ultimately it is our adaptation to suffering that hides behind the facade of civilization. It is our capacity to suffer that reflects the subtlety of integration of body, mind and spirit. It is an individual person's capacity for fundamental relationship to feeling that collectively forms the basis for society and culture.

Just as naming a pelican does not really help us know the bird (except in the abstract), so too, naming and perhaps explaining inner psychical states such as fear, does not necessarily help us know ourselves. Is there a Self to know? It is paradoxical that if someone is not truly present they will have a persona that gives the illusion of substantialness, while in reality such a person is quite insubstantial. But if a person is truly present, open to Infinity, there is little persona there, but much more spaciousness—and this *is* quite substantial. What we are is not something that can be known in any finite sense. Do we really know ourselves better because we can label our feelings or give reasons for their cause? Yes and no. The first time we make a feeling or dynamic conscious we have become more self-aware. It is the subsequent times we are conscious of these feelings that are the crucial moments. In the case of fear, having become conscious of fear even once implies self-awareness that is prior to the experience of fear.

200     After all, if I know that I am afraid, who or what is it that knows? The next time we are afraid, do we treat the fear as something already known, pull out last week's (or a past lifetime's) interpretation and label and split off in endless explanations and defense? Or do we realize that I am is prior to any fear, and any

lifetime? I-amness remains and is untouched. With this understanding there is less need to resist fear and it becomes a doorway into a new universe of feeling. Entering this doorway, passing into immediacy with fear (or any feeling or emotion whether pleasant or unpleasant) is, I believe, the very fuel that drives incarnation in human beings. It is in this way that we refine the intuition of our relationship to the Universe and step by step evolve into Cosmic Consciousness.

We might well ask an important question: Is the great cerebrum, the biological basis of intellect, a means to defend against or escape feeling and the body, or is it perhaps the servant of conscious evolution? If the latter is the case than the whole import of the First Miracle is not to escape through abstractions, but to remain conscious and present in the midst of feeling. The cerebrum may not be Nature's effort to transcend our core brain, but the very means of making our feeling-relationship to existence ever more conscious.

There is an enormous range of responses to the stimuli and situations that generate suffering. Some people despair and feel victimized, others find dignity and generosity of spirit. The real issue is not that we suffer, but whether we accept this as one of the difficult initiations that Existence requires of us as incarnating organisms. The work of spiritual practice is to learn to approach this initiation wherever it arises in life, in whatever its guises, as disciples of our deeper nature and all that it holds.

When we see a man tormented by remorse, we are witnessing a miracle of the highest order. Does an amoeba suffer remorse, or a cow, or a primate? We complain about emotions and feelings that have taken countless millions of years to become part of the repertoire of Life. What of sorrow, guilt, shame, rage? And what of awe, reverence, compassion, and the sense of the sacred? Is it possible to reach a level of complexity in which we can experience the latter and not the former too? Each of these flowers with a step forward on the Incarnational journey. Each is miraculous.

If we cannot be the disciple of the feeling of remorse, if it is too unbearable, perhaps the emotion expressed will be guilt or

201

shame. If guilt or shame are unbearable, perhaps outrage and blame will be expressed. With each step away from the immediacy of our feeling we, in a manner of speaking, disincarnate into a psychological universe of ever greater complication, confusion, contingency, and necessity. We have become the victims of our feeling and its cause will inevitably be perceived as outside of us; thus we are disempowered. On the other hand, if a man can submit to his remorse, he may witness his heart opening to the suffering that is everywhere and he will awaken to compassion. Incarnation is the amount of reality we can bear. What we cannot bear we will think about, or via various mechanisms relegate to unconsciousness. This is why, I believe, Mother Teresa says, "The suffering people of the world mediate for us with God." When we do not blind ourselves to our own genuine suffering or the suffering of others our organism stands and breathes at the threshold of Infinity. If we can bear what we feel, not in the sense of successfully defending ourselves from it but conversely, in being shaken beyond reason to the very roots of our being without closing down in reflexive self-defense, Infinity can take deeper purchase within our organisms.

This is the mystical fire in which we must burn if we are to take another step forward in Incarnation. This is conscious suffering and it requires faith even as it bestows it at the same time. Faith is perhaps the most profound of human capacities. Faith implies a positive relationship to the Transcendental Reality, a direct relationship to God unmediated by symbols and ideas. It is a Yes to more and more of all that is. It is Yes not merely with our intellect which can, albeit abstractly, acknowledge the interconnected wholeness of existence. The Yes of faith is a whole-bodily opening and submission to the immediacy of life in all its indescribable feeling. It is a Yes that is the very sacralization of our whole being. It is as though we are standing before a precipice and "without the least idea whether we shall be utterly quelled or defeated," we open unconditionally to Now.

When we suffer consciously we become like a window on the Infinite. In this sense it can be said that we "mediate" between the Finite and the Infinite, between Earth and Heaven. When we stand with another, open to infinity, the suffering we can bear is the heart we can share. Through this heart shines the Divine radiance that restores each moment to Mystery.

I am not ennobling suffering. I simply call us back to our fundamental condition that is prior to suffering. When we are self-indulgently repeating the litany of our troubles, wearing our suffering like a cloak, a precious badge of identity, this is avoiding relationship to a deeper condition of being, a deeper possibility for ourselves. When we turn Reality into a parent who is to care for us and protect us, we live in a fantasy about life and in this fantasy we are infantilized. When we try to help others before we ourselves have deeply submitted to our own suffering, we are really hiding. We are not truly meeting the other. Beneath these defenses there forever beckons a far deeper, far more inscrutable state of being. Descend to this. Bear what you can. Submit to it. Let it consume you. "You" is always a relative self-concept. This self-concept is ever preceded by a more fundamental dimension of Self…endlessly. We must come in the deepest humility to our own suffering and the suffering of others. It must humble us. This is the journey of Incarnation. It is like a spiral in which we return, again and again, to our feelings and penetrate them a little further, submitting a little more each time. We submit because we know that nothing that we are conscious of is ever what we, ultimately, are. This knowledge is faith. We submit because we have faith and we have faith because we have submitted. Ultimately, it is our incarnation that determines what we can experience, what we can bear, and it is our faith that allows us to bear a little more…each time.

The evolution of consciousness is an incarnational movement, it is the embodied capacity to express the Great Intelligence of the universe. Ultimately, it is the obligation of each of us to become disciples of this intelligence within our own organisms. This is happening whether we are conscious of it or not, but if we are conscious of this obligation we have achieved what, I believe, is the truer sense of liberation. We are not liberated in the sense of being immune to, or beyond, suffering. Nor are we exempt from

203

the capacity to make mistakes and shame ourselves. Liberation means that we are no longer victims of this suffering, nor of our own ignorance, foolishness, and error. We are the disciples of every moment. Living rooted in our wholeness as conscious organisms, every moment brings the empowerment of insight. Humiliation is part of this; the embarrassment of our egos is essential to our evolution. No matter what, there is opening and learning. This would be another disguise for narcissistic self-involvement if it were not for the recognition that being a disciple of the Great Intelligence is to be the servant of Life's deepest impulse. Herein we are honored and humbled. Without any ambition or intention we become mentors to, and servants of, the Awakening Impulse, helping others to live this more consciously.

Respecting our own incarnation is the closest we can ever come to recognition of the Great Intelligence. It is our touchstone for healthy, intelligent behavior. It is through the refining of our feeling that we recognize the truth or falsehood of our participation with life.

To become a disciple of the Great Intelligence is equivalent to what the Buddhists mean by becoming a bodhisattva. The bodhisattva is an enlightened servant of the awakening consciousness. This service is summed up in the very beautiful bodhisattva vow, also known as the Quan Yin vow, or the vow of compassion:

> "Never will I seek nor receive private, individual salvation. Never will I enter into final peace alone. But forever and everywhere will I strive for the redemption of all creatures, throughout the world."

Of course, if the ego sees such a vow as a decision to serve life, we are speaking of just another ploy of the ego as savior, the ultimate do-gooder. But this vow is not a vow made by the ego, it is an avowal of the condition of life itself. To me, it is one of the greatest affirmations of relationship ever expressed by the human heart. It is the recognition that there is no salvation, no enlightenment, no final peace outside the whole community of existence. The higher realization is forever the servant of learning, growth and evolution, for this is the very nature of our universe. Nothing evolves independent of anything else. Recognition of this is liberation. Recognizing oneself as the servant of this awakening is joy.

1. I recommend *The Meaning of Christ for Our Age,* Llewelyn, 1984, (now out of print) and *The Pilgrim's Companion,* Element, 1992, by Aster Barnwell.

# CHAPTER 15

# THE ENNEAS
# MANDATE

*The Inner Teacher, Outer Teachers and*
*The Community of Consciousness*

I n the journey of awakening, two complementary dynamics are essential. The primary movement comes from within. It is the enlightening impulse of the universe expressed through the soul of each of us. I refer to this as the inner teacher. The secondary movement comes from without. It is made up of the individuals who, through whatever means and in whatever relationships, strongly influence our understanding of ourselves. But it also includes those situations through which our lives are transformed. These are the outer teachers.

The inner teacher, as I use the term, is a metaphor for the fundamental spiritualizing impulse that is evolving within us all. It is not an inner guide in the popular sense—some kind of wise guardian subpersonality that tells us what to do. As spiritualizing impulse, it is equally immanent in our personal pain or happiness, our personal success or failure, as it is in our infinite nature that is forever prior to these concerns. The inner teacher is the complement to the outer teacher. Together they are the essential force for the comprehension of the First Miracle dilemma and a doorway toward the infinite, uncreated source that is the awakened self.

As a person becomes established more and more in his I-amness, it is the inner teacher that is awakening. Yet, paradoxically, as we begin to respond to the call of the inner teacher, we may, as well, hear the call of the outer teacher—wherever he, she, or it may be. In effect, the two cannot be separated and so the question of inner and outer teacher becomes a matter of psychological maturity. The attraction to any outer teacher reflects radical intuition. When our spiritual intuition is young, the outer teacher must be extraordinary, larger than life, perhaps demonstrating special psychic powers in order for us to perceive and rely on his or her spiritual authority. Simultaneously, there is the temptation to rely too much, with the consequent danger of psychological regression and infantilization. As our intuition matures and we become more and more referent to infinity, the outer teacher becomes someone calling us to our fullest potential as human beings in the fullness of ordinary life. This relationship gradually becomes universal, reflected in everyone, and in the extraordinary invitation life places moment by moment. A person who denies the outer teacher risks denying the inner as well, and vice versa. He may rationalize that he is listening to his inner teacher and therefore reject any relationship with an outer teacher, but it is just as likely he is objectifying his own ego in one of its infinite disguises as spiritual and psychological sovereign. On the other hand, the individual who deifies the outer teacher and unquestioningly submits himself to the guidance of that teacher, is again objectifying his own ego in the form of the specialness of the outer teacher. In either case I-amness is betrayed.

This is not just a problem in spiritual teachings; this is the fundamental dilemma throughout life. If we do not know ourselves, we are in poverty and attempt to enrich ourselves by unconsciously submitting our own I-amness to thoughts, feelings, people, careers, and so on. They become, in a sense, the gurus of one or another aspect of our own egos. Even apparently enlightened teachers can become sacrificed, to the collective transference of their devotees and risk betraying their own evolving I-amness.

Enlightenment may mean the transcendance of the First Miracle ego position, but no matter the claims to the contrary, there is no person whose evolution is complete. Consciousness is relationship, and relationship within the vastness of our universe, as well as in the day-to-day living of life, has no end. We are all continuing to evolve in the great emergence of consciousness.

As a Western man, I stand in a tradition of strong individualism, but as a conscious man, I recognize I am the fruit and expression of many relationships and will forever be so. I am ever grateful for the outer mentors who have been instrumental in my growth. I am also indebted to many people who I know only through their writings, or through contact in dreams. But I have never been able to submit fully to any relationship in which my own spiritual intuition was compromised. I have found that it is life, itself, and every relationship I encounter that is the guru and the path of my awakening. Every relationship in which I withhold my full attention, in which I defend against naked availability and am no longer referent to infinity, reveals the growing me and, paradoxically, restores me to infinity. As this has been my path, it is, first and foremost, the relationship to the inner teacher that I seek to awaken in the people with whom I work. It is to the inner teacher in the reader that I direct this book.

A commitment to consciousness is a way of life, not an escape from suffering, or a reward, or a path of salvation. It is, purely and simply, service to what is potential in us, and this is seen, ever and always, in the mirror of our relationships to each other. For nearly everyone this will mean a commitment to a path of study, and therefore a relationship to one or a number of teachers who help to reflect us back to the fundamental relationship. Ideally, the path is one in which the teaching is the servant of the awakening impulse within every member, students as well as teacher. But in actuality, the form of such a relationship is complex, and very challenging to live.

Second Miracle consciousness cannot be taught like a subject in grade school; the teaching is, in essence, the quality and integrity of all the relationships: teacher to students, students to each other, and the whole community to the world at large. At the heart of these relationships there is a direct transmission of the unspeakable, first between teacher and student, but eventually between everyone. It is a process that could be described as energetic induction. It is an alchemical transformation precipitated within the student by the presence of the teacher whose attention, at least while he or she is teaching, is rooted in Infinity.

Creating the context of such transmission is the heart and soul of a spiritual teaching. There are techniques that invite new insight and an increased potential for energetic availability, but more essential is the overall consecration of the relationships. Spiritual teaching requires a high degree of openness and availability between teacher and student and this means a genuine respect and honoring that must be mutual. At its best, this is a relationship of great beauty and wholesomeness, but is also highly vulnerable to distortion and abuse. The integrity and wisdom with which the honoring between student and teacher is invited is crucial to whether the teaching flowers in psychospiritual maturity or whether it creates unhealthy dependency on the teacher and diminishment of the student's connection to his own inner wisdom.

The availability of the student to the transmission of the teaching requires softening of the student's own ego boundaries. It is this opening of the First Miracle ego to the deeper Ground that invites the possibility of awakening into the Second Miracle. As ego boundaries become porous there is an increased receptivity to energetic induction. Simultaneously, there is also regression of basic egoic defenses. Almost inevitably this has the liability of a temporarily diminished capacity for discernment and judgment. This makes the student highly vulnerable to manipulation, not only by an unscrupulous teacher but by the unconscious shadow forces lurking in the community of the teaching. Here is where real vigilance and honesty is demanded of each and every member of a spiritual association.

Another equally important consideration is that as ego-boundaries soften there is vulnerability to psychic phenomena of all kinds. In the gap between the intact First Miracle ego and the healthy establishment in Second Miracle beingness there exist powerful extra-egoic forces. It is these extra-egoic forces that are the basis for much of spiritual and religious imagery and symbols. While the ego is intact they have virtually no conscious reality and minimal psychic relevance. But when the ego has been transiently weakened, they become potent forces indeed. This is the realm of the archetypes, and of angelic and demonic entities that can now easily overwhelm the First Miracle personality.

This is precisely when a teacher is most needed. This teacher can come from within as one's own deepest intuition. It can appear in dreams and visions, often as one of the great spiritual adepts of the past. Or it can be the presence of a wise and experienced living teacher to mirror back the inner intelligence. In general, if a person knows himself well, he has knowingly or unknowingly honored his inner teacher and can pass through this stage relatively safely. But if he does not and has no access to a capable outer teacher, there is real danger. In effect, it is the role of the outer teacher to instill within the student a profound sense of love and wholeness. Paradoxically, this will mean presenting him not only with his true beauty and soul qualities, but equally with every place where the student is non-relational, where there is withholding, self-deception, lack of integrity, and self-delusion, in essence the structure of his First Miracle shadow-self. These must be made conscious and eventually forgiven so that there is no unconscious hook in the student's psyche by which to be captured by the extra-egoic forces. Now, if an opening occurs, that student has the inner clarity and self-knowledge to pass safely through this potentially dangerous stage.

Many years ago when I spontaneously entered into this state of unboundedness between First and Second Miracle consciousness, I had already done a great deal of psychological work on myself. To me the true value of psychological work is that it is a form of self-inquiry where we learn about our own personal areas of potential self-disception and distortion. Therapy alleviates some suffering, but this, to me, misses the point of its real value. Psychotherapy is a means of approaching the fundamental question:

Who am I? Measuring whether this makes us happier or not is less relevant; self-knowledge is what is important. Recognition is transcendance; whatever we perceive about ourselves implies the existence of the Self in which this awareness is occuring. Psychotherapeutic insight prepares us, albeit often indirectly, to gradually disidentify from personal psychological dynamics that, during awakening, can be dangerously amplified and act as attractors for difficult psycho-spiritual forces. Insecurity, for example, if it has not been addressed, becomes the attractor for power. Abandonment fears become the attractors for unhealthy submission to codependent relationships, including with spiritual teachers. Having undertaken a good deal of ego level work in myself (is it ever done?), when I was suddenly plunged into a flood of nearly overwhelming energy, visions, and sensations, while feeling quite overwhelmed, I did not tend to see these as my own personal psychological problems. While I was still quite naive about spiritual awakening, I realized that these were forces from deeper within the psyche, and I had the insight to ask within myself, "Who has been here before and mastered this territory?" Immediately, I knew that Jesus had done so, even though in the whole of my life I had only read the New Testament Gospels once. Synchronistically, this single reading had occurred about one month prior to this opening. I remember crying at certain points of the text while I read, without really understanding why. The insight to intuit the consciousness Jesus had embodied is an example of the inner teacher. By pointing my intuition toward Jesus, I was inviting a previously unconscious level of spiritual integration that led me though this period and continues to enrich my life and work.

It is highly seductive to First Miracle consciousness to desire that the presence of a living spiritual master bestow instant enlightenment. First Miracle man is used to being able to take on centuries of hard-won knowledge by mere memorization, so he imagines that he can have a short-cut to the Second Miracle as well. Certain teachers can precipitate powerful psychospiritual phenomena in some of their students and this easily fits the expectation of instant enlightenment. These teachers may, at times, be absorbed in genuine higher states of consciousness, and from the perspective of these states no longer be concerned with conventional social and material values. For First Miracle people who have been mired in conventional self-reflection, there is a tendency to consider this a demonstration of true freedom and to project even more specialness on the "enlightened" master, further amplifying the perceived gulf between the master's authority and the student's inner authority. But absorption in the Infinite can be failure of the capacity for relationship at the personal, human, and material level of reality, equally as much as absortion in personal and material concerns can be a failure of relationship to the Infinite.

Powerful psychic openings and energetic experiences, despite their intensity and wonder, are a far cry from mature, embodied Second Miracle consciousness. Second Miracle consciousness, itself, is very new on the evolutionary stage, at least as far as humans are concerned. Buddha lived a mere twenty-six hundred years ago, Jesus but two thousand. To imagine that the present early demonstrations of such consciousness can automatically be lived in the fullness of complex social and cultural relationships is a profound arrogance. It is an arrogance that pervades many spiritual teachings and communities, an arrogance that, I believe, rests upon the pivotal hubris that enlightenment is a final state, a final achievement of conscious evolution. We would, I feel, do better to discard the whole notion of enlightenment except as a process of ever-growing individual and collective embodiment, or capacity for consciousness. When examining any spiritual teaching and any teacher, we must ask whether the teaching environment and relationships are generating a mature capacity for consciousness in the people who subscribe to it, and emphatically this must be reflected in psychological maturity. In short, what is the capacity for relationship? Spiritual experiences and powers such as visions, altered states, and strong energetic sensations are meaningless unless there is a true capacity to embrace the fullness of daily life and earthly human relationships in all of their complexity. Escape into the mysticism of the subjective pole of consciousness—the world of spiritual experiences and powers—is no more likely to save us than escape into the mysticism of the objective pole, the world of science and what it promises. These must meet in each of us where they become two sides of the same coin of wholeness.

><

There is an intelligence in the universe that is undeniable. This understanding is the very gift of human consciousness as we reach out and perceive the nature of the universe we are in. We see this in the formation of galaxies, in the creation of Earth's atmosphere, in the balance of ecosystems—literally, it is everywhere. Whether we know it or not, each of us is being formed within this intelligence and as we learn how to listen, we can allow our lives to become more and more the expression of this intelligence. We are never really alone, never really isolated. For anyone who is an observer of the unfolding of individuals in their spiritual journey, this intelligence is nothing short of miraculous.

Often, as I've said, this intelligence is expressed directly to us in dreams and visions. One dream, in particular, has powerfully influenced my life and has had a strong ongoing influence in all that I teach. The dream occurred a few months prior to Easter in 1987. As I discuss this dream, I will be recounting the progression of insight in about the same way it grew in me in the years since:

> *A Master Musician is going to give a performance. In the dream I do not have a body or any specific locus of awareness; I am just a witness. I observe the technical preparations being made on the Master's instrument. The instrument looks like a giant violin or cello that fills the whole front of the amphitheater or concert hall. It is lying on its back with the strings facing upward. The neck of the instrument is exposed just above the ground, but the body is embedded in the earth. I see that as the strings are plucked or bowed, the vibration conveys itself into the Earth through the body. Technicians are working to ready the instrument and to tune it. I sense that as they tune it the sound resonates through all the Earth and that, in turn, the Earth is tuning the instrument.*

*Suddenly, the Master Musician is standing immediately in front of me, looking directly into my face. He is white-haired, neither stern nor friendly, a very commanding presence. He says: "Jesus was an Enneas. He never tried to do good. He never tried to heal anyone."*

*Immediately the Master Musician's face is gone and everything disappears. An awareness happens that is very difficult to describe. There is nothing, no local sense of being, just a movement like falling through space or emptiness, as if between dimensions. There is no feeling, just awareness. Then a voice that is everywhere—it may be my own, or God's, or the Master Musician's—says: "How can I heal you?" With this question, which is also somehow a statement, I surface into waking consciousness.*

My first impression on awakening was of mystery, but the reverberation of the question, "How Can I Heal You?" troubled me. At that time I was forty years old and going through a delicate period with my health. There had been a great deal of difficult change both inwardly and outwardly. So this question made we wonder what it was I was expecting from existence. Did I think I was ill? Was I wanting healing? It is one thing to speak about suffering in the context of my teaching, but now I realized that I had begun to identify myself with my own suffering. The dream made me begin to once again look through the mirror of my experience.

The dream posed another, perhaps even more important question: Was I still, at some level, trying to do good, to heal others? Was calling others toward awakening consciousness a variation of this same impulse? I say, at some level, because I had long ago set aside healing as an objective in my work, though it continued to happen around me. Nevertheless, the desire that my work truly serve people's lives often caused me to lose the sense of being referent to infinity. Alleviating suffering and awakening consciousness often became a finite yardstick for the value of my work. Thus the statement in the dream, "Jesus never tried to do good. He never tried to heal anyone," was a stunning declaration of something I already intuitively believed, but had not fully trusted in my own life. Seeing that healing happened out of a spontaneous and unobstructed aliveness, that it was as much grace as the result of some specific effort, I had for a long time cautioned against making healing a goal for spiritual work. But denying it as a goal is not the same as affirming the deeper root of healing.

The most mysterious aspect of the dream, for me, rested in the assertion that Jesus was an Enneas. At first I was not able to even spell the word. I wrote it down as En-yus and Aenyeus in my journal. I have many dictionaries, but under these spellings and other variations I could not find it. Then several months later I was browsing through a new edition of *The Gospel According to Thomas.* This particular edition contained interpretations of the Gospel, as well as related essays by other authors. As I read, I came across some unfamiliar words and turned to see if there was a glossary. In that moment I knew what I was going to find. Sure enough there, under E, was the word Enneas. The glossary said: "Ninth, a plane or dimension of Being, therefore an Aion." Enneas comes from the Coptic language, a mixture of ancient Greek and Egyptian that flourished in the early centuries A.D. in the area of Alexandria. The original Nag Hammadi Library, of which *The Gospel According to Thomas* is a part, was written in Coptic.

Immediately, this definition plugged into my dream: Jesus was "a plane or dimension of Being, an Aion." An Aion is the first level in which God, the Absolute, the Uncreated can begin to be intuited or symbolized in any way. Aion is a level of manifestation of the Absolute prior to Jahweh, the God of the Old Testament. Some years after the dream I read Jung's work *Aion*. But while I found his thoughts interesting, they did not enlarge my intuitive feeling of the dream. It remains sufficient for me to continue to, again and again, yield my own actions and motivations to the intuition of Jesus' consciousness as a condition from which goodness and healing spontaneously arise.

The crucial gift of the dream is the insight that wholeness begets wholeness out of its own nature. First Miracle consciousness will forever attempt to manipulate situations and create some

215

modification of experience that attempts to approach some imagined ideal of wholeness. Here is the ego hiding in acts of kindness and goodness, and especially in the guise of the healer and even in the guise of teacher as well.

It is questionable whether goodness is even possible at the level of First Miracle consciousness. Consciousness of goodness is possible, but not the ability to be good or do good. Realizing this again and again shocks me back into faith. In the midst of my teaching or as I reach toward someone who is suffering, something yields within me and the attention becomes open, listening. This is what I call Sacred Attention. I continue to act, but the actor has become conscious and is, moment by moment, being yielded to Infinity. I am not denying that we have an obligation to honor each other and to treat each other with dignity and caring, and that this involves actions taken on behalf of the wellbeing of others. But this obligation is not a moral imperative to which to conform our behavior. It is recognition of our true nature as individual parts of an interconnected wholeness. This recognition begets wholeness.

When we create the other as an object of need, we simultaneously create ourselves as the object of goodness: the helper, friend, healer, humanitarian, philanthropist, and so on. Once again, we are living an incomplete relationship both to the other and to ourselves. The consequence of holding healing and goodness as goals of a spiritual journey again and again invites and reinforces the fundamental egoism that is forever seeking safety, security, answers, rightness, and so forth. As I have argued throughout this book, First Miracle behavior is essentially Godless. Self-consciously directed goodness is inevitably a trespass on the innate wholeness of whoever is the receiver of this supposed goodness. As Goethe said, "If you treat a man as he appears to be, you make him less than who he is." And it is a trespass against ourselves. We become subtly defined in such actions not only in terms of generating a false identity as helper or teacher, another false "place to rest our heads," but also in the perpetuation of the dualism of good and bad that then begets the next generation of ideals and goals to which the ego becomes committed and self-substantiated. To break this cycle, we must begin to at least be willing to concede the possibility of our own self-serving ends and be willing to live in the tension of not really knowing who or what we really serve with our efforts.

So how do we act for the goodness of the whole? I am not sure we can know how, but learning about ourselves and moving as much as possible from our own wholeness is probably the best place to start. We have to stop pretending that we are good people. Walt Whitman made this comment: "Showing the best and dividing from the worst, age vexes age." It is not that we are bad people either: It is just that our consciousness both of ourselves and of our world is limited. We, ultimately, do not know what is good or bad. This is why Jesus admonishes that we must not resist evil. He was not speaking about tolerating a Hitler. Hitler had to be stopped because he was violating every principle of life. Jesus' remark was, I believe, directed to an inner dynamic in which resisting evil actually ends up affirming the basic First Miracle consciousness that will forever generate good and evil. I was recently told that Thomas Merton used to ask the question, "What was Adam's sin?" The answer Merton gave was that Adam tried to do good. Adam thought he could make things better. In our own inner lives, when we feel something that frightens us about ourselves, once we resist it, we have committed ourselves into an infinity of judgments and reactions that can forever obscure our perception of a more fundamental level of our own wholeness. To not resist requires intuition of something beyond any self-perception. To not resist implies a deeper faith. If we are to treat each other well then we must first enter that level of consciousness in which "our neighbor is ourself." This is our evolutionary destiny.

In the meantime, we will undoubtedly make many mistakes. We already recognize that government welfare programs are just as likely to reinforce impoverishment as to support human dignity. The impulse is right, but the objectification of people is the problem. The impulse to care for each other emanates from our Second Miracle nature. But when we attempt to institutionalize programs and objectify both need and altruism we run into problems because we objectify people instead of creating real relationship. We do not, as yet, address the issue of suffering in such a way that really empowers people, so the problem returns, again and again. On a personal scale that all of us have experienced or will experience, what kind of relationships do we want from others in response to our own suffering? If a person is very ill they know, whether they outwardly show it or not, that visitors who make small talk and act as though everything is normal are often just protecting themselves. This dissembling is avoidance of relationship, which diminishes the potential to be uplifted in each other's presence, "where two or three or more are gathered." Even acts of direct caring, such as cleaning and feeding a sick person, can be a form of self-protection, an avoidance of real relationship. I have spent a good deal of time with people in the last phases of their lives and often they have confided to me how deeply they are drained by any kind of dishonesty. Any kind of behavior that tries to disguise death and suffering demeans the real relationship that brings us together at such times. We simply do not honor another if we see him as an object that is poor, or sick, or frightened, and will not look squarely into our own finite frailty. We must together suffer the embarrassment and humiliation of our egos in the fierce invitation of life, if we are to drink together of the fountain of relationship breathed to infinity.

This is why I feel the example of someone like Mother Teresa as a spiritual hero can sometimes do as much harm as good. Without realizing that her behavior is mandated organically from the Enneas dimension—her profound relationship to the Beloved, Jesus, in herself—our egos objectify her good acts, making them part of a noble ideal. While the Enneas dimension is potential in all of us, it is not reached through idealism. When Mother Teresa, or other deeply consecrated individuals are enobled because of their heroic lives and then emulated out of an idealistic notion of goodness, we have not really seen through to the deeper wholeness. What level of relationship to ourselves and our own inner beloved are we really obeying? Without realizing it we have chosen sides in the ancient polarity of good and evil. Idealism is one of the great plagues of the human soul. We must find our own authentic expression of the Enneas mandate by living deeply and with total integrity and not take refuge in ideals, even the most noble ones. Is someone who cares for the poor, the ill, and the outcast any more heroic than someone who works to mature a long-term marriage or any long-term, committed relationship? In my life, it has seemed to me far harder to sustain and evolve these intimate relationships than it ever was to tend to the needs of suffering strangers as a physician, or even in my teaching work now. The range of these latter relationships, even when deeply consecrated, is intrinsically narrower in terms of the repertoire of emotional and psychological issues that must be addressed and the degree of paradox and tension within them, than in a mature marriage of equals likewise consecrated to Infinity.

A marriage is a relationship that reflects us back to Infinity day after day, in the midst of all the human issues that arise between people. Marriage generally begins as ego fulfilling, a choice for happiness that will protect us from suffering, and when we are "in love" in the romantic sense, this is surely the case. But over time, if a marriage is to become a mature spiritual relationship, it will begin to call us into ever deeper levels of revelation of our unconsciousness and potential for self-deceit and capacity to cause suffering to the other and ourselves. It holds up the possibility of a mirror in which we can ruthlessly behold how we avoid true relationship to ourselves, God, and each other. When we grant to our spouse equal physical, mental, emotional, and spiritual authority as we imagine for ourselves and become Guru and Shakti, teacher and beloved to each other, calling each other back, again and again, to Infinity, this to me is truly heroic.

Mother Teresa is a hero not because of what she does, but because of who she is and how she came to her vision and service to life. While "by their fruit they shall be known" speaks to the ultimate inseparability of who we are and what we do, we have to be able to look past the form alone. The ego constantly seeks an image of itself or others that forestalls its true submission to the wound of consciousness. How many people quietly struggling in spiritual marriage are regarded as heroic? To me, it is not Mother Teresa's acts in themselves that make her admirable and worthy of emulation, but the question of whether she is expressing her deepest authenticity and the Enneas within her. This is for her alone to know. But making her and other people like her into an ideal, such as First Miracle consciousness does, can just as easily imprison the believer as liberate him toward the full possibility of conscious relationship.

The image of Jesus travelling around and performing healings has never rung true for me. I have no doubt that he was a profound healer and that some of the stories in the Bible are true, yet I am certain that Jesus never wanted this aspect of his ministry to be prominent. I imagine that every time healing happened of itself he was astonished and came to more deeply understand the nature of the changes that had happened in him. He had become referent to infinity, and infinity sheds its blessing, which is the blessing of the universe's innate intelligence. But I suspect that when Jesus felt the need to perform a healing for the sake of his followers' faith, which would have been a near-impossible temptation to deny at times, that something inside of him cried out in anguish.

The dream was a blessing for me. During my life and in my teaching I have come to crucial points where the energy was changing and needed a new consecration. If I remained within the old consecration, the energy would, like "new wine in old wine skins," become sour. I had, years before, learned through another dream that I had to stop doing conferences. So after a great deal of soul searching I did stop doing them. I began to *be* them. I took on associates, taught them, learned with them, and by lightening my load was able to flow in beingness rather than doingness. My health returned and the work flourished. But the ego always reasserts itself; there is always the danger of having it co-opt even the clearest insights leading, once again, to crystallization.

Through the dream of Enneas, I began a whole new level of putting down baggage. Every time I would catch myself wanting anything at all to happen in my work I recalled, "Jesus was a plane or dimension of Being. He never tried to do good. He never tried to heal." This insight, like a song or mantra, has carried me ever deeper into radical faith. More and more I simply do nothing. I remain present, let the words come when they want, enjoy people, and the whole play and dance of our discovery together. I take responsibility for when my ego interrupts simple, unobstructed service to the Unobstructed Moment...and yield once again. The most crucial mirror for me in all this, as my above remarks suggest, has been my marriage. As it becomes more honest, so does my teaching, and I experience, more and more, the nearness of God.

As time goes on the meaning of the vast cello-like instrument embedded in the Earth becomes more and more significant. What kind of music can we play? What kind of consciousness can we access that isn't embedded in Gaia, in all of Nature? The instrument has come to symbolize, for me, my organism. I am embedded in Nature and, specifically, in this Earth and when I am played by God, the Master Musician, it is the Earth that tunes me even as I tune Her. My teaching has progressively returned to the sense of organism as an expression of the whole complex dynamic of relationships we call life. This dream helped me understand where the real grounding of the transcendent must take place: here, in our embodiment, in our organism, in our Earth. Instinct is our friend and benefactor. It is the distilled expression of countless relationships embodied over billions of years. There is connectedness and wisdom here beyond our comprehension. Sensuality is the movement of God and Nature in our feeling. It is God feeling. It is God feeling pain or joy in us. But it is also all of Nature in our joy and our suffering, all of Nature in our experience of sentience. How we play the instrument of our organism reflects our attunement to Nature and will always in turn tune Her.

I realized through this dream that God does not know how to heal us. "How can I heal you?" God is a movement of attention forever into infinity, forever through the mirror of now into the root of consciousness itself that cannot be known. If God has any intention, that intention is our own. The voice that was my voice, and also the voice of God, arises in a space that is prior to any

221

sense of self or any notion of space, time, or other. We are, our-selves, God and we do not, in fact, cannot, heal ourselves. Healing is the texture of God, the intelligence of the universe expressing in us. We do not do this. When medicine is a manifestation of our God-ing it does heal us because we are expressing an Intelligence that is already present and innate. When medicine is merely conse-crated in trying to do good, it is improper science and it does as much harm as anything else. When we are God-ing in our dance and song and touch, then we are also tuning the instrument of the universe even as it tunes us. The dream took so much of what was alive in my life and gave it back to me in a way that even now deepens my worship and my faith.

For years I believed that I had never heard of the word En-neas, and then one day I remembered that I had studied a system of human personality analysis called the Enneagram back in the early 1970s. The system describes nine fundamental human per-sonality types, their strengths and weaknesses, their unique pat-terning. The root of Enneagram teaching is said to have been passed down from ancient mystical sources. In the last decade this system has become quite popular in the West.

When I was studying the Enneagram, I thought there was valuable insight about the nature of different personality types, though making such separations has always felt contrived to me. I felt kindred with every type and felt attracted to all the types, more or less. This, the instructor insisted, meant that I must be afraid to limit myself to one type. By default, then, I was labeled a fear type. I can accept that, at the level of my First Miracle nature, this may have been, and still may be the case, but in my Second Miracle nature there is a home for all types.

As I contemplate the dream, I see Jesus as an Enneas: one in whom all the variations of human personality are included. Much in the same way that white light becomes the spectrum of color when passed through a prism, Enneas when passed through the prism of incarnation becomes, among many things, the full spec-trum of human personalities. We can look at personality types as fundamentally different, and appreciating these differences can be helpful in resolving misunderstandings about each other. In other words, however we label ourselves becomes the basis for deeper relationship, and not a rationalization for the avoidance of relationship. In addition, lest we get lost in believing that we are a type and have one more place to rest our First Miracle heads, we might consider that Second Miracle consciousness is that state in which these fundamental differences work together as an organic whole. Our Second Miracle self has access to and, in actuality, can express the fundamental energy of each of these types. Not only are they resolved within the Second Miracle, but I have repeatedly observed in my group work that as individuals deepen and the energy of the group heightens, paradoxically, rather than being divided by our differences, we are united. Rather than becoming similar, there is a growing authenticity and uniqueness. True individuality is the basis for communion with others.

Oddly, in the period preceding the dream, I was actually countering my own innate rapport with people and my own humanness by emphasizing the universal impersonality of higher energy. But higher consciousness places an equal demand on our capacity to recognize each other and meet each other personally. My wife, Ariel, who came into my life a few years before this dream, could see this distortion. She had been encouraging, even demanding, that I let myself be more natural. Becoming a step-parent to a six-year-old son and twelve-year-old daughter, certainly left little room for the quality of extended attention and impersonal indifference that I had cultivated. The heightening of attention that had become so natural to me in the context of being a teacher did not let me easily shift between personal and impersonal levels of relating. In short, the ego had co-opted the experience of higher energy and had made it a way of avoiding relationship rather than embracing all of life. I now feel that the dream, in emphasizing the naturalness of being, was saying not only, "Don't try to heal or do good," but as well, "Don't try to hold one state of attention as higher or better than any other. Live in faith so that every moment is as full of inception as every other." And as I live, so this is what I experience.

223

# LAST WORDS

I have been aware throughout this book that my sense of the readerchanges. Most of the time I am speaking to all of us who realize that we are being called to a new destiny, that we cannot afford to delay, that for our own sake and for the sake of our world we are making a commitment to consciousness. Sometimes I am expressing insights aimed specifically at those who work in a service role, those who are therapists, healers, teachers, and leaders, people who bear the karma of assisting others to move forward in consciousness. But today I was speaking to Kaye, a close friend in spirit, suffering what feels to be the Dark Night of the soul. I realized that I have been writing to people like her, people who have, from the fullness of dedicated lives, entered this territory almost impossible to describe, a place where we struggle to find faith in our own emergence, a place of unspeakable misery and grace. Here we are the children of evolution, the alchemical vessels of incarnation. Though no one can remove this suffering until the inner alchemy has been fulfilled, the soul rejoices in companionship and takes respite in being seen.

There is no medical or psychological interpretation for this place, no treatment, whether from Western medicine, or from Eastern medicine, energetic, homeopathic, herbal, or naturopathic. There is only listening, rest, and faith. This is a wound the ego cannot heal, a place we explain or rationalize at our own risk. To merely label it suffering or depression is to deny God's agency in our souls. No one is called to this place before his time, and all those who have found themselves at this place have, already within them, the means of making the passage. When the time comes in true ripeness, we all have the means. Jesus said, "I will chose one in a thousand, and two in ten thousand, and they shall be as a single one" (Logia 23). These, I believe, are among the one in a thousand or two in ten thousand that Jesus was speaking of, but there are many of us being called now. We live in such a process with only the dignity (it largely feels like indignity) of the waiting. With enormous courage and faith we keep our hearts open. From time to time, we are blessed with a dream that may instruct us and renew our faith in the intelligence of spirit. In this territory we are each ultimately alone, but we also implicitly recognize those who have been there too. Just being met in silence, a silence pregnant with unknowing, a silence only faith can teach us, can seem life-saving. Indeed, that someone can meet us in faith, that someone, in trusting our process, urges us onward and is confident in us— without really saying a thing—is a joy difficult to measure. While my intent has been to speak to people at all stages of the journey, I have hoped that the silence behind some of these words has been for these brave souls as well. This vigil that we hold for one another in the dark crucible of transformation, more and more of us hold for our world in this time of global passage.

My first book took nine months to write, in the days before computers. Many friends spent many hours typing each new round of editing and changes. I do not remember how long the second book took, a few months shorter I think, but I do recall that *The Black Butterfly* took only ninety days. I was proud of that then; it seemed that the balance and focus of my life had reached an apex. Everything was in place, all the support I could want.

Perhaps it was the culmination of a cycle, because shortly there-after all hell broke loose. The man I thought I was received a lesson that, when life wants to, it throws us a curve ball and faces us with what we really need for our spiritual growth—like it or not.

Ready or not, I accepted. I followed my heart, remarried, became, as I have already told, a step-father, left behind the land I loved and moved in search of a better situation for the children. Life has never been the same since, nor, in some ways, as uncom-plicated as it was then, nor as rich as it has become. This book is part and parcel of that change. It has taken more than two years to write. I have grabbed a few hours here, a few days there in the midst of so many distractions, so much of the trial, ache, and wonder of daily life, of family fun and feud. I have written parts in one coun-try, parts in another, parts at home, and parts in the homes of friends and even strangers. I have written outside on the porch, while my son, Andreas, and his friend were playing in the pool so that I could hear their laughter, and so that they could sense me near and call to me and tell me of their adventures.

A few years ago this would have been impossible. I would have needed a special environment for the creative process. But somehow, and I think many people will understand this, especially mothers and business people who juggle many hats, there is no ideal time for creativity, or truth, or wholeness. We take it all together as part of everything, or maybe life passes us by. When our hearts learn to flow with this there is a great sense of freedom. When we can, we work; when we can't, we are full in whatever else life calls us to; there is no space that is more or less holy and rich than this one, now.

I think this has to be learned. Perhaps the most important thing we have to learn to do for ourselves is to slow down so that we can listen to our hearts, so that we can be guided and informed by our deeper nature. Does it seem contradictory that I, who has just confessed the busyness and distractions amid which this book has been created, should speak of slowing down? It is not so for me. I have come to feel the timelessness in ordinary living; I have come to feel that spirituality is meaningless until it reaches into

226

our simple daily activities. Divine ordinariness: Life is filled with paradox. Being a servant of the awakening impulse and earning a living at it has often felt painfully contradictory. Being an itinerant spiritual teacher, with all the demands of that way of life, and being a family man at the same time, is no small thing to sustain either. Modern life is ruthless in the tensions it asks us to reconcile in our hearts and in our living. In the integration of such tensions, taking time to listen deep in our bodies is the great elixir. Our bodies understand such tensions…if only we don't live too fast. Slowing down is the key. Perhaps this was not true in the past; perhaps we had to speed up, to use our minds as cleverly as possible in order to survive. But this adaptation no longer serves us today. We need to give our minds a rest, to take time with ourselves to meet the Beloved in our hearts. "Slow down" is the great cry coming from our souls, and it is not easy to accomplish in our modern world. The paradox here is that it is not necessarily doing less; it is the place where our doing comes from. Are we the disciples of fear, or of wholeness and love?

Time for our souls is so precious. Unless we truly understand how to feel the timeless presence in the fullness of our often hectic daily lives, then finding time is our first priority. Buying time is more like it. We buy time when we spend less money, stop leveraging our future with debt, when we aren't seduced by the fancy car, when we make do with the smaller house, when we share more instead of accumulating such a redundancy of things. What we save we must invest in ourselves, in our spiritual growth. We must learn a new Yes, a radical selfishness that says, "If I have lost the sense of the Beloved in myself, I cannot be the disciple of love in my work or my life. I cannot make wise choices or be the servant of the deeper intelligence." As we take off some of the financial pressure, and discipline ourselves to release other pressures to keep doing, saying no to weekend work and yes to open time, unplanned time, we become wealthy inside. This is true wealth. This is wealth that doesn't overburden our environment, that won't destroy our world. Something is waiting for us when we make the space…after we pass though our fear of emptiness. It is spiritual richness, a richness of the heart. I feel it more and more as I sense my own life becoming more and more honest. Walt Whitman writes that, "the unseen is proved by the seen." My prayer for each of us is that our relationship to the fullness that is God will be seen in the integrity of all our relationships, in how we make space in our lives to let spirit come so deep into our every breath, in our capacity to be fulfilled with very little. I am not always the best example of this, but every time I see myself substitute some unnecessary activity or material purchase for a deeper connection to myself, I gently remember, "This is not the way." Our modern world mercilessly conspires against this and we must be vigilant. But with each step we take into true spiritual integrity we are rewarded with the living presence. We are carried by an invisible current and want less and less for anything else.

Not long ago, I found myself in Hamburg giving a talk, or rather, that was what I was supposed to be doing. I was finding it very difficult to speak. It was an uncomfortable silence for me; I felt the audience expected me to give a lecture as planned. But I had said what I could say and it was simply this: "If we could feel and really trust that what had brought us to that auditorium was already working in our lives, that hearing me was only a pretext for our gathering, that we were actually there together in obedience to a deeper intelligence, already disciples of the new possibility, we might not feel complete, or saved, but we would know ease and peace in our hearts." And we would stop being afraid and, perhaps, stop being so spiritually grandiose. I could sense that this was just too simple, that for many people it has to be more complicated and more extraordinary than that. The journey is still so narcissistically focused, so much about personal attainment, personal enlightenment. Well, why not? We are human. But until we see our personal attainment as service to a larger process, none of our attainments will really set us free.

I had spoken this understanding from the deepest place in me, and my heart was breaking; I could say no more. Then suddenly a woman stood up and spoke of the work she had done with me a few years before. She spoke about discovering the courage to be alive, one day at a time. She spoke of learning that fear and hope were both lies. Now she just lived the truth of her experience each day. Then I recognized her as a woman with advanced breast cancer who, at the time of our meeting, had been told she had only months to live. But there she was, still alive and bringing such a gift back to me. After she finished a man stood up next to her and said he was her partner. He said that her health was still frail, but that living with her now was always a completely new experience, that she had become an inspiration in his life. He, too, personally thanked me. Around the auditorium a few other people stood up and said similar things. I almost couldn't take it in. They really were disciples of the Teaching. Together we had pointed a way, and there I was on the stage and they in the audience, each of us living the work and being transformed in the living.

We need each other for this journey; we need to meet each other in the fullness. We can no longer be the disciples of fear. When we feel ourselves hurrying, feeling pressured to do ever more, we can be assured that fear has crept into our hearts. Love is forever calling us to slow down in ourselves. When we do, we are blessed by peace. The bigger the energy, the more silence we must feed it, then our knowing becomes vaster, and we accomplish more without trying. When we don't we find ourselves outwardly accelerating faster and faster, needing more and more, doing more and more, and feeling empty and anxious. For those of us who have learned to listen, the way gets simpler and simpler. That it is a demanding path is of little matter. My prayer would be that it demand ever more of us and that we give it with an open heart.

In the coming years, we will see more and more change at every level of our lives. The quickening of spirit will continue to increase. Because it is universal energy, it will enliven everything, the best and the worst of us. It will enlighten some, and depress others. Heal some, and sicken others. It will make us selfish or selfless according to whether we are the disciples of fear or love. This is its grace and our hope. It will carry us toward wholeness, one way or another, challenging every structure and every form. We will either be disciples who are enriched or victims who are run over. Some years ago as I was struggling with all the changes in my life, I realized I might not be able to integrate such tremendous personal change and all the stress of it without developing a disease. Yet, even as I had this anxious thought, I understood that our deeper being will not choose disease unless it is the best or only path left available to it. If this were the case, I had the faith that it would be the most intelligent effort possible to bring me toward a new integration. I opened my heart to Mystery and left the how to God and my soul; the fear evaporated.

In the coming years, there will be few outer signposts or structures stable enough to navigate by—except the environment. Businesses, governments, churches, social organizations will all be in tremendous flux. Only the environment will show us, with implacable honesty, whether we have become true disciples or are continuing our collective ego-trip. We must, as best we can, steer by the environment; what is healthy for the Earth is healthy for us. In this effort we will continue to be plagued by self-interest, and our differing abilities to respect the intuition we are all feeling about the health of the environment. But whether we choose to listen and obey of our free will, or are forced to by Earth changes, we will eventually have to accept our obligation to nurture the whole planet.

With all the outer change, the one stable incontrovertible truth that we each will have today, next year, and in the decades to come, will be our own bodies and our capacity for feeling and consciousness. We must learn to listen to ourselves, listening through the seemingly chaotic turbulence of changes, to the deeper I-amness. Like the Earth environment, it may not tell us what we want to hear, but it will never lie to us. It is the core that puts fear behind and is the disciple of love. Its deepest truth is intimacy. Intimacy and diversity is the heart of our universe. It is the intimacy of hydrogen and oxygen atoms that make water which, in turn, formed the oceans in which life was born. Ancient traditions recognized the intimacy of the four elements, air, water, earth, and fire. We now have a much more comprehensive understanding of

230

these elements, but we have lost the sense of integration between them. As we look to our own discipleship, we will, again and again, have to ask of our personal capacity for intimacy, our capacity in healthy timing, to open our hearts to the great diversity of life and of each other. Biological survival in the battle with Nature is no longer the issue; our future hangs on psychological maturity. Whatever spirituality we profess, it must call us toward the wisest psychological adaptations. This is a good question for us to use as a lens through which to examine the ceaseless choices we will need to make in our lives: Does this choice, this action, this behavior, invite the greatest psychological maturity?

The basis for all future psychological adaptations begin with the family. A healthy family is the best environment for setting the stage for higher life. I am not talking about an ideal family. As modern life challenges the family structure, we must not polarize into issues of right or wrong; there is no ideal family. As soon as we find ourselves speaking about ideals, anywhere, we can be sure that we are in our intellects, not our hearts. Could we truly have become conscious of the sacred value of the family if we had not violated it so? I don't think so. As we finally recognize the consequences of broken families, we will seek to listen to the health of our families and communities. And here, I think, is an essential guiding light for business.

The successful businesses that rise to prominence in the next centuries will be attracting the most intelligent people because they honor and support the intelligence of body and family. These enlightened organizations will increase vacation time, for a rested person is as close to his genius as he will ever be. They will provide a minimum of one year of maternity leave and excellent child care so that every employee knows that today's work is not done at the expense of the next generation's wholeness. Enlightenment areas will be created for meditation, music listening, body-mind exercises, or just simply for rest. Creative inspiration is born at such times.

231

It will not be long before spiritual values will be openly discussed and govern every aspect of the work environment. The heart of spirituality, as I have said, is our capacity for relationship. For this reason the successful businesses of the future will, in one way or another and with varying emphasis, be addressing four foundational dynamics.

1) **The individual.** No business can ultimately succeed unless it is committed to the empowerment of every employee. The question to ask in our hearts in order to focus this issue is: Do I like what is happening to me in this environment? Do I like how I am being invited into relationship with my co-workers? Businesses, as spiritual environments, will support the highest level of individual authenticity, intelligence, and aliveness in every person. To do this requires understanding the second dynamic.

2) **Group energy.** Every organization is essentially a group, and usually groups within groups. If we don't understand the dynamics of group energy and how to maximize the positive potential of this energy, we will not be able to create the environment most conducive to empower the intelligence and creativity of each individual. Since the one is never separable from the whole, the questions to ask in our hearts to guide this principle are: Is our corporate culture, or group identity, united around sufficiently universal and inspirational principles and values? Are we flexible enough to encourage individual authenticity and focused enough to generate unity of purpose? For this principle to be fulfilled, the third dynamic must also be respected.

3) **The larger collective.** No organization exists outside of relationship to a larger collective that it serves and is, in turn, served by. The questions to ask in our hearts to guide this principle are: Does our work here serve real needs within the larger collective? Does our work help to heal our communities? Life knows what is good for it; nothing in Nature exists that doesn't somehow support the integrity of the whole. But the human ego often ignores this truth. Selling products and services by seducing egos and by manipulating desires, when authentic needs are not also being addressed and fulfilled, ultimately weakens everyone. If individually or collectively we achieve success by compromising or weakening others, we will eventually fail.

4) **The Earth.** The consideration that governs this principle is the health of our environment, both locally and globally. All human activity has environmental impact, but negative impact can be lessened and positive impact encouraged. Consciousness of this is growing, but this consideration must be part of the equation in every decision we make.

The role of education will also need to be re-examined. While the subjective and objective sides of our subject-object awareness are equal in importance, we live in a time in which, for many centuries, too much value has been placed on objective knowledge at the expense of subjective knowledge. Objective knowledge is information; subjective knowledge is essence. When these go hand in hand, we are wise. But perhaps for the first decade or so of life we should let the subjective side take more of the lead. This amounts to teaching our children to live, first and foremost, from the inside out, to learn to listen to their feelings, to learn to live in their bodies, to meet their world with their hearts. Later they will seek the information they need to express their hearts and will acquire objective knowledge without losing touch with their souls. As we look at the thousands of laid-off individuals in our modern societies who seem helpless to find a meaningful life, we are seeing the consequences of people trained to live from the outside in, people who unconsciously fitted themselves into the expected mold, without first learning to listen to their deeper essence. In the future there will be few expected molds to depend upon. The current rush to increase math and science studies to be competitive in the high-tech market will only serve us if the people who move toward these areas have already taken healthy purchase of their hearts.

All of these thoughts are broad strokes that mark a few crucial trends for the future. Obviously they require a major shift in social values. But this is precisely what is happening. The Second Miracle is upon us and will continue to permeate every aspect of human life and expression. Sadly, or perhaps not, because this is who we are, the old patterns will not be released until they have brought us to greater suffering. It is in the crucible of suffering

233

that the past can be re-experienced, forgiven, and honored, even as we make room for a new intelligence and new behaviors. The future will be marked by increasing entropy within all the structures built from our old consciousness. This is not because they are wrong, only that we have become unconscious within them so that they have ceased to grow. We have to reinvent them once again, from birth to death and everything in between, so that there is room for the emergence of a new capacity for consciousness. Entropy, the creation of fragmentation and disorder, is always easier to cause then the creation of greater coherence and interrelatedness. Perhaps this is why so many films exploit our fascination with explosions and destruction, and why war is easier than peace. The art of the future, as it has always really been, is the art of intimacy, of seeing God in ourselves and each other, the art of creating new and ever-more complex interconnectedness.

In a mature person conscious attention is worship. To behold our world, ourselves, and each other with an open heart is the most powerful thing we can do. There is great wholeness that permeates our universe, but when we live and act with worshipful attention we have the power in our very attention to amplify this wholeness. This is how miracles happen; the quality of our attention has the power to bring about healing and wholeness, not only of ourselves and each other, but of our whole planet. Our greatest challenge will be to not be seduced by fear and contract away from the fullness of our fundamental relationship to God. Our individual lives will be over soon, but the possibility of the future will stand on our courage to trust the depth of our feelings, to see the world as it is, to open our hearts and live in faith. This is what we do when we make an incontrovertible commitment to consciousness.

**Richard Moss** received his Doctorate of Medicine in 1972, but after a few years of general practice a life-changing realization led him to his true calling: the exploration of spiritual awakening and its integration in daily life. His books, *The I That is We, Surgery, Self-Healing and Spirit* and *The Black Butterfly* have been translated into five languages and speak with exceptional clarity and insight into what is the grace and obilgation of this pivotal time in human evolution. For twenty years Dr. Moss has been working intimately with groups, helping people all over the world to touch their deeper essence and thus transform their lives. He lives with his wife and has three step-children.

For information on seminars, talks, audio cassettes and other materials in the U.S. contact: **Richard Moss Seminars** 1-800-647-0755. In Australia contact: The Vine and the Branches, 27 Bonds Rd, Lower Plenty, Victoria 3093. Phone 03-439-8248. In Germany contact: Orgoville International, Eisenbuch 8, 84567 Erlbach. Phone: 08670-1669. In France contact: Deborah Bacon, 24 Blvd de Reuilly, 75012 Paris. Phone: 01-4344-6118.